HEAVEN
ON
EARTH?

HEAVEN ON EARTH?

The Social & Political Agendas of Dominion Theology

Bruce Barron

Zondervan Publishing House

Academic and Professional Books

Grand Rapids, Michigan

A Division of HarperCollinsPublishers

Requests for information should be addressed to:
Zondervan Publishing House
Academic and Professional Books
Grand Rapids, Michigan 49530

Library of Congress Cataloging-in-Publication Data

Barron, Bruce.
Heaven on earth? : the social and political agendas of dominion
theology / Bruce Barron.
p.   cm.
Includes bibliographical references and index.
ISBN 0-310-53611-1
1. Dominion theology–Controversial literature.
2. Evangelicalism–United States–Controversial literature.
3. Fundamentalism–Controversial literature. 4. Church and social
problems–United States. 5. Christianity and politics–Protestant
churches. 6. United States–Church history–20th century.
I. Title.
BT82.25.B37 1991

230'.046–dc20   91-34815
                                                                             CIP

Edited by Leonard G. Goss and Tom Raabe
Cover designed by Terry Dugan

Printed in the United States of America

92 93 94 95 96 / AM / 10 9 8 7 6 5 4 3 2 1

• Contents •

• Abbreviations •

BOOKS OF BIBLE

Old Testament

Ge	Genesis
Ex	Exodus
Lev	Leviticus
Nu	Numbers
Dt	Deuteronomy
Jos	Joshua
Jdg	Judges
Ru	Ruth
1Sa	1 Samuel
2Sa	2 Samuel
1Ki	1 Kings
2Ki	2 Kings
1Ch	1 Chronicles
2Ch	2 Chronicles
Ezr	Ezra
Ne	Nehemiah
Est	Esther
Job	Job
Ps(s)	Psalm(s)
Pr	Proverbs
Ecc	Ecclesiastes
SS	Song of Solomon
Isa	Isaiah
Jer	Jeremiah

La	Lamentations
Eze	Ezekiel
Da	Daniel
Hos	Hosea
Joel	Joel
Am	Amos
Ob	Obadiah
Jnh	Jonah
Mic	Micah
Na	Nahum
Hab	Habakkuk
Zep	Zephaniah
Hag	Haggai
Zec	Zechariah
Mal	Malachi

New Testament

Mt	Matthew
Mk	Mark
Lk	Luke
Jn	John
Ac	Acts
Ro	Romans
1Co	1 Corinthians
2Co	2 Corinthians

Gal	Galatians	1Jn	1 John
Eph	Ephesians	2Jn	2 John
Php	Philippians	3Jn	3 John
Col	Colossians	Jude	Jude
1Th	1 Thessalonians	Rev	Revelation
2Th	2 Thessalonians		
1Ti	1 Timothy		
2Ti	2 Timothy		
Tit	Titus		
Phm	Philemon		
Heb	Hebrews		
Jas	James		
1Pe	1 Peter		
2Pe	2 Peter		

Versions of the Bible

KJV	King James Version
NASB	New American Standard Bible
NIV	New International Version
RSV	Revised Standard Version

• Acknowledgments •

When I began the research that led to this book, my specialty was the contemporary charismatic movement. But the charismatics I wanted to study were politically active, and thus to put them in proper context I had to study other politically inclined ideas and thinkers. The scope kept getting broader, and before I finished I found that I had entered a totally new field—in my full-time career as well as in my writing.

This roundabout process meant that I had a lot to learn along the way, in areas to which I had not given much thought previously. I am especially grateful to those persons who spent untold hours helping me grasp the issues and debates into which I had wandered and who treated me with unfailing charity even when I seemed very slow to catch on, or when I never quite came to see things their way. Gary DeMar of American Vision; Gary Amos, Joe Kickasola, and Herb Titus of Regent University; and Mark Rodgers, my mentor in Christian political thinking and now my colleague on a congressional staff, deserve particular appreciation in this regard. Tom Atwood, Jerry Bowyer, Michael Cromartie, Steve Fitschen, Jim Garlow, John Gimenez, Os Guinness, Anne Kincaid, Steve McDowell, Mike Patrick, Earl Paulk (along with numerous members of his church staff), Dennis Peacocke, Ralph Reed, Tommy Reid, Guy Rodgers, John Seel, Jim Skillen, and Bob Slosser furnished valuable and insightful interviews and comments. Many of these people reviewed early drafts of the manuscript, as did Gary North with his distinctive wit and unbounded vigor.

This work was initially my Ph.D. dissertation in religious studies at the University of Pittsburgh. I am deeply indebted to my advisers, John Wilson, Tony Edwards, Doug Hare, and Sam Hays, all of whom graciously brought their expertise to bear on movements outside the scope of their normal pursuits. Their probing questions greatly sharpened my work. I am also grateful to Alex Orbach of the Pitt religion department for enabling me to develop my musings about dominion theology into a viable research topic.

Len Goss and his colleagues on the Zondervan editorial staff have shown extraordinary support of this project.

My wife, Nancy, freely accepted my professional evolution—and the resultant shift from theological to political debates at the evening meal—while remaining an able, resilient, challenging discussion partner and an indispensable sounding board.

• 1 •

Re-Christianizing America
The Onset of Dominion Theology

T he 1980 American presidential election featured the reappearance, after a half century of relative hibernation, of evangelical Protestants as a significant force in national politics. If any single event captured and symbolized that reemergence, it was the National Affairs Briefing Conference on August 21–22 of that year. On those two days eighteen thousand evangelicals assembled in Dallas to hear leaders of the (then genuinely new) New Christian Right discuss campaign issues and call the flock into political action. Having billed itself as nonpartisan, the gathering could not formally endorse Ronald Reagan, the one presidential candidate who addressed the conference; but Reagan enthusiastically endorsed the evangelicals, and in so doing he baptized them into legitimacy on the Republican scene.

As the Christian Right took shape and began growing, previously little-known names became national political players: Falwell, Robison, Jarmin, McAteer, LaHaye. The name of Rousas John Rushdoony, however, remained unknown. Thus it may seem strange that Robert Billings, a leader in Jerry Falwell's Moral Majority organization and later a member of the Department of Education under President Reagan, is said to have remarked during a moment backstage at the National Affairs Briefing, "If it weren't for [Rushdoony's] books, none of us would be here."[1]

Just what had Rushdoony done? Since the late 1950s he had

been churning out books and speeches on the relevance of the Bible—particularly biblical law as found in the first five books of the Old Testament—to culture, education, politics, and government. Though not one of the direct catalysts in the reawakening of the Christian Right in the late 1970s, Rushdoony had been stimulating Christians to think politically for over two decades. His ponderous writings were not widely read, but those whom he influenced transmitted many of his ideas to wider audiences.

If Rushdoony did help the Christian Right get off the ground, these higher-visibility political activists have effectively, albeit unintentionally, returned the favor. By reawakening evangelical interest in impacting politics and culture, they have broadened considerably the market for books like Rushdoony's, and several of his colleagues and disciples, more given to popular styles of writing than Rushdoony himself, have seized the opportunity. Now, after thirty years of prolific writing, Rushdoony is no longer a solitary voice crying in the wilderness; he is the recognized founder of a distinct movement known as Christian Reconstruction.

Reconstruction has affinities with the Christian Right, but its scope and goals are broader. Whereas the Moral Majority affirmed political pluralism, agreeing that persons of any religion or no religion have equal rights to participate in government, Reconstruction just as openly rejects pluralism and cites "the moral obligation of Christians to recapture every institution for Jesus Christ." To Rushdoony, pluralism is a false ideology that infringes upon the total sovereignty of God: "The church of the twentieth century must be roused out of its polytheism and surrender. The crown rights of Christ the King must be proclaimed."[2] Unlike the Christian Right, Reconstruction is not simply or primarily a political movement; it is first and foremost an educational movement fearlessly proclaiming an ideology of total world transformation.

The Reconstructionist vision, which promises Christians that they will regain dominion over American society (and eventually the world) and direct it in accordance with biblical law, may seem hopelessly unrealistic; but it will not fade from view quickly. Its intellectual substance, internal coherence, and heavy dependence on Scripture have helped Reconstructionist philosophy win a hearing in many sectors of the Christian Right.

The idea of Christian dominion, though with less emphasis on biblical law, has been echoed within the charismatic movement, that segment of American Christianity identified by its free-spirited, demonstrative worship and its practice of spiritual gifts such as tongue speaking and prophecy. Several prominent charismatics, including presidential candidate Pat Robertson and Virginia Beach pastor John Gimenez (initiator of the gigantic "Washington for Jesus" rallies in 1980 and 1988), have called on conservative Christians to retake America's cultural leadership.

Perhaps the most distinctively "dominionist" figure on the contemporary charismatic scene is Earl Paulk, who packs some eight thousand energetic worshipers each Sunday into services at Chapel Hill Harvester Church in suburban Atlanta. Paulk's books and tapes, prominently endorsed by many important charismatic leaders, have spread across the country his message that charismatic Christians must apply their faith to the task of reshaping American society. Although Paulk is one of many currents of sociopolitical activism within the charismatic movement, many have come to perceive him, as they have Rushdoony, as the father of his own social movement within evangelical ranks. Paulk and his ideas are usually identified as "Kingdom Now" because of his central theme that Christians should strive to demonstrate the kingdom of God on earth now rather than wait for Christ's second coming.

While differing from Reconstruction in many ways, Kingdom Now shares the belief that Christians have a mandate to take dominion over every area of life. The similarities between the two movements are strong enough that many observers have grouped them together under the more encompassing rubric of "dominion theology."

THE CONTEMPORARY SIGNIFICANCE OF DOMINION THEOLOGY

This book seeks to examine carefully the various brands of "dominionist" thinkers in contemporary American evangelicalism.

There are several reasons why these Christians deserve careful attention and rigorous analysis.

First, Reconstruction and Kingdom Now are distinctive ideologies that have grown in popularity during the past decade and have the resources and potential to grow further. The dominionists stand out recognizably in contrast with society, with other evangelicals, and often with each other. If we describe them superficially or lump them all together, as others have done, we will fail to understand their goals and motivations. Their visible participation as evangelicals active in public life makes them worthy of serious, careful study, very little of which they have received thus far.

Second, the sudden rise of Pat Robertson, whose 1988 presidential candidacy surprised most of America by displaying extensive, well-organized grass-roots support, makes understanding the dominionist style of social thought still more important. Robertson would not call himself a "dominionist," and he has stated publicly that he is not a Reconstructionist,[3] but his ideas and visions have definite affinities with the worldviews of both Reconstruction and Kingdom Now. As we will see, Robertson's explicit emphasis on the need to restore Christians to leadership roles in American society mirrors what we will call a dominionist impulse in contemporary evangelicalism.[4]

But furthermore, beyond their identifiable size and their similarity with one national politician, Reconstruction and Kingdom Now carry a broader significance as a reflection of the position of evangelical Christians in American society. The debate over dominion theology illustrates evangelicals' uncertainty over how to answer the most important question they have faced in the fifteen years or so since their resurgence became undeniable: how they should interact with the increasingly secular society around them.

Sociologist James Hunter exposed the foundational importance of this question when he argued, in a 1987 book, that American evangelicalism, even while appearing to grow numerically, was crumbling on the inside. Hunter pointed out signs that evangelicals were losing their distinctives and tending to blend with the rest of American society in many areas of theology, morality, family, and politics. In the political realm, Hunter suggested, most evangelicals had cultivated an "ethic of civility," offering acceptance to virtually all religious and cultural groups and seeking only to be accepted themselves as equal partners in society.[5]

But can evangelicals extend this civility in a broadly pluralistic sociopolitical context while upholding their own religious tradition's exclusive, conversionist truth claims (i.e., that salvation can be obtained only through Jesus Christ)? Most evangelicals say yes; most dominionists vigorously dissent. In doing so, the dominionists have selected the path of resistance, openly confronting both the prevailing culture and the fellow evangelicals they accuse of having accommodated to that culture. Therein lies the core definition of a dominionist, a definition that unifies the many variations of dominion theology.

WHAT IS A DOMINIONIST?

The name "dominion theology" derives from Genesis 1:26–28, which presents the Bible's first statement about God's purpose for man:

> Then God said, "Let us make man in our image, after our likeness; and let them have dominion over the fish of the sea, and over the birds of the air, and over the cattle, and over all the earth, and over every creeping thing that creeps upon the earth." So God created man in his own image. . . . And God blessed them, and God said to them, "Be fruitful and multiply, and fill the earth and subdue it; and have dominion over the fish of the sea and over the birds of the air and over every living thing that moves upon the earth." (RSV)

But not everyone who refers to Genesis 1:26–28 as humanity's dominion mandate can be classified a dominionist—not in the sense in which we will be using the term, at least. After all, to move from the Genesis passage on human dominion over nature to a claim that contemporary Christians should be taking dominion in civil government is not an obvious step (though, as we will see, the dominionists' arguments from Scripture extend far beyond their use of this particular text). In fact, others have derived contrary political applications from the same text. For example, Paul Marshall, an evangelical for whose political philosophy Genesis 1 is also important, differs from most dominionists in affirming political pluralism and in considering non-Christians equally suited as Christians for the task of governing.[6] Others seeking the contemporary relevance of Genesis 1:26–28 have deduced primarily a call to protect the environment and the natural resources over which God has set humanity as stewards.

What, then, is a dominionist? In the context of American evangelical efforts to penetrate and transform public life, the distinguishing mark of a dominionist is a commitment to defining and carrying out an approach to building society that is *self-consciously defined as exclusively Christian*, and dependent specifically on the work of Christians, rather than based on a broader consensus. While the contemporary evangelical discussion is far too complex to be reduced to a rigid dichotomy, there is nevertheless a great divide separating, on the one hand, those who seek to work together with many other groups to improve society and culture from those who, in contrast, believe that meaningful improvement of society can come only on Christian (or at least predominantly Christian) terms. It is this division that separates Paul Marshall's claim that one cannot solve political problems "merely by encouraging large numbers of compassionate evangelical Christians to go into politics" from Pat Robertson's advocacy of just this solution.[7] All socially active evangelicals agree in theory that society should conform as much as possible to a biblical worldview, but dominionists go a step further by urging evangelicals to take on in essentially single-handed fashion—with little or no partnership with other groups—the task of infiltrating, radically transforming, and even taking over social institutions. Many evangelicals want to change the world, but only the dominionists insist that they must run it.

In calling the dominionist agenda one of "radical" transformation of society, I do not intend to imply the existence of any subversive or violent tendencies in dominion theology. Rather, I have selected this term to denote the dominionists' desire for sweeping, fundamental change, not just readjustments, in the social system and in its directors. They are radicals in the same sense as the "radical feminists," or the Black Power "radicals" who scorned the more moderate methods of Martin Luther King during the civil rights movement. Within evangelicalism, the dominionists are the "radicals" who, while by no means uninvolved in the current political system, are less likely to settle for moderate reforms or compromises and more likely to seek the establishment of alternative social structures. (This is why Reconstruction does not see itself as primarily a political movement: it aims not at partial political change but at building a new society.) This all-encompassing agenda puts them at odds with those more moderate evangelicals who work for social change yet still affirm the pluralistic nature of a society in which all ideas—be they Christian or anti-Christian, derived from or opposed to biblical law—have an equal right to be heard and to compete for public acceptance.

This great divide between two styles of Christian involvement is often easier to recognize than to define. Michael Cromartie, research associate at the Ethics and Public Policy Center in Washington and an astute observer of evangelicals in politics, has summed up the two positions in this way:

> Some evangelicals argue, and in fact insist, that the only way for society to be pleasing to God is for Christians to run things, especially evangelical Christians. They insist that we must work to get Christians elected, appoint Christian judges, and vote only for Christian candidates. Then we will see a righteous society.
> Others take a different approach. They argue, and I think correctly, that those who are in rebellion against God (the unregenerate) still have the native capacity to do good things. They can perform good deeds and they can be concerned about traditional family values; but the doing of these things *will not* bring them redemption and salvation.[8]

Cromartie's summary needs refinement, because most dominionists would not deny that unbelievers have a "native capacity to do good things." Nevertheless, the dominionists do tend to believe that only Christians (or, in an alternative formulation, only those persons committed to a Christian base for law) are qualified to be leaders.

And this tendency has frightened others—even fellow conservative Christians—who fear that by making such exclusive claims to social power the dominionists are setting the stage for serious conflict with those who do not want to live in a Christian society. Richard Neuhaus, a prominent commentator on religion and politics in contemporary America, thinks that if our society does not resolve the tension between those who desire a Christian social takeover of some sort and those who fear it, "We are headed for religious warfare in America. I think it is not alarmist to say that this society could unravel and we would have our own version of the wars of religion of the seventeenth century."[9]

POINTERS TO A SOCIAL TREND

Few are as alarmed as Neuhaus that dominion theology could ultimately threaten the stability of American democracy. But with American evangelicals and the secular state clashing repeatedly over questions of public morality, education, family rights, and religious freedom, it is not inconceivable that the United States could be entering a period of extended church-state conflict of a magnitude and depth normally associated with repressive atheistic regimes. If so, the dominionists are well positioned to enter the conflict with grim, unflinching determination. They boldly proclaim that Christianity (as they understand it) and the modern state are incompatible, that the clash between them is inevitable, and that the peacemaking evangelicals who believe they can avert the conflict through friendly negotiation with society are woefully misguided.

In addition to awakening conservative Christians to political matters, evangelical political activity since 1975 has generally exhibited two traits that tend to make the dominionist alternative more tempting. The first is *limited success*. The new breed of repoliticized evangelicals has been described as a group who has said, "We're mad as hell and we're not going to take it anymore,"[10] but in reentering the public square the evangelicals have discovered that the "it" they wish to eradicate will not give way easily. Their welcome by the party that holds the White House has translated into little implementation of their agenda. Prayer remains out of schools, moral relativism seems to receive greater legal protection than does traditional Christianity, and expanding, uncontrollable drug wars suggest a society in continuing moral decline despite the evangelicals' best efforts. Left wondering what more they can do, many evangelicals are confident of only two aspects of the answer:

(1) they must do more, and (2) neither the Republican party nor any other standard political approach can serve as the vehicle.

This combination of the perceived urgency of change plus dissatisfaction with available avenues of change has led some evangelicals to consider larger, more exclusively Christian visions of change—such as those offered by dominion theology. Reconstruction and Kingdom Now represent logical alternatives for conservative Christians who have repudiated otherworldly escapism but who remain caught between big dreams and limited opportunities.

Secondly, however, dominion theology also represents an alternative to the *internal ambiguities* present in those manifestations of Christian Right political activism that have tended, in practice, to become more "moral" than openly "Christian." The initial surge of the evangelical return to politics in the late 1970s saw groups like Christian Voice and the Moral Majority move beyond their Christian subculture to make common cause with non-Christians who shared their social goals. But while these organizations' membership remained overwhelmingly Christian, their rhetoric and their coalition building blurred religious divisions. Jerry Falwell declared that "Moral Majority, Inc., is not a religious organization" and affirmed partnership not only with conservative Catholics but also with Jews and even Mormons, while others in the Christian Right accepted aid from that allegedly cultic nemesis of true Christianity, Sun Myung Moon.[11] It is noteworthy that among the three prominent political strategists with whom the Christian Right worked hand in hand, Howard Phillips was Jewish, Paul Weyrich Catholic, and only Billings a fellow Protestant.

This effort to emphasize the connection between morality (*not* religion) and politics, while downplaying right religious belief as a prerequisite for either moral or political truth, diverged from the traditional fundamentalist view that the Gospel of personal salvation in Jesus Christ was the first and only priority. The Christian Right now asked believers to accept, for political purposes, an unequal yoke with unbelievers, welcoming non-Christians as equal colleagues and saving the spiritual message for another time. Its religious and political goals seemed incompatible; to seek either one hindered pursuit of the other. Thus Bob Jones II (of Bob Jones University in South Carolina), an unshakable militant fundamentalist whose insistence on the primacy of the religious goal never wavered, could in 1980 call his former ally Falwell "the most dangerous man in America."[12]

Dominion theology, in contrast to the Moral Majority's scheme of broad political cooperation, reduces this religion-versus-politics tension by proposing an explicitly Christian agenda in which only fellow believers in the binding nature of God's revealed law are invited to participate. Within the ideologies of Reconstruction and Kingdom Now, political action is no longer an interruption of the Great Commission to preach the Gospel, but an integral part of it, one of the multiple means Christians must use to "disciple the nations" (Mt 28:18–20).[13]

WHAT'S AHEAD

In chapters 2 and 4 we will examine in detail the ideology, history, key leaders, and impact of the Reconstructionists and the charismatic dominionists, respectively. Between these two chapters we will look at another branch of evangelical thought that, while not clearly dominionist by our definition, does have some affinity with Reconstruction and is better positioned to make a mark on American society: the stream of thought emanating from the College of Law and Government at Pat Robertson's Regent (formerly CBN) University in Virginia Beach, Virginia. This discussion will also clarify the often-misunderstood relation of Robertson himself to Reconstructionist thought. (Because the ideas are so complex, chapters 2 and 3 may seem difficult reading at times despite my attempt to explain concepts in nontheological language. A glossary of essential terms is provided in the back of the book.)

Having described Reconstruction and Kingdom Now as the two branches of the dominionist impulse, we will turn in chapter 5 to the relations between them. We will see not only the similiarities between the two groups, but also the differences that prevent them from combining into a single force. We will then look at two persons and one organization who have sought to expand the appeal of the essential dominionist agenda on which Reconstruction and Kingdom Now do agree. The individuals are Dennis Peacocke, a strategically minded activist respected by both dominionist branches, and Pat Robertson, whose presidential campaign embodied key aspects of the dominionist worldview. The organization is the Coalition on Revival, whose agenda for social change bears some resemblances to dominion theology.

After understanding the dominionists themselves, we must next relate them to their cultural context. Chapter 6 begins this task by examining dominion theology's relationship with evangelicalism in general. To describe this relationship we will use the symbols of "badge" and "reform." We will see that dominion theology qualifies as evangelical because it accepts, with only a few uncommon twists, the two "badges" required of those wishing to be considered evangelical: the need for personal commitment to Christ, and belief that the Bible is the infallible Word of God. But we will also see several "reforms" the dominionists have sought to encourage within evangelicalism and the opposition they have aroused as a result.

Though fought on different fronts, the various dominionists' efforts to "reform" evangelicalism reflect their greater dissatisfaction with contemporary American society and the place of evangelicals within it. Chapter 7 reinforces that theme by investigating the impact of dominion theology, especially its Reconstructionist subset, on American evangelical political activity.

Many of the conflicts between evangelicals over dominion theology arise from the great dilemma of applying the Bible to modern life: our world poses questions the biblical writers did not face and thus did not answer directly. Chapter 8 looks at several of the specific conflicts in Bible interpretation. I will argue that the conflicts result from the different evangelical groups' use of different and irreconcilable principles of interpretation. This conflict shows that other sources in addition to biblical exegesis are needed as a foundation for contemporary political philosophy.

Finally, chapter 9 offers general reflections on dominion theology and sets forth the basics of my own philosophy of Christian sociopolitical involvement.

WHY CHRISTIAN SCHOLARSHIP?

To combine careful, responsible study with God-honoring application to real life, as I seek to do in this book, is the unique task of genuine Christian scholarship. This concept deserves a brief explanation, as it is often poorly represented and inadequately appreciated even in Christian circles.

On one hand, much of modern Christian thought is not scholarship. Best-selling author Dave Hunt's book on dominion theology, *Whatever Happened to Heaven?*,[14] provides a good example. (I could almost as easily cite many of Hunt's ideological foes as illustrations.) Hunt shows a deep, sincere zeal for the Christian Gospel and, in each of his books, delivers many reliable insights regarding the primacy and meaning of that Gospel. But his analysis of dominion theology falls short in many respects. He apparently has not read Reconstructionist material in sufficient depth (Rushdoony is cited in just a single footnote) and shows no sign of having grasped its philosophical foundation. As a result many of his criticisms are inaccurate. He charges that dominionists place political goals before spiritual ones but does not discuss Reconstruction's insistence that politics must be integrated with evangelism; it is Hunt's own guidelines for limited political activity which, like those of the Moral Majority, struggle to combine the two goals. Nor does Hunt cite the passages where Reconstructionists themselves affirm that personal, spiritual salvation must always be primary. He criticizes dominion thinkers for concentrating on earthly rewards but fails to discuss contrary evidence, such as Reconstructionist affirmations that spiritual blessing, Christian duty, and heavenly reward are their main motivations or Earl Paulk's frequent insistence that a mature Christian must be ready to die for Christ.

Hunt makes no effort to find any common ground with the fellow Christians who take the brunt of his attack. He has, it seems, investigated dominion theology not to interact with it but to refute it. His work is Christian in that it proclaims the primacy of the Gospel of Christ; but even though it entailed substantial research, it is not scholarship.

On the other hand, there exists plenty of scholarship that is

not Christian. Many fields of higher education remain inhospitable to Christian thought, and the canons of "scholarly objectivity" force even Christian scholars to conceal their faith commitment and use only the analytical tools acceptable in their academic discipline when writing articles for professional journals or books for university publishers. (One looks in vain in my Ph.D. dissertation, written for a secular department of religious studies, for any discussion of "Christian scholarship" parallel to the present remarks.)

But what value does Christian scholarship have? Why should a Dave Hunt care about being a "Christian scholar" when he already has his own developed theological views and knows he doesn't like dominion theology? Why should a reader prefer "Christian scholarship" over books like Hunt's?

For several reasons. First is the matter of *truth*, which is essential to a Gospel that announces, "The truth will set you free" (Jn 8:32). Inadequate research leads to inaccurate conclusions and in turn to inaccurate applications of those ideas to Christian life.

Second, only Christian scholarship enables readers to think for themselves. Hunt admirably urges readers to evaluate everything he or anyone else says and make their own independent judgments; but by misrepresenting opinions other than his own he effectively prevents his readers from understanding the options and drawing intelligent conclusions.

Third, Christian scholarship best strengthens the body of Christ by minimizing disunity among believers. Christians, to be sure, must recognize that unity at all costs is a false unity that overlooks truth: some so-called Christian beliefs are dangerously wrong, and some so-called Christian teachers are actually wolves in sheep's clothing. Division is sometimes necessary to protect the truth from unacceptable compromise. But if Christians must divide, it should be over actual differences of opinion, not failure to listen to or understand each other.

Fourth, Christian scholarship is the path of humility. Christians who acknowledge their own shortcomings and imperfections are thus open to learning from all sources, though submitting everything to the preeminent authority of the Scriptures and the Spirit of God. They freely enter dialogue with persons of other persuasions, presenting their own criticisms with integrity while also offering their own views for critique and considering attentively the responses they receive. Such dialogue does not reduce participants to a least common denominator of agreement (as feared by those Christians who revile even the concept of dialogue with other religions), but identifies disagreements openly while improving mutual understanding and provoking sharper, more precise thinking on all sides.

I am hardly so brash as to claim that this book perfectly meets the ideal standard of Christian scholarship. I have, however, made every effort to be accurate, gentle, and fair. I have spoken personally with most of the key figures in this story, and many of them have reviewed the manuscript, checking for factual accuracy and providing constructive criticisms.

LOOK OUT, WORLD

What little attention dominionists have received from secular writers has more often than not been designed to convince the general public that dominionists are extremist, fanatical, and downright scary. Indeed, many Americans may wish to "look out" for dominionists because these evangelicals would like to reshape society in sweeping fashion. But at the same time, Americans have another reason to "look out," for our society is courting disaster in many of the areas the dominionists have sought to address.

I do not identify myself with any of the various dominionist agendas, and I especially fault their tendency toward overconfident, dogmatic, even brash certainty concerning the rightness of their proposals. But I believe that many signs—the crumbling of traditional sexual and family values; the spiraling of government expenditures; the declining sense of personal responsibility seen in both social welfare programs and our criminal-justice system; the seduction of our youths' minds and morals by drugs, crime, sex, and television—are warning this civilization that it is floundering without foundations. And a society without foundations, like a house built on sand, will soon collapse. The dominionists may be right less often than they think, but they force all of us to ask what our own foundations are. That is ample reason to listen to them.

• 2 •

God's Law for the Twenty-first Century
The Reconstructionist Worldview

Y ou can't beat something with nothing," says Gary North repeatedly.[1] And indeed he and his Reconstructionist colleagues practice what they preach. Critics have attacked Reconstruction on many points, but never for having nothing to say. In over a hundred books, its main proponents have sketched a brand-new society—though they might prefer to say they are reconstructing an old one, based substantially on the pattern God gave Moses four thousand years ago.

The Reconstructionists' intricate, complex program weaves together three levels of ideology. First comes their underlying claim that the dominion mandate of Genesis 1 remains in effect and that it is thereby "the moral obligation of Christians to recapture every institution for Jesus Christ."[2] Next come their three key theoretical foundations: biblical law, postmillennial eschatology, and presuppositional philosophy. These foundations, in turn, direct the whole Reconstructionist worldview: its theology, sociopolitical agenda, tactics, and optimistic hopes. In explaining the structure of Reconstructionist thought, I will address the three ideological levels in this order.

THE GOAL: DOMINION

"The creation mandate was precisely the requirement that man subdue the earth and exercise dominion over it. There is not one word of Scripture to indicate or imply that this mandate was ever revoked."[3] With this thesis Rousas J. Rushdoony, the father of Christian Reconstruction, summarizes the introduction to his magnum opus, the ponderous *Institutes of Biblical Law.* He thus also embodies the ultimate goal of the Reconstructionist quest: to establish godly rule throughout the earth before Christ returns.

This, Reconstructionists say, is the climax toward which human history leads. Jesus Christ reinforced this dominion mandate (also called the "cultural mandate" because it seeks to transform human culture) with his postresurrection command that his disciples should go into all the world and "disciple the nations" (Mt 28:18–20). Adam's fall made the task more difficult by bringing God's curse upon humanity and nature and forfeiting Eden's paradise in exchange for hard work; but God expected his people "to continue working out the implications of man's dominion assignment."[4]

Christ's atonement then restored God's people to their place of "legitimate dominion."[5] Christ expressed the centrality of this mandate in his prayer "Your will be done on earth as it is in heaven" (Mt 6:10), "a prayer for the worldwide dominion of God's Kingdom."[6]

Christians are to carry out their dominion assignment in every sphere of life, bringing the world "into captivity to Christ" and under the law of the kingdom of God. "Christ is to be acknowledged as Lord everywhere, in every sphere of human activity. . . . Our goal is world dominion under Christ's lordship, a 'world takeover' if you will." To achieve this goal the Christian church must preach a "full-scale gospel" that declares not only God's expectations for individuals, families, and churches but also his "holy standards of civil rule." "The message of the Bible is simple in principle: *comprehensive redemption.*"[7]

THEORETICAL FOUNDATIONS

The Game Plan: Biblical Law. One cannot take a neutral position regarding the law of God, Reconstructionists say: one endorses either God's law or human autonomy. If God's law is not honored, unchecked rule by either the state (totalitarianism) or by the individual (anarchy) will result. Reconstruction contends that it alone "takes seriously the law of God."[8]

What about all the other Christians who claim to follow God's ways? They fall short because they deny "the continuing validity of Old Testament law in exhaustive detail." While the New Testament does supersede the Old in some respects, it "does not teach any radical change in God's law regarding the standards of socio-political morality." On the contrary, "*one* basic covenant of grace," anticipated in the Old Testament and realized in the New, characterizes all of God's dealings with humanity. Since the God of Scripture does not change, his "grace and law remain the same in every age."[9]

Biblical law "constitutes a plan for dominion under God," a covenant or "peace treaty" God offers to humanity.[10] Just as Moses promised in Deuteronomy 8 and 28, those who obey the law will, in general, experience its blessings.[11] Over time, "under biblical law, wealth ultimately passes to those who are exercising dominion under God."[12]

Reconstructionists agree that applying the Old Testament to modern society is a complex task requiring considerable "exegetical and theological homework,"[13] but they maintain that Christ surpassed only the ceremonial sections of Old Testament law, leaving its moral and civil guidelines intact. God's method of administration has changed under the new covenant, but his moral character has not. One cannot distinguish civil from moral law within the Old Testament law codes, for they are intertwined; nor can one find any unique feature of Old Testament Israel that would invalidate the law's relevance to modern society.[14] The New Testament rejects the law as a means of justification but retains it as a standard for sanctification.[15]

Reconstructionists differ on the degree to which the central figures of the Protestant Reformation endorse their program. While Greg Bahnsen states "The Reformers recognized quite clearly that the law had not been abolished . . . [and] set down the law's proper functions,"[16] Rushdoony focuses more attention on areas where they erred. Rushdoony quotes Calvin's statement that a nation can be well governed while neglecting Mosaic law; he calls this idea "heretical nonsense" and gives Luther even less gentle treatment.[17]

In contrast, the Reconstructionists are unanimous in their admiration for the Puritans, whose adherence to biblical law-order marked "a resolute return to the fundamentals of Christendom."[18]

While the Reconstructionists affirm in principle the binding nature of Old Testament law, they are sometimes flexible in their interpretation. David Chilton says the Jubilee law, which required restoration of all land to its original owners every fifty years, fits under the ceremonial category, since "it was a symbolic prefiguring of the work of Jesus Christ," and is therefore no longer applicable. On the other hand, Chilton interprets the Old Testament's insistence on "just weights" in financial transactions quite literally, as a prohibition of paper money.[19]

Cause for Confidence: Postmillennialism. The concept of a Christianized America, let alone a Christianized world, may seem inconceivable—but not to Reconstructionists, because of their eschatology (i.e., theory of how the world will end). With Reformed thinkers of earlier times (such as American theologians Jonathan Edwards and B. B. Warfield), and in contrast to nearly all of contemporary evangelicalism, the Reconstructionists are postmillennialists; that is, they believe that Christ will not return to this earth until after (*post*) the restoration of the ideal society (the *Millennium*) foreseen in Revelation 20.

The Reconstructionists' "theonomic" (i.e., based on God's law) ethics is not logically dependent on postmillennialism, but this eschatology provides important psychological motivation by making the theonomic effort relevant to human society's expected future.[20] Also essential in reinforcing the Reconstructionists' optimism is the traditional Calvinist doctrine of predestination, which asserts God's absolute, direct sovereignty over all things and thus denies that any force can interfere with God's program of ultimate victory. Predestination is sometimes distinguished as a fourth theoretical foundation of Reconstruction.[21]

Gary North has gone so far as to sketch a scenario by which he believes worldwide regeneration might occur. He expects that the prosperity and blessings experienced by Christians who adopt Reconstructionist principles will cause societies to place these believers in positions of prominence. In this way whole nations will discover the blessings of living out a Christian social order, in turn provoking other nations to imitate the practice until "the kingdom of God becomes worldwide in scope."[22]

The Reconstructionists' defense of postmillennialism includes exegetical, theological, and logical arguments. Exegetically, they take literally the biblical passages that speak of world renovation and the uprooting of God's enemies. The "Magnificat" spoken by the Virgin Mary in Luke 1 promises that "history would see a mighty reversal of things because of her Son's birth. . . . All this would be in fulfilment of the prophecies to patriarchs and prophets."[23] Isaiah 65, one of those key prophecies, foresees that "new heavens and a new earth" (v. 17) will come to pass at a time when death and sin still exist and other normal human activities continue; therefore this event must precede Christ's return.[24] Premillennialists (who deny that this restoration can happen before the second coming of Christ) cite passages in the Gospels and the book of Revelation that speak of future calamity and of a world-deceiving antichrist figure, but Reconstructionists respond that these predictions were fulfilled in the destruction of Jerusalem in A.D. 70 and have nothing to do with the end of history.[25]

On a broader theological level, Reconstruction argues that salvation and sanctification have three stages: definitive (through Christ's completed work), progressive (a gradual process taking place throughout this age), and final (in the Last Judgment). These three stages, they claim, must apply to institutions as well as to individuals if God's redemption is to be comprehensive.[26] Similarly, the parables of gradual growth, recorded in Matthew 13, represent a slow but steady process of historical continuity by which Christians will transform the earth before the end of time.[27]

Along with these exegetical and theological arguments, Reconstructionists also draw on philosophical logic to support their postmillennialism. To believe that culture will decline until Christ returns would imply, North states, that Jesus is "a loser in history," a possibility clearly unacceptable to Christianity. Rushdoony similarly endorses postmillennialism on the basis that, in a world ruled by God, the church cannot travel a path "from victory to defeat."[28]

The Reconstructionists expect God to win, but they do not believe he is in any hurry. Chilton (perhaps in jest) concludes, based on a reference to a "thousand generations" in Deuteronomy 7:9, that history must have at least 36,600 years left (i.e., 1,000 generations times 40 years for each generation, minus the 3,400 years that have passed since Deuteronomy was written). Gary DeMar, temporarily shifting the emphasis from God's predestination to human responsibility, says Satan's temporary authority will last only "a few generations . . . unless Christians voluntarily give him more time by retreating into cultural irrelevance." North, even while expressing hope that major revival could begin in his lifetime, fully expects to die before the end and describes his work as "a long-term investment in intellectual capital."[29] He and other Reconstructionists believe that the current humanistic system is bound for crisis, and they hope to be ready to offer their program when, "on the far side of some disaster," other people start paying them more attention.[30]

Since they do not expect the restoration of a godly culture immediately, Reconstructionists appeal to Christian duty and eternal reward to motivate adherents of their social program. They admit they may not see in their lifetimes the cultural transformation toward which they toil (though they will experience *personal* blessing by obeying God's law), but "their obedience to Christ in history also produces fruit in eternity."[31] Dutiful and resolute, they usually avoid inflated promises of immediate success and instead inspire their followers with a simple motto of commitment: "Get to work."[32]

The Reconstructionists' patient tactics reflect their postmillennial confidence as well, as they refuse to take matters into their own hands by engaging in active rebellion. Reconstructionists do engage in "Christian resistance" tactics designed to defend their freedoms against government intrusion, such as defiance of state regulations imposed on Christian schools, but they reject violence as a means of social change.[33] Bahnsen assures his readers that theonomists "are not advocating the forcible 'imposition' of God's law on an unwilling society. . . . We do not advocate any modern 'holy war' or use of force to compel submission to God's standards."[34] James Jordan similarly rejects revolutionary tendencies and praises those Christians who "submitted and also worked for change."[35] North echoes that dual command: "Faithful Christians are not to preach perpetual contentment with moral evil . . . [nor] instant liberation through revolution and violence."[36]

The Reconstructionists may be awaiting humanism's demise with bated breath (in an especially hopeful vein, Rushdoony has said that "we are in the last days of humanistic statism"),[37] but they do not seek to hasten the crisis. Instead, they rely on conversion, education, and prayer, hoping that a majority of citizens will eventually be persuaded to let Reconstructionists "take over at the wheel" and guide society. Until this happens, "Christians must be content with only partial reconstruction, and only partial blessings from God."[38] In the meantime, weekly small-group meetings are recommended for educating believers and spreading the truth to friends.[39] It is appropriate to pray that God's enemies "either repent or be destroyed," and even to pronounce the curses of the imprecatory psalms against the wicked, but the act of vengeance must come from God, not by unlawful "sneak attacks."[40] The great reconstruction can come only by democratic means and must therefore be accompanied by massive spiritual revival.[41]

On the other hand, North occasionally hints that, once on top, Reconstructionists might not be as cooperative or pacific. Christians will change their style, he suggests, once they escape "civil impotence": "Remove [the ungodly leader's] power, and the battered Christian should either bust him in the chops or haul him before the magistrate, and possibly both." Once Reconstruction begins spreading its reformation across the globe, North says, societies that refuse to come under God's authority "are to be destroyed."[42] In contrast, David Chilton, while admitting he has also used such "takeover" language, now says it scares him.[43]

Especially in view of their minority role in the struggle against humanism, Reconstructionists are willing to enter coalitions with fellow Christians who do not share all their principles. Rushdoony, North, Chilton, and DeMar all have joined the steering committee of the Coalition on Revival, an organization that seeks to unify and mobilize evangelicals to transform American society. As master strategist North puts it, "We simply don't have the funds to be hyper-exclusive. We also don't have the bodies."[44]

Philosophical Certainty: Presuppositionalism. The third theoretical prong of Reconstruction is presuppositionalism, a "philosophy which argues that the conclusions men draw from all evidence [are] governed by their operating presuppositions concerning God, man, law, and nature."[45] In evangelical thought presuppositionalism is the main alternative to *evidentialism*, which seeks to prove the truth of Christianity to the unbeliever by appealing to "evidences" such as the historicity of Christ's resurrection or the internal consistency of Scripture.

Two biblical passages are most commonly cited as support for presuppositionalism:

> The heavens declare the glory of God;
>> the skies proclaim the work of his hands.
> Day after day they pour forth speech;
>> night after night they display knowledge. (Ps 19:1–2)

> The wrath of God is being revealed from heaven against all the godlessness and wickedness of men who suppress the truth by their wickedness, since what may be known about God is plain to them, because God has made it plain to them. For since the creation of the world God's invisible qualities—his eternal power and divine nature—have been clearly seen, being understood from what has been made, so that men are without excuse. (Ro 1:18–20)

From these passages presuppositionalists argue that the truth about God has already been placed in every heart and therefore does not require intellectual defense based on appeals to human reason. Each person either acknowledges "the self-attesting truth of an infallible Bible" or rejects it, as a matter of "humanist faith," in favor of contrary presuppositions. It is fruitless to present evidences of Christianity to the unbeliever, because he will misinterpret them unless his false presuppositions are exposed first.[46]

The main practical implication of the Reconstructionists' presuppositionalism is their rejection of any "natural law" based on human reason. "For the Bible, there is no law in nature, because nature is fallen and cannot be normative."[47] Thus the believer and unbeliever have essentially nothing in common, no shared convictions on which to build a law-order. Presuppositionalism uses this radical denial of common ground to declare all humanly devised social systems invalid; in place of these false systems, Reconstructionists assert the divinely revealed, binding nature of biblical law.

Reconstruction faults Christian political efforts like the Moral Majority for seeking to appeal to a "common morality" and for failing to challenge the humanistic myths of pluralism, religious neutrality, and practical compromise based on reason. North has no plans to settle for a morally favorable but still religiously neutral civil government: "Let the God-despisers get back into their closets and keep silent. They will be silent on that final day; they should begin practicing early."[48]

PRACTICAL APPLICATIONS

All three legs of this theoretical tripod provide essential support and motivation for Reconstruction's extensive, systematic efforts at conceiving a new society. Biblical law supplies guidelines, principles, and even specific legislative commands. Postmillennialism (bolstered by the Calvinist belief in God's predestinating sovereignty) delivers the confidence that the Reconstructionist undertaking, even if destined for short-term frustration, will receive God's blessing and will ultimately bear fruit. Presuppositionalism justifies the Reconstructionists' boldness in demanding radical social transformation while paying relatively little attention to the claims and counterarguments of those who do not share their religious presuppositions.

Armed with this theoretical ammunition, Reconstructionists have set forth a complete system of "biblical blueprints" for modern society. Their political philosophy begins by calling for multiple spheres of government, interrelated but with no one sphere occupying uncontested preeminence. ("Government" here carries the broad meaning of "jurisdictions or authorities to which we must all submit." Civil government is only one of these jurisdictions.)[49] In this system, free from domination by church, state, or any other single entity, resides true liberty. The approach has a definite, acknowledged affinity to James Madison's *Federalist Papers* and to his conception of a government whose multiple branches hold each other in check.[50]

Though Rushdoony sometimes speaks of numerous spheres, each with its own authority,[51] Reconstruction generally separates society into four domains, which must be reformed from the bottom up. First and most basic is individual self-government, without which no social improvement or stability is possible. "A people cannot legislate itself above its level" of personal faith and morality. Renewal must begin with individuals, not social structures, for no institution can survive by coercion alone.[52]

A second basic sphere is the family, which is "designed to extend God's visible sovereignty. . . . The family is the chief agency of dominion."[53] Families, not civil government, should be responsible for educating children and caring for the aging. Since family ties are stronger motivators than is a vague concern for humanity in general, a family-based welfare system is more effective than a state-operated bureaucracy. Since property belongs to the family, and to encourage responsible stewardship and investment, families should be able to pass their holdings from one generation to the next, without liability to estate taxes.[54] Especially in contemporary America, where the public school is the main source of indoctrination into secular, humanistic thinking, parent-financed Christian schools are an indispensable aspect of Christian reconstruction. The book of Deuteronomy requires education based on biblical law, so "anything other than a Biblically grounded schooling is thus an act of apostasy."[55] Since the dominion mandate calls us to "be fruitful and multiply," and since the Old Testament promises long life, high birth rates, and low miscarriage rates as blessings for the faithful, population expansion is desirable. Overpopulation is a false fear contrived by humanism; food shortages generally stem from the cultural values and lack of productivity ensuing from pagan religious faiths.[56]

A third governmental sphere is the church, which, contrary to common misunderstanding, does not control the state in Reconstructionist theory. The church teaches its members how to behave in every area of life; it assists the (reconstructed) state in interpreting biblical law; it governs itself, settling disputes internally so that Christians will not take their differences to secular courts; it protects doctrinal truth and excommunicates heretics (but does not execute them: only the state can inflict civil punishment, and then only for unlawful actions, not for false beliefs). The church is responsible for administering welfare for members whose needs their families cannot meet; this ministry to the poor is not enforced by the state but is an important obligation to God, who cares about the poor.[57]

Finally comes the state, whose function in Reconstructionist thought is carefully circumscribed (and, in comparison to the modern American bureaucracy, greatly reduced), limited essentially to dispensing civil justice and restraining evil. The state may levy a tax for its services, but it may not require more than one-tenth of its citizens' income, for it cannot set itself above God, who alone can require a tithe.[58]

The state should interfere in the economy only to prevent illegal activity or unlawful gain. Any other involvement is "state socialism," "covetousness by majority vote." State-run welfare, education, and social security, state-imposed racial integration, minimum wage laws, antidiscrimination laws, progressive taxation, foreign aid, tariffs, and trade unions are all anathema to Reconstruction.[59] Reconstructionists appeal to history as well as theology in documenting "the obvious, proven superiority of the free market" but believe that free-market capitalism by itself cannot work without the values and attitudes inculcated by Christianity.[60]

Just as the state must not infringe upon the other spheres of social authority, so state power itself must also be decentralized; this is the only way to avoid the twin dangers of totalitarianism and anarchy. Neither judges nor legislators should seek to build a perfect society through endless proliferation of laws; the perfect society is an impossible goal, an illusory product of the myth that humanity can be perfected by social engineering.[61] Rushdoony, who derives extensive social and political implications from early church creeds, calls the Council of Chalcedon in A.D. 451 the "foundation of Western liberty" because, in declaring that there was no confusion or intermixing between the divine and human natures of Christ, it made clear that salvation can come only from divinity and not from human sources. Chalcedon thereby, Rushdoony says, disallowed "messianic claims" by any humanly devised state. "Is God or the state man's savior? The answer of Chalcedon is emphatically for God and liberty."[62]

Although "God has not prescribed a particular administrative form for political government,"[63] some Reconstructionists are understandably attracted to the pattern this nation followed in its early years under the U.S. Constitution before power became increasingly consolidated at the federal level. Reconstructionists often point out that many of the state activities they regard as intrusions into family or church authority did not exist in early America. Thus they can speak of America as having a "Christian heritage," though the nation gradually lost its way as it abandoned biblical standards and "increasingly deified the state."[64]

Contrary to frequent misunderstanding, the Reconstructionist endorsement of the Constitution even includes the First Amendment, which prohibits federal establishment of religion. This endorsement, however, derives not from any tolerance of religious pluralism, but from their (historically accurate) view that the First Amendment barred religious establishment only at the federal level, not the state level.[65] Since different religions promote irreconcilable concepts of law, total religious toleration is "neither possible nor desirable."[66]

Reconstructionists rail against a criminal-justice system that, in their opinion, blames society for crime and pities criminals when it should be doing just the reverse. Humanism errs grievously by attributing crime to the criminal's environment, whereas the Bible holds the criminal personally responsible.[67] Reconstructionists do not flinch at Old Testament penal sanctions, which prescribe the death penalty for severe transgressions such as rape, witchcraft, and homosexual behavior. All punishments should reflect the principle that crime requires restitution, to God and to the victim. Those guilty of noncapital crimes should be sentenced to restitution, not prison, since "in Biblical law the goal is not punishment but restoration."[68]

God continues to judge nations as well as individuals, and those that fail to carry out God's judgments will ultimately feel God's wrath. "Societies have fallen in great numbers for their defiance of God, and they shall continue to fall as their violation of God's order continues." Since Christ's lordship covers all areas of life, civil government should be explicitly Christian. "There is a jurisdictional separation between church and State but not a religious separation. Jesus is King of *all* the nations."[69]

THE ROOTS OF RECONSTRUCTION

Since Reconstruction strikes many observers as a quixotic attempt to rebuild a "Christian America" that never was, it may be surprising that Reconstructionist philosophy's roots are more Dutch than American. The social theory Gary North tirelessly popularizes today is a third-generation descendant from that of Christian statesman Abraham Kuyper, prime minister of the Netherlands from 1901 to 1905.[70]

Kuyper (1837–1920), after a riveting conversion from tame Protestant liberalism to staunch Calvinism, embarked with boundless energy on the task of relating that Calvinism to every sphere of life. Kuyper wrote voluminously (including over twenty thousand newspaper articles), edited two political newspapers for half a century, founded the Free University of Amsterdam (where he also taught theology), and served as leader of his political party for forty years. All this effort derived from his conviction that true Calvinism should transform all of culture.

As the theoretical base for his critique of competing worldviews, Kuyper argued that, since one's response to God determines how one lives, *all* human behavior is ultimately religious; therefore, wrong opinions can be traced back to false religious presuppositions, while correct presuppositions (if logically and accurately applied) will guide the believer toward proper thinking about all of life. Buttressed by this presuppositional philosophy, Kuyper advocated the formation of Calvinistic schools, newspapers, political organizations, even hospitals. Though his belief in the principle of common grace permitted carefully considered political cooperation with other groups, Kuyper insisted heavily on the "antithesis" between Christian and non-Christian thought. Warning that the expansion of a centralized state would endanger personal liberty, he coined the phrase "sphere sovereignty" to describe his own theory, which circumscribes the regions of state authority (though not as strictly as his Reconstructionist descendants would do).[71]

While his star was rising in Holland, Kuyper visited America, delivering a series of lectures at Princeton Seminary—then the primary bastion of Calvinist theology in America—in 1898. But his ideas did not take hold right away in this country, largely because they clashed with the philosophy then predominant in American intellectual life: common-sense philosophy.

Contrary to Kuyper, common-sense philosophy posited a large realm of common ground shared by all human minds. Its main developer, eighteenth-century Scottish philosopher Thomas Reid, had applied to epistemology (the study of how we think) the empirical (i.e., based on observable facts) approach Bacon and Newton had used in natural science. Reid asserted the basic reliability of human sense perceptions, both physical and moral. Rejecting the skepticism of the British philosopher David Hume, Reid said common sense tells us that our intuitive judgments generally agree, and he argued that this agreement could not be possible without an underlying unity in human perception and thought.[72]

The unhesitant trust with which common-sense philosophy accepted the reliability of human perception fit well with the optimism that pervaded American society during the postrevolutionary period. By the early 1800s common sense had become the prevailing philosophy in America. Later in the nineteenth century, the two towering theological giants of Princeton Seminary, Charles Hodge and B. B. Warfield, would invoke common-sense presuppositions in presenting an evidence-based defense of the Christian faith that, they believed, would convince anyone who examined the facts squarely of the truth of Christianity. In other words, one could reach the right conclusions by honest inquiry; it was not necessary to start with the right religious presuppositions. Warfield, in whom the Princeton method reached its culmination and who can be considered the father of modern American evangelical apologetics (i.e., defense of the faith), insisted that all persons attain knowledge in fundamentally the same way and that, while apologetics alone could not make anyone a Christian, "Christianity has been placed in the world to reason its way to the dominion of this world."[73]

Kuyper, then, flew in the face of his hosts' tradition when he opened his 1898 Princeton lectures by stating that, in Christianity's attempt to protect the foundations of Western culture against the assaults of modernism, "apologetics have advanced us not one single step."[74] United with Kuyper in Christian faith yet separated by a wide philosophical gulf, Warfield and the Princetonians listened cordially but quizzically. Presuppositionalist philosophy would not take hold within American Protestant thought until three decades later—delivered, ironically, by a Dutch immigrant, Cornelius Van Til.

Van Til came to the United States as a child but read the work of Kuyper and his fellow Dutchman Herman Bavinck while studying at Calvin College and Seminary in Grand Rapids, the mecca of Dutch Reformed thought in America. A brilliant, philosophically minded scholar, Van Til completed his seminary training with high honors at prestigious Princeton and returned there as professor of apologetics in 1928.[75] But he never shifted his philosophical allegiance from Kuyper to Warfield.

Quite possibly the religious context in which Van Til lived reinforced his sense that evangelical apologetics required a new direction. Evangelical theology no longer dominated American thought, and the foundations of conservative theology were crumbling, especially within the northern Presbyterian Church, the denomination to which Princeton was related. Hodge and Warfield's old confidence in their ability to demonstrate the Bible's reliability by rational argument seemed less tenable when more persons, even within the church, were reasoning their way to other conclusions.[76]

The old Princeton theology's reign collapsed in 1929 when the Presbyterian church's General Assembly, by reorganizing the Princeton Seminary board of trustees, stymied conservatives' efforts to halt liberalizing trends. Van Til and three other Princeton professors immediately resigned and subsequently joined the faculty at Westminster Seminary, hastily founded in Philadelphia to maintain the faith the evangelicals felt Princeton had discarded. Van Til would teach there for nearly half a century.[77]

Van Til finely honed presuppositionalism into a rigorous philosophical system, relying on the absolute authority of Scripture and the nearly absolute antithesis between the thinking of believers and unbelievers. Since God, Van Til argued with classic Calvinist logic, fully and sovereignly determines all history and defines all truth, humans can find truth not by thinking originally but only *analogically*—that is, by discovering and following what God has already thought. Christianity is the only belief system that makes sense of the world; all other systems, by introducing an element of human autonomy, negate the Christian principle that God has defined all things and imply instead that the universe is irrational, pervaded by chance. No mediating position is possible; "a little autonomy involves absolute autonomy."[78]

Van Til relentlessly insisted that other Christian philosophies (including common-sense philosophy) falsely grant epistemological autonomy to unbelievers by encouraging them to evaluate the evidence for Christianity by their own reason. "We cannot subject the authoritative pronouncements of Scripture about reality to the scrutiny of reason," Van Til declared, "because it is reason itself that learns of its proper function from Scripture." The true Reformed apologetic, "consistently Christian in its starting point and methodology," denies that the believer "can, at any point, approach the non-believer on a neutral basis." The only common ground believer and unbeliever share is the knowledge of God, a knowledge that sinful humans seek to suppress. Relying heavily on Romans 1, Van Til insisted that "deep down in his mind every man knows that he is the creature of God and responsible to God." The Christian should grasp non-Christian methods of reasoning well enough to demonstrate their inevitable internal inconsistencies; once this is done, one can present the Reformed methodology, which unabashedly "presupposes the truth of Christian theism."[79]

In other words, one does not submit proofs for Christianity; rather, one demolishes all alternative presuppositions and then insists that Christianity must be presupposed before one can think straight. (Once one has the right presuppositions, every fact in the universe fits logically and thus provides further evidence of the truth of Christianity.) Against objections that this method blindly assumes the divine nature of Christianity rather than demonstrating it, Van Til answered that it is impossible *not* to start from *some* assumption. To assume that one can attain truth by starting from a so-called neutral standpoint, he argued, is itself a nonneutral presupposition that presumes the Christian methodology to be false.[80]

Following Kuyper's doctrine of the strict antithesis between believer and unbeliever,[81] Van Til declared that "the natural man . . . must be hostile in principle at every point to the Christian philosophy of life." Unbelievers can participate in scientific progress, but only to the extent that they violate their own irrationalist philosophy by presuming that the universe is unified and predictable.[82]

Both Van Til's philosophy and his practical applications laid essential groundwork for Reconstruction. Although Van Til did not advocate postmillennialism or theonomy, he carried on Kuyper's commitment to consistently Christian thought that encompasses all of life; he affirmed the dominion mandate; he deemed Christian schools a necessity, since knowledge of God is basic to all knowledge; and he placed the absolute truth of Scripture beyond the reach of any questions human reason might raise.[83] It seems almost inevitable, in retrospect, that a disciple of Van Til should apply his theory to the field of law, insisting that there too all pretensions of human autonomy must give way to God's absolute, self-attesting truth as revealed in Scripture.

RUSHDOONY AND HIS FOLLOWERS

The transformation of presuppositionalist social theory into consistently theonomic ethics, as well as the birth of the Reconstructionist movement itself, was the work of Rousas John Rushdoony. The son of Armenian immigrants (his father had been an Armenian Protestant pastor in his homeland), Rushdoony was impacted by the Armenian church's strong reverence for the Old Testament.[84] He received ordination from the Presbyterian church and served as a missionary to Native Americans in Nevada; there his struggle to give his converts a solid Christian foundation convinced him that Christian evangelism, in order to be successful, would need to go beyond preaching a conversion experience and create a Christian culture as an alternative to a declining Western civilization.[85]

While a pastor in California, Rushdoony discovered Van Til's philosophy, which he lavishly praised in his first book (published in 1959). Rushdoony left pastoral work three years later to join a private foundation, under whose auspices his prodigious writing and speaking career accelerated. In 1966 he formed Chalcedon, Inc. (subsequently the Chalcedon Foundation) to support and promote the program of research, teaching, writing, and cultural renewal he had by then begun to call Christian Reconstruction.[86]

Gary North, who had met Rushdoony in 1962, joined him at Chalcedon. North initially specialized in conservative economics, completing his doctorate in economic history in 1972. He married Rushdoony's daughter the same year. North got a taste of politics in 1976 when he served on the Washington staff of Ron Paul, a Texas congressman who favored extremely limited government. As he watched Paul gain minimal support in Congress for his attempts to reduce the size of government, North concluded that "those who believe in political salvation at a national level are certain to be disappointed."[87]

Rushdoony and North became estranged in 1981, supposedly after a dispute over an article North wished to publish in Rushdoony's *Chalcedon Report*.[88] The main result of their separation was an increase in Reconstructionist output, as North moved his Institute for Christian Economics (ICE) to Tyler, Texas, and expanded his productivity. He also broadened his name recognition in evangelical circles by debating Ron Sider, author of the influential *Rich Christians in an Age of Hunger*. North showed up at the debate with copies of the diatribe against Sider he had just published, David Chilton's satirically titled *Productive Christians in an Age of Guilt-Manipulators*.[89]

Driven by an intense sense of mission into which they have unwaveringly channeled their intellectual and material resources, Rushdoony and North have created a social movement essentially by themselves. It could be argued without much exaggeration that these two men—one imposing intellectual and one ingenious popularizer—are a sufficient explanation of why Reconstruction is now a widely recognized option in evangelical social theory. North has contributed not just his life and his intellect but a large amount of hard cash to the cause: as a successful and respected economic forecaster, he has had substantial capital available to invest in his ideological commitments. His Institute for Christian Economics paid David Chilton to write *Productive Christians* and has subsidized wide distribution of its books, often at extremely low cost.

One can trace Reconstruction's emergence through the series of critiques it provoked. Through the 1970s Reconstruction could stimulate a response only within the rather insulated circles of conservative Presbyterian and Reformed thought, and even then only reluctantly.[90] In 1981 Francis Schaeffer, a crucial but less overtly radical instigator of evangelical reentry into public life, felt a brief dismissal of "theocracy" was adequate.[91] In early 1987 veteran evangelical spokesman Carl Henry unequivocally affirmed, "To be sure, not all Old Testament ethics is meant for today. The Hebrew theocracy is gone, along with the laws that were reserved for it."[92] But by then a different spirit was emerging, as Reconstructionists were making too much noise to be ignored as simply an inadmissible option. *Christianity Today*, evangelicalism's flagship magazine, devoted a cover story to the topic in February 1987, and other critical responses soon followed.[93] By 1989 Henry, while no more sympathetic to Reconstruction, felt compelled to acknowledge and briefly refute, rather than simply dismiss, their position. The topic had attracted so much attention that Westminster Seminary's professors could find a market for their papers on theonomy at Zondervan, a major evangelical publisher.[94]

The third major Reconstructionist writer, Greg Bahnsen, learned from both Rushdoony, whom he met while still a teenager, and Van Til at Westminster Seminary, where he became the first student to complete both the M.Div. and Th.M. degrees within three years. According to North, Van Til hoped Bahnsen would succeed him in his chair at Westminster. Now a pastor in California, Bahnsen subsequently earned a Ph.D. in epistemology and has authored the movement's most analytically rigorous defenses of theonomy.[95]

Bahnsen's theonomic convictions apparently contributed to his dismissal from Reformed Seminary in Jackson, Mississippi—another bastion of conservative Presbyterian scholarship, where he taught from 1976 to 1978—but not before they made a major impact on several of his students. Four of them have become important figures in the movement: Kenneth Gentry, a leading defender of postmillennialism and trenchant critic of the dispensational premillennialism in which he was first trained; David Chilton, later North's associate; James Jordan, who moved to Texas with North and has since specialized in applying Reconstructionist thought to liturgy and ecclesiology, though moving away from a strictly theonomic position; and Gary DeMar, who writes prolifically for an Atlanta-based educational ministry called American Vision. Author of a three-volume series on *God and Government* and a prominent player in the Reconstructionists' eager refutations of popular critic Dave Hunt, DeMar has also gained respect among evangelicals for his favorably received work on other issues of more general interest, such as *Surviving College Successfully.*[96]

Two other figures worthy of mention are Joe Morecraft, a theonomist pastor in suburban Atlanta and unsuccessful Republican candidate for Congress in 1984, and George Grant, who seeks to show both the workability of Reconstructionist economics and the compassionate side of his movement by developing church-based programs to combat poverty. Grant, who directs community ministries at D. James Kennedy's Coral Ridge Presbyterian Church in southern Florida, has like Jordan distanced himself from a hard-line commitment to theonomy.[97]

INTERNAL DIVERSITY

Up to this point, the description might imply that Christian Reconstruction is a united movement whose distinct ideas are unanimously held by a close-knit group of highly intellectual evangelicals. But some of its major figures have denied that there is a Reconstructionist movement at all or have argued that it has splintered since 1985 and is now profoundly fragmented.[98] Nevertheless, the internal disagreements that have left even insiders uncertain as to how to define a Reconstructionist have also helped to enhance the movement's influence.

The trivial nature of the official explanation given for the best-known squabble between Reconstructionists—the feud between Rushdoony and his son-in-law North—has appeared to critics as a compelling symbol of Reconstruction's rigid dogmatism and stubborn inflexibility. It should also have led them to probe more deeply for larger differences commensurate with the severity of the rift. James Jordan has pointed out a far more substantial cause of the movement's division into Vallecito, California (Rushdoony), and Tyler, Texas (North), factions: Rushdoony sees the family but North sees the church as the most important social institution. This difference has considerable implications; for example, North and Tyler see the church as a microcosm of society and emphasize strict church discipline, while Rushdoony minimizes the importance of the institutional church. Jordan calls these "two radically and comprehensively different" approaches to biblical authority and social transformation and sees this divergence as the source of the radical split within Reconstruction, which became unmistakable by 1985.[99]

But there are other differences as well. While most Reconstructionist leaders are postmillennial, Joe Kickasola, professor of public policy at Regent University and an important disciple of Bahnsen, declines to take a firm eschatological position, saying the biblical data are insufficient. Others, such as Jordan and Grant, have distanced themselves from theonomy. Bahnsen, the rigorous exegete, takes issue with Jordan's interpretive methods.[100] Practical applications divide the group further; for example, Reconstructionists have disagreed on whether the confrontational antiabortion tactics of Operation Rescue represent a justifiable form of civil disobedience.[101]

In the short run, however—and perhaps the long run too—these differences offer the same benefit to Reconstruction's key ideas as does the vigorous denial that Reconstruction is a "movement": both developments free those ideas from the stigma often attached to the word *Reconstructionist*. Since theonomy, postmillennialism, and presuppositionalism are all minority opinions within American evangelicalism, few evangelicals have become hard-core disciples of Reconstructionist ideology. But the loosening of these ideas from their Reconstructionist label and the appearance of moderated "semi-Reconstructionist" or "soft-core" versions enable each concept to be considered on its own merits and to become a more respectable option than if it remained inextricably tied to a movement many evangelicals have branded extremist.

As a result, all these ideas are now independently infiltrating evangelicalism, attracting many who would vigorously disavow the label "Reconstructionist." And all of them, whether separately or together, further the Reconstructionists' ultimate goal: to popularize and implement a distinctly Christian vision of building society. Any one of the three main concepts, even without the other two, tends logically toward the dominionist position: theonomy encourages radical, Bible-based reforms in law and government; postmillennialism encourages Christians to aim for total victory in society; and presuppositionalism denies common ground with unbelievers. It is through this trickle-down form of influence—not because of any formal organization, membership, or specifically defined platform—that Reconstruction is an important social movement, the impact of whose ideas extends far beyond the relative handful of American evangelicals who would identify themselves as Reconstructionists.[102]

EVALUATION OF THEONOMY

Any critique of Reconstructionist social theory must center on the case for theonomy, presented most formidably by Greg Bahnsen in *Theonomy in Christian Ethics*. Bahnsen is to be commended for his complete, measured, exhaustively argued presentation, so firmly rooted in Scripture that no policymaker who claims to be a Christian can simply ignore it.

Space limitations prohibit extensive exposition of Bahnsen's argument for theonomy. However, his main line of argument can be summarized as follows:

1. God communicated his perfect law to Israel in the Old Testament.
2. The Old Testament shows that God held Gentile nations to the same ethical and moral standards as Israel.
3. Christ canceled the ceremonial portions of the law but confirmed the moral law, including its civil precepts.
4. Therefore the law given by God in the Old Testament remains in force and binding upon all nations today.

A superb logician, Bahnsen presents his case sensitively and without overstatement. He acknowledges that "theonomists certainly do not 'have all the answers!' " (p. xx), since disagreements will persist in exegesis, reasoning, and application and over precisely which laws should be considered ceremonial.

While I share Bahnsen's reverence for God's law, I believe his theonomic ethic has two flaws that seriously affect its application to modern cultures. First, his division between moral and ceremonial law puts far too much material in the former category, inadequately considering the unique status of Old Testament Israel as God's exclusively chosen nation.[103] As part of his attempt to show that Israel's civil order was not unique, Bahnsen notes that it was not a pure theocracy, since church and state were separate entities. However, this formal separation does not alter the fact that Mosaic law authorized civil punishment for religious offenses, such as apostasy, sorcery, and false prophecy (see, e.g., Lev 20:1–5; Dt 13:1–18; 17:2–7). Still other Old Testament capital sentences, including those for blasphemy (Lev 24:14–16) and Sabbath-breaking (Nu 15:32–36), appear more related to the protection of Israel's spiritual purity than its civil order.

Under the new covenant, God's people are a nation only in a spiritual (1Pe 2:9), not a governmental, sense; thus no nation has the same mandate to punish religious offenses that Israel had. Further, once it is established that Old Testament law was designed to maintain religious as well as civic righteousness, the equity of all other punishments in non-Israelite cultures must be reconsidered. Murder, as a heinous and violent crime, may still merit capital punishment, but the sentence for deviant sexual behavior (if it be considered a civil crime at all) should almost certainly be softened. Bahnsen appears to overlook the implications of this Old Testament–New Testament discontinuity when he asserts that "when God says homosexuality (for instance) warrants capital punishment, then that is what social justice demands" (p. 441).

The second flaw is Bahnsen's claim that God held Gentile nations to the same standard as Israel, even in Old Testament times. The Old Testament passages Bahnsen cites (in chapter 18) show that all rulers are accountable to God, that sin is a disgrace to any people, and that God brought judgment on Gentile kings and nations guilty of idolatry or sexual aberrations; but these are sins that any person could be expected to recognize *by nature*. Nowhere are non-Israelites judged by criteria approaching the exactitude of the law given to Israel. Bahnsen's claim that one should expect Gentiles to be under the same law because God is no respecter of persons (p. 340, citing Ro 2:11–12) also fails; Bahnsen has already granted that God held some persons responsible for the ceremonial law and not others, so there is no reason why God could not do the same with regard to civil law while still acting equitably.

Bahnsen correctly observes that the New Testament essentially reaffirms the Old Testament conception of the civil magistrate (p. 398); but, as we have just seen, this Old Testament conception is not what Bahnsen believes it to be. He attempts to find New Testament confirmation of his view in Mark 7:6–13, but again his logic fails. In this passage Jesus chides the Pharisees for claiming to obey the law while they ignore the provision stipulating that anyone who cursed his parents should be killed. Bahnsen says the continuing validity of this law is "simply assumed" by Jesus (p. 256). But Jesus cited the law to prove to the Pharisees that they were not living up to their own professed standards, not to reconfirm the provision for New Testament times. The logic is similar to that of the parable of the minas, in which the master's statement to the wicked servant, "You knew . . . that I am a hard man" (Lk 19:22), is a reference to the servant's own opinion and does not mean that the master (who signifies God) is actually unjust.

Unquestionably Old Testament law embodies many timeless principles from which every society can benefit. But the unique interrelation of civil and religious spheres present in Israel was *not* intended for replication by Gentile nations. For this reason, a Christian approach to law must sensitively reexamine, not simply co-opt, Old Testament law. Mosaic law lacks the differentiation between civil and religious dictates that must be developed before one can appropriately transfer these prescriptions to a New Testament context. This perspective on law informs the further points of critique that follow.

EVALUATION OF RECONSTRUCTIONIST THOUGHT

Reconstruction's leading writers have self-consciously adopted the role of *educational*, not political, activists, preferring for the most part to tantalize their readers with ideal social theory rather than to focus on what can be immediately achieved in the political sphere. This tendency is especially visible in those Reconstructionists who, since they expect Western humanism to collapse and open the door for widespread adoption of totally new paradigms, believe that trying to influence the current system step by step is an unwise tactic. As a result, Reconstruction functions more effectively as a stimulating set of theoretical principles than as a guide to action in the real world. In sticking so closely to its blueprints for an ideal society, Reconstruction often seems to overlook the real-life problems, resulting from human selfishness and sin, that those ideal structures would not ameliorate.

Reconstruction's distaste for unions is one example. Nearly everyone would agree that in a world characterized by nonadversarial relationships and generous employers, labor unions would be unnecessary. In an imperfect society, however, laws prohibiting industrial monopolies and guaranteeing labor's right to organize are necessary provisions that reduce eminent injustice.

Similarly, it is quite possible that responsible Christian parents could often provide more effective education, with a clearer moral base, than America's public schools currently offer. But in a society marred by rampant family disintegration, in which many parents are neither Christian nor responsible, dismantling the public schools might only intensify the chaos. To advocate this step, without acknowledging that it could work only if preceded by a long period of healthy social change, may cause more harm than good.[104]

This does not mean that the Reconstructionist critique of the expansion of state power carries no plausibility. Ameliorative measures such as state-financed welfare not only limit individual liberty (through increased taxation) but also begin the gradual process toward the idolatrous presumption that the state can best solve all our social problems. I can testify to the predominance of this error in contemporary America, for in my college years I never even heard the argument presented that reducing the size of federal welfare and social-service programs could actually be an act of compassion. (Admittedly, I majored in humanities, not economics.) Nevertheless, in rigidly limiting the state's role Reconstruction would in many cases replace new injustices with a return to the old ones. Unless human nature has improved, expelling the state from many of its current regulatory functions would likely restore the evils that occasioned those regulations in the first place—and perhaps in even worse form, since American public morality has, if anything, declined in the past century as the influence of Christianity has dwindled.

Here, as in general, I find fault not with Reconstruction's reverence for biblical law but with how it proposes to apply that law to a complex society far different from Old Testament Israel.[105] Others have noted that modern society is far more complex, with many different sectors of activity, than the world of the Old Testament (agrarian Israel had no need for zoning laws, for instance) and faces new problems that only the state can address (e.g., curbing pollution to protect our water supplies or the ozone layer).[106]

Of course, a Christian would be hard pressed to justify government involvement in these areas if the Bible explicitly forbade them. But while the Bible warns (e.g., in 1Sa 8) against overdependence on the state, it nowhere limits the scope of state involvement as explicitly as Reconstruction does. In fact, in one case the Bible approved a major state-run social program: Joseph's nationalization of Egypt's food production so as to store up reserves before a famine (Ge 41). This was an extreme case because the danger of starvation was severe, but it proves that God is not rigidly constrained within Reconstruction's principles of limited government.

Reading biblical law with sensitivity to changed historical and theological circumstances means combining biblical principles with a dependence on the Spirit who guides us into all truth. Gary North may call this flexibility "fighting something with nothing," but actually I believe the problem is that North and other Reconstructionists have an overly rigid philosophy of law. One example of this rigidity appears in an article on tithing in which James Jordan argues that the ten-percent minimum giving established in the Old Testament remains binding today. Jordan says that to teach people simply to give the amount God moves them to give "places men in bondage, for they never know when they have given enough."[107] The possibility that one can receive assurance of moral righteousness through the sense of a clear conscience, rather than through legal observance, seems not even to have occurred to him. (Let me hasten to add my own belief that most American Christians, as residents of the world's richest nation, should probably be giving *more* than ten percent, not less.)

Jordan's rigidity exemplifies the Reconstructionists' implicit assumption that without a fixed, written law one cannot know when one has done right. Rushdoony unintentionally betrays the weakness of this position when, in one passage in his *Institutes*, he admits the existence of another option: "If the law is denied as the means of sanctification, then, logically, the only alternative [for believers] is Pentecostalism, with its antinomian and unbiblical doctrine of the Spirit."[108] Rushdoony may find them unbiblical, but Pentecostals insist just as loudly as Reconstructionists that they seek holiness God's way. The main difference is that Pentecostals, without denying the validity of the Old Testament, believe Christians should look mainly to the New Testament and to the direction of the Holy Spirit for guidance in life. (This is one reason why Reconstructionists and charismatic or Pentecostal Christians often have difficulty in relating to each other even when they share the goal of Christian social dominion.) Ironically, Rushdoony himself exhibits the interpretive flexibility I am describing—though in this case I differ from his conclusions—in expanding the limits of permissible divorce beyond the limits set forth in either the Old or New Testament.[109]

WHAT MAKES A CHRISTIAN SOCIETY?

When Reconstructionists give historical examples for their confidence in Christianity's appointed task of transforming civilization, one begins to wonder just what transformations they envision. Chilton praises the attitude of the New World's first explorers, who "came *expecting* that the New World would be Christianized. They were certain of victory, and assumed that any obstacles they met had been placed there for the express purpose of being overcome."[110] The explorers did win the land, but they never won the hearts of their human "obstacles," the Native Americans. Similarly, few will challenge Chilton's claim that "the whole rise of Western Civilization" is intimately related to the impact of Christianity;[111] but he does not address the irony that many of the changes Christianity wrought have subsequently tended to make modern culture more secular rather than more Christian.[112] Christianity's belief in a God-ordered world, for example, inspired modern science and medicine, but the success of these pursuits has led much of society away from conscious dependence on a supernatural being. Having received with gratitude the impetus toward progress Christianity has provided, the modern West now believes it can get along fine on its own.

Those Reconstructionists who advocate a religious test for holders of public office also go astray. When we need our kitchen sink repaired we do not ask whether the plumber is a Christian, though we do look for both professional skill and ethical integrity. We should do the same with our lawmakers. We should not discourage them from reading the Bible, but we should judge them primarily on their principles and their abilities, not their religious commitment. Christian politicians are not always the most principled or the most competent, any more than Christians are always the best plumbers.

THE AMISH EXAMPLE

One thing Reconstruction has done very well is to put politics in its place. As Gary North puts it: "Politics fourth!" Christians should recognize that individual, family, and church renewal are more integral to cultural transformation than is political action.[113] It might be interesting to compare Reconstruction's vision with the work of a Christian group that is successfully building a harmonious, numerically increasing community by going to the opposite extreme and totally divorcing itself from culture and politics: the Amish.[114]

Though totally unconcerned with exercising civil leadership, the Amish are successfully doing much of what Reconstructionists propose. Their birth rate of over six children per family, combined with skillful socialization that keeps eighty percent of their youth within the Amish fold, enables them to grow in numbers as fast as the Israelites under Pharaoh. Their clear, all-encompassing expectations and tight discipline avoid divided allegiances and build bulwarks against competing worldviews. They have no need for state welfare programs because they consistently care for each other, first within the family (with three generations often living side by side) and then, if necessary, through mutual-aid services (such as the proverbial Amish barn raisings) at the church level. They have remained as independent as possible not only socially and culturally but politically too. They have prospered financially even while paying millions of dollars in taxes for schools they do not use and a social security system in which they do not participate.[115]

Reconstructionists will not increase their numbers as quickly as the Amish through these means, however, as they would have trouble convincing women whose preferences have been shaped by general society to follow the Amish example of bearing six children. The comparison between the two groups suggests that a religious group wishing to achieve a truly reconstructed society, as opposed to just bits and pieces of legislative change, must intentionally separate itself so as to form and gradually expand a distinct society of its own. Substantial social reconstruction is probably unattainable among persons whose values and lifestyles have been formed not in the seclusion of a sectarian colony but in the midst of American society with its unprecedented opportunities for freedom, leisure, and self-fulfillment.

Of course, Christians could not assume that withdrawing into Amish-type enclaves would make it easier for them to pass Christian values on to future generations. As Gary DeMar points out, the Amish are free to live as they do only because other Christians remain in the civil sphere to help protect freedom of religion.[116] Nevertheless, Reconstruction cannot commend itself as an alternative Christian ideology worthy of serious consideration unless it can show that its ideas foster harmonious relations among communities of Christians. Such potential is genuinely resident in the Reconstructionist social vision, even if—for Reconstructionists as for all of us—the flesh is often weak.

SOMETHING FOR EVERYONE

The all-encompassing nature of the Reconstructionist program makes it hard to swallow and easy to criticize. I questioned here the assumption that the Old Testament civil structure was intended to hold the permanently normative status Reconstruction grants it.

Likewise, those who do not share the movement's eschatology will usually not accept its goals or tactics. And those who do not share its presuppositional philosophy will tend to reject its often confrontational attitude toward unbelievers. Reconstructionists have boldly addressed so many areas of theology and social policy that there is something for everyone to get upset with.

But in that unpopularity also lies Reconstruction's usefulness: even those who find its assumptions or methods invalid can still discover in Reconstruction some of the most extensive, solidly researched, and carefully constructed Christian social thought available. Non-Reconstructionists can draw selectively from Reconstruction's insights in developing their own biblical framework for sociopolitical transformation. In the next chapter we will meet one particularly important group of evangelicals that has done just that.

• 3 •

The Quiet World Changers at Regent University

While the Reconstructionists promote their provocative agenda through a flurry of literature, a group of less flamboyant evangelicals is quietly increasing its influence. This group also envisions a reconstruction of sorts—but of 1787 America, not 1620s Puritanism or Old Testament Israel. They believe the founding documents of the United States, the Declaration of Independence and the Constitution, derive from biblical foundations of law, but that subsequent developments have obscured that foundation. Thus they urge that America return to the original intent of those documents.

This "constitutionalist" position has been espoused by Christian law professor John Eidsmoe, author of *Christianity and the Constitution*. John Whitehead of the Rutherford Institute, known for defending religious freedoms in the legal arena, advocates similar views as well. But the most productive center of constitutionalist thought is the College of Law and Government at Pat Robertson's Regent (formerly CBN) University. This college, which includes graduate programs in law and public policy, receives little attention, largely because its professors seldom publish; to understand its significance I had to make two trips to Virginia Beach, conduct a series of interviews, and delve through a mountain of unpublished articles and class notes. But Regent is teaching its law and public-policy students distinctive principles of government and, furthermore, is successfully placing its graduates in federal government agencies, think tanks, and other influential locations. It is surprising, especially in view of the presidential aspirations of Regent's chancellor, that this college has not received greater scrutiny.

REVIVING THE AMERICAN REPUBLIC

Regent University does not spoon-feed its students a narrow orthodoxy regarding law and government. Its public-policy department has room for both the theonomic Joe Kickasola and the Dutch-born Philip Bom, who takes a less restrictive, Kuyperian view of the state's proper role. This breadth reflects the university's educational philosophy, which requires students to be committed to receiving a Scripture-based education but not necessarily to hold any specific theological or sociopolitical dogmas. But there is an identifiable core of public-policy thinking at Regent, and it lies between Kickasola and Bom. That core is represented primarily by Herb Titus, dean of the College of Law and Government and professor of the main course that presents a biblical perspective on law, and Gary Amos, who teaches the courses on government.

In direct contrast to the Reconstructionists, who claim that the only available options are theonomy and humanistic, "autonomous" natural law, Regent's core professors affirm a third option, the "laws of nature." This stream of thought, they believe, derives from the apostle Paul's references in Romans 1–2 to the law written on all persons' hearts. They trace this biblical influence through the development of English common law, particularly in the work of thirteenth-century legal theorist Henri de Bracton and eighteenth-century statesman William Blackstone, whose *Commentaries* became the basic text for early American jurisprudence. Amos and Titus argue that the Declaration of Independence's invocation of the "laws of nature and of nature's God" reflects Blackstone's dependence on God-inspired reason and revelation, respectively, as coexpositors of God's absolute, unchangeable law. The eighteenth-century understanding of "laws of nature," they assert (again following Blackstone), must be carefully distinguished from the concept of a "natural law" perceptible by reason alone; in contrast, "laws of nature" refers specifically to the generally perceptible knowledge that affirms the special revelation provided by "nature's God" *through Scripture.*

Amos therefore states that an eighteenth-century reference to "laws of nature and of nature's God" would have intentionally and recognizably signified both reason and Scripture-based revelation as source of these laws; revelation is needed, he says, because sinful humans cannot accurately perceive the laws of nature by reason alone. This line in the Declaration, then, "incorporates by reference the moral law of the Bible into the founding document of our country!"[1] The Constitution, in turn, rests upon the Declaration's recognition of absolute law; therefore the original intent of its authors is crucial to the document and must not be obliterated by the nonabsolutist approach of legal relativists who believe law must evolve along with changing circumstances.[2]

On many practical issues, the constitutionalists and Reconstructionists line up closely. Though the former group tends to quote Jefferson and Madison while the latter turns directly to Scripture, they join in calling for decentralized government, a reduced federal bureaucracy, limited power of taxation, and a judiciary that interprets, not creates, law.[3] The two groups part sharply, however, with regard to the use of Old Testament law today. Citing Aquinas, Calvin, and Locke as allies, Amos says the moral but not the judicial sections of Mosaic law apply under the new covenant.[4]

Herb Titus's personal biography sheds further light both on the mission of the university he serves, as dean of the College of Law and Government, and on the ways in which he and Amos resemble yet also diverge from Reconstruction. After becoming a Christian in 1975, while teaching law at the University of Oregon, Titus learned from reading Rushdoony, whom he found "stimulating and comprehensive," about the relationship between Christianity and law. Inspired to investigate the early history of American law, Titus then discovered Blackstone—whom he had never been required to read while earning his law degree at Harvard. Blackstone's references to the book of Genesis, combined with Titus's emerging discontent with the evolutionary nature of contemporary jurisprudence ("I found that lawyers took Darwinian theory more seriously than the scientists did"), led him to see Genesis as the foundational framework for law for all nations, and thus to depart from the Reconstructionist reliance on Mosaic law as the only adequate basis for civil order. With Amos, Titus sees the law of Moses as God's specific prescription for the holy, chosen nation of Israel; he cites the establishment of nations in Genesis as proof that one can build a nation on a foundation other than Moses.[5]

Hoping to play a role in training the next generation of Christians "to think rightly about politics and law," Titus shared his vision for a Christian school of law and public policy with Pat Robertson in 1978. He subsequently taught at Oral Roberts University's new law school but was not fully satisfied with its approach: in accord with Roberts's emphasis on healing, ORU was stressing the lawyer's role as an interpersonal healer and reconciler, whereas Titus wanted to articulate a new perspective on the very principles of law. He became CBN University's founding dean of public policy in 1982; four years later the opportunity to mold a law school in accordance with his vision unexpectedly landed at his doorstep, as financially strapped ORU transferred its whole program to CBNU and Titus was named its dean as well.[6]

THE REGENT PRINCIPLES

The single principle of law and government Regent instills most incessantly is the need for an absolute foundation. The building of a healthy society, states Herb Titus, "must begin with the very foundations of law. Not surprisingly, God has revealed those foundations in the very first book of the Holy Scriptures."[7] Titus forthrightly affirms—to the astonishment of secular law school professors—that he looks to the book of Genesis to discover the meaning of law, and he hastens to point out that Blackstone did the same.[8]

Whatever the topic, from affirmative action plans to the Supreme Court's obscenity standards, Titus reiterates the grave danger of replacing God-created absolutes with evolving human conceptions as the source for law. This insistence on absolutes causes him and his Regent colleagues, even while they teach their students how to succeed in a secular legal-political system, to return frequently to Scripture as their criterion by which to judge whether the current system is ultimately right.

This return to Scripture, however, is much less often a return to Mosaic law for the Regent constitutionalists than it is for the Reconstructionists. In addressing affirmative action programs, for example, Titus looks to Acts 17:26, and its statement that God "hath made of one blood all nations of men" (KJV), as well as to Genesis for the principle that all humanity is a single race. Therefore, he concludes, no legal distinction between races is legitimate, not even if intended to remedy prior racial injustices.[9]

Titus also relies heavily on the principle of jurisdiction. Rigorously searching the Scriptures to determine what forms of jurisdiction God has delegated to humankind, Titus finds that God has permitted the civil authorities to judge and punish criminal acts but not to compel deeds of love. From the Mosaic law through the parable of the good Samaritan, he argues, God has always considered our obligation to help the needy a moral, not a legal, requirement; for this reason publicly financed social welfare programs "violate the law of love." Similarly, Titus finds both in Jesus (Mt 28:19–20; Jn 18:35–37) and in James Madison's *Memorial and Remonstrance on the Religious Rights of Man* the denial that the state has authority to teach what is the truth. "God has denied to the state any jurisdiction over men's hearts and minds," he states; education is the task of the family and church, and therefore public education is illegitimate.[10] Not all Regent professors criticize public education in such sweeping tones as Titus, but when I visited the university I was told that all the law professors with young children were home-schooling them.

Because they work from a broader application of biblical principles and with less rigid adherence to Mosaic norms than do the Reconstructionists, the constitutionalists remain somewhat more flexible regarding permissible government involvement. For example, Gary Amos readily justifies federal action in environmental control or economic policy as matters of national security and stability. But this freedom is circumscribed by Regent's insistence that the national constitution is a civil covenant, binding on future generations and modifiable only in those ways sanctioned by the original covenant itself. "The commonwealth covenant is not an open-ended agreement that is designed to change to accommodate changing conditions!"[11]

Regent's commitment both to God's law and to religious freedom relies on what Amos has called the "Creator-Redeemer distinction." As he states it, "God ordained some things in the creation of the world . . . that are not changed by the coming of the gospel."[12] One of them is the proper structure of civil society. Christians are called both to bring individuals to a knowledge of Christ as Redeemer and to restore civil society to the pattern set forth by God the Creator. Only Christians can perform the former task, but non-Christians can participate in the "cultural mandate" of establishing civil justice, since this is a matter inherent in the "laws of nature"—the creation order—and unaffected by the coming of Christ.

The Creator-Redeemer distinction yields an analogous juris-dictional principle: the Great Commission is within the church's jurisdiction, but civil government is the state's jurisdiction. Thus the state should not establish religion and the church should not use the state's resources to propagate the faith. Civil law should reflect God's timeless principles, but civil government should in no way coerce the individual's religious conscience.

This set of principles leaves the Regent constitutionalists rejecting Reconstruction's limitations on civil tolerance for religious liberty yet equally adamant in rejecting societal consensus as a sufficient basis for law. Only the law of God, they say, provides a foundation on which society can be built. This principle is so central to Titus that he declined to sign the Williamsburg Charter, a document that sought to unify as broad a segment of American society as possible behind a shared commitment to religious liberty (see chapter 6 below). Titus felt the language of the charter, consciously designed to appeal to believers and unbelievers alike, implied the adequacy of human reason rather than divinely revealed truth as a basis for law. Even though he too supports religious liberty, he considered the charter's reluctance to ground that liberty explicitly in the law of God to be too important an issue for practical compromise.

HOW THEY'RE PULLING IT OFF: THE REGENT PEDAGOGY AND ITS IMPACT

To say that Regent's College of Law and Government concentrates more on instilling principles than on a specific list of proposals, or to note their apparent lack of interest in disseminating their ideas more widely through publications, would give the impression that the school is relatively unconcerned about making an immediate, practical impact. Such would be a very erroneous impression. On the contrary, the school is strategically focusing its efforts in accordance with the university's stated mission of "training leaders who will prepare the United States and other nations for the coming of Jesus Christ and the establishment of His Kingdom on earth."[13]

Regent's public-policy students are required to take a "biblical principles" course in each of five subareas: law, history, natural science, government, and economics. In each area students are expected to grasp foundational, central concepts before they move on to questions of policy. But following these introductory courses the curriculum emphasizes application of principles to current issues. Professors consistently describe both the current state of affairs and the ideal state of affairs they derive from their biblical foundations; they then challenge students to consider how policies could be implemented that would move from the current to the ideal state. Steve Fitschen, a Regent student who has analyzed the school's pedagogy from within, has noted the resulting combination of reactionary and radical elements: while predominantly favoring a return to an earlier political order, Regent stresses at the same time the need for new and creative solutions to contemporary problems. Fitschen sums up Regent's approach as emphasizing "retrogressive foundations and progressive applications."[14]

Regent's students are encouraged to think big, as befits "world changers." The faculty uniformly believe that their pedagogy will produce foundational, analytical graduates capable of making an impact in whatever field they enter. They often cite examples of alumni who have taken Regent's ideas into strategic positions.

There are many such examples. The U.S. Civil Rights Commission has employed two graduates—an especially interesting match in view of Regent's firm opposition to affirmative action. Another graduate holds a prominent position at the Heritage Foundation, perhaps Washington's most influential conservative policy think tank. The State Department has hired a Regent alumnus to work in the Bureau of International Organization Affairs, assigned to matters concerning the United Nations. Others have taken leadership positions with major political-action organizations devoted to traditional values, such as Concerned Women for America, the Pennsylvania Family Institute, Concerned Charlotteans (of Charlotte, North Carolina), and the Tennessee Coalition for Traditional Values. Several have joined the conservative National Legal Foundation. These are only a few of many examples, as half of Regent's graduates have moved directly into public-policy positions.

Not surprisingly, many Regent graduates have gone on to work for Pat Robertson. Eleven percent have taken jobs with his Christian Broadcasting Network or affiliated organizations. Several grads became staff members for Robertson's presidential campaign. Others have joined the two new organizations Robertson has formed since his return from the campaign trail: the Christian Coalition and the American Center for Law and Justice. The Christian Coalition is involved in grass-roots political action; the ACLJ (just a slip of the pen away from ACLU) deals primarily with First Amendment issues, filing lawsuits and providing legal counsel in cases involving religious freedom. Time will tell, but both have the potential to become important players.

TONED-DOWN RADICALISM

Regent's commitment to being practically effective, and not simply a consciousness-raising educational movement like Reconstruction, raises a dilemma the Reconstructionists need not face. The Regent thinkers cannot simply rail against society, as Rushdoony and North do, and prepare for its predicted collapse; rather, they must present their transformative vision in ways acceptable to the gatekeepers who control entry to the legal-political system. Regent's tactically skillful response to this dilemma is best illustrated by its law school's three-year quest for accreditation by the American Bar Association (ABA).[15]

The Regent (then CBN) law school came into existence in 1986 after evangelist Oral Roberts, in an unusually lavish demonstration of his "give and God will bless you" motif, gave his university's law program, including a one hundred eighty thousand-volume library, to Pat Robertson. However, the ABA did not agree to transfer the Oral Roberts University law school's accreditation to CBNU. Thus began CBNU's battle for ABA accreditation, an essential mark of approval since forty-three states normally permit only graduates of an ABA-accredited school to take the bar exam.

In twice turning down CBNU's application for accreditation, the ABA cited concerns about the university's limited endowment and financial instability, but even when those questions were resolved the ABA remained suspicious of the effect of CBNU's self-proclaimed religious mission on academic freedom. When queried on this matter by an ABA committee, Dean Titus sought to stress the similarities between CBNU and any other law school. "Every law school in the nation has a common faith from which they address every question," he averred. "And there is no difference between us and any other law school except that our common faith is different."[16] Titus assured the committee that a student could endorse *Roe v. Wade* without being kicked out of the CBNU classroom, that an unbeliever who understood what kind of education he or she would be getting at CBNU would be most welcome, and that CBNU was far from the only law school where professors expressed their disagreements with prevailing law. He had to return to yet another hearing, assuring ABA representatives that the university's statement of faith did not limit faculty or student freedom of opinion on any legal issue, before provisional accreditation was finally granted in June 1989.

The contortions Titus and his law school were forced to undergo in achieving accreditation reflect the struggles their form of Christian worldview thinking faces in addressing its "central challenge . . . to move from cultural isolation to cultural leadership."[17] Herb Titus and his Regent colleagues, while not nearly as confrontational as Gary North, at the same time insist heavily on the need for a biblical foundation for law and government. But before the ABA Titus was compelled to downplay this distinctiveness, instead assuring his questioners that the CBNU statement of faith is compatible with any position on any legal issue. If that is really the case, one might wonder just what is the practical content of the Christian worldview CBNU's Bible-based law school proposes to communicate.

Nevertheless, this situation is consistent with the Regent understanding of Christian worldview thinking. The university requires its students to adopt a way of thinking (one with Scripture at its foundation), not to assent to a set of do's, don'ts, and dogmas. This is why Regent can describe its commitment to Scripture as a foundation, not a limitation, of intellectual freedom.

Of course, the Regent law school has not been overrun by ideological diversity—not yet, at least. It is clear that the College of Law and Government, while not requiring its students to subscribe to any specific legal or political views, does instill a distinctive core of concepts and perspectives. Although Dean Titus has assured the ABA that members of the Regent community are free to endorse *Roe v. Wade*, it is virtually certain that no one has done so. It is equally certain that Regent does not publicize in its fund-raising efforts the fact that, in theory at least, an abortion-rights advocate could progress through the Regent law program without ever being commanded to repent.

At this point Regent appears to have addressed the dilemma of how to present itself by alternating between two images. When promoting itself within the evangelical community, Regent aspires to world-changing status, resisting secularist inroads as part of its mission to "prepare the United States and other nations for the coming of Jesus Christ." However, when addressing a broader audience Regent plays down this normative streak, offering endorsement of this pluralistic society as long as that society accords Regent the same measure of religious freedom enjoyed by other groups. As Dean Titus told the ABA's questioners in defending his law school's right to exist: "We're talking about America. We're talking about a nation that encourages pluralism, that encourages diversity, and we're saying this has a place in American legal education."[18] This is not duplicity, but behavior exhibited by many special-interest groups who, although they would love to remake the whole world in their own image, know that in order to maximize their effectiveness they must cooperate with the system and learn to settle for partial victories.

In other words, while Christian worldview thinkers like those at Regent may have ultimate designs of overturning the world, in their public presentation they just ask not to be stepped on. This self-presentation as underdogs finds an interesting parallel in another organization that has emerged from the same source as Regent: the Christian Coalition, founded in 1990 by Pat Robertson to help (conservative) Christians regain a greater voice in American government. The Christian Coalition, seen by some observers as the primary group moving to fill a leadership vacuum in the Christian Right, is committed to long-range, systematic, effective action. As one of its regional directors put it, the coalition is "teaching people to develop a lifestyle—a consistent Christian worldview that includes citizenship." As such, it embodies the spread of Christian worldview thinking and of increasing political sophistication among evangelicals.[19]

And how is the coalition presenting itself? Its executive director told the evangelical magazine *Christianity Today*, "We think the Lord is going to give us this nation back one precinct at a time, one neighborhood at a time, and one state at a time." That sounds like a plan for eventual cultural dominance. However, painfully aware of the angry responses that have ensued when evangelicals have been perceived as envisioning a political takeover, the coalition proclaims as its public theme, "American Christians are tired of being stepped on." As a result, other Christians have criticized the group for behaving as if what has historically been the dominant religious culture in America now needs a Christian antidefamation league.[20]

PINNING DOWN PAT

Now that we have outlined the philosophy of the Regent group, pointing out both the similarities and differences with Reconstruction, we may be better prepared to interpret the views of this university's prominent, controversial chancellor. Pat Robertson admits to an appreciation of many Reconstructionist ideas, particularly the focus on the dominion mandate,[21] but his own position is much closer to that of Titus, whose "insight and assistance" he acknowledged in his most political book, *America's Dates with Destiny*.[22] Most significantly, though he asserts that God must be the source of civil law, Robertson is no more theonomic than were Washington and Jefferson. He briefly argues that the principles of the Declaration of Independence are biblical, claims the Constitution was built on the foundation of the Declaration, and thenceforth develops his political views from the nation's founding documents, not from Scripture. He also vigorously and repeatedly rejects civil establishment of religion and assures his readers that evangelicals are as "deeply committed" to pluralism as anyone else.[23]

Many of Robertson's policy stances endeared him to Reconstructionists, but his outpouring of admiration for pluralism reflects the political necessities faced by an evangelical candidate who was seeking to position himself as the best hope to continue the Reagan revolution.[24] Some of his earlier statements, such as his claim that only Christians and Jews are fit to govern America and his 1984 vision that God's people would soon hold sway in Washington, had dug him a diplomatic hole from which even repeated assurances of moderation could hardly extricate him.[25] Once Robertson chose to work through the Republican party, he was forced to eliminate all tinges of radical-sounding dominionist rhetoric in order to gain practical influence.

Robertson still appears to dream of a purely Christian social takeover. In early 1991 he laid out a scenario according to which, he projected, "a coalition of Evangelicals and pro-family Roman Catholics" would take over the grass-roots rebuilding of the Republican party after a 1996 Democratic presidential victory, and that by the year 2000 this conservative coalition would have enough strength to win the presidency and a majority in Congress.[26] But when Robertson himself was a candidate, political exigencies kept him from talking about Christian dominion in the decisive terms characteristic of recognized dominionists. Reconstructionists, many of whom at first endorsed Robertson, thus found him less appealing the longer he ran.[27] Their dissatisfaction reflects their greater

reluctance to compromise ideological purity for the sake of short-term victory.

EVALUATING THE REGENT PROPOSAL

Regent's constitutionalists have constructed essentially a two-pronged defense of their political philosophy: they argue both historically (that their position largely echoes that of the Founding Fathers) and normatively (that their position echoes the ultimate, unchanging law of God). This dual foundation enables them to present their policy arguments with equal integrity following either the norms of public or of evangelical discourse—that is, using either secular-sounding or Bible-based reasoning. This approach is possible because Regent, for the most part, does not adhere as Reconstructionists do to the narrow version of presuppositional philosophy that treats large sectors of knowledge as reliably accessible only for the Christian believer.

Nevertheless, Regent's historical argument tends to beg the question, because their appeal to the authority of the founders holds up only if one assumes that the founders' ideas carry some form of permanent, normative status. The founders certainly studied Blackstone, whose legal philosophy rested on Scripture, but the basic rights and freedoms embodied in the Declaration of Independence and the Constitution are also compatible with eighteenth-century Enlightenment thought. For this reason it is not clear that James Madison, if transplanted into today's religiously pluralistic America, would insist with Titus and Amos that the Declaration of Independence has incorporated Scripture as part of the common law. On the contrary, Madison and the other founders, given the intellectual options available today, might be quite willing to accept any social consensus, whether acknowledging a biblical foundation or not, that continued to honor the Bill of Rights.

Ultimately, therefore, Regent's policy thinkers must prove not just that they are reiterating what Jefferson or Madison said two hundred years ago, but that their philosophy of government is the only acceptable one. Here there remains room for further debate on specifics, even among those who consider the Bible authoritative. For example, one can argue that, as part of its God-given responsibility to maintain social order, government is justified in compelling that all youths receive adequate education and in establishing public schools to meet that need. To state that parents hold responsibility for training their children does not categorically exclude parents from selecting a non-Christian, publicly financed institution as the provider of some of that education—whether that institution be the township soccer club, a local music program, or a public school.

On a broader level, Titus's application of the principle of jurisdiction may be overly rigid at points. He has rightly noted that social welfare is a moral and not a legal duty in biblical law; but does this jurisdictional principle universally take precedence over concern for persons with disabilities, even if the level of voluntarily contributed resources in a society is seriously inadequate? As I will argue more fully in chapter 9, I believe a more sensitive balance of limited government with practical concerns is needed.

Nevertheless, even if one disagrees with some of Regent's policy applications, it is hard to fault their methodology. Their policy development is principled and thoroughly Christian in derivation, yet it avoids three traits that hinder Reconstruction's effectiveness. First, it fuses principle with practical necessity in a way that encourages constructive engagement with the prevailing system. Second, its use of Scripture is less dependent on theological assumptions that are not widely accepted among Christians (especially regarding the applicability of Old Testament law). And third, Regent denies that Christians should compel religious belief in their leaders or seek to formally Christianize the state.

The differences between the Regent constitutionalist approach and Reconstruction are sufficiently substantial that each group sometimes views the other as an adversary—as both Gary North and Gary Amos have pointed out to me. But the underlying link is that Regent's professors, partly inspired by Reconstructionist thought, have dedicated themselves to developing and applying an explicitly Bible-based approach to public policy. The moderating traits that keep Regent's program from being genuinely "dominionist" in our sense of the term may also be the very traits that will help this group achieve greater success in implementing its agenda within American society.

• 4 •

"I Feel It in My Spirit"
The Kingdom–Now Worldview

W e could be devastated," Don Paulk moaned to his wife one evening in 1982. "He just said there was no rapture."

Denying the existence of a rapture might not seem an earthshaking event, but it can be if one is trying not to offend the membership of one's Pentecostal church. Thus Don Paulk, associate pastor of Chapel Hill Harvester Church in suburban Atlanta, had good reason for concern. His brother Earl, the church's head pastor, had just preached a sermon denying that Christians should look forward to being removed from the earth ("raptured") before the Great Tribulation that would conclude human history. For many Pentecostal Christians the Rapture was not simply a barren doctrine but a treasured hope that heaven could materialize at any moment. Would Earl Paulk's new stance cause the congregation to desert them?

Earl had greater reason for confidence than Don, for he believed God had specifically instructed him to reread the book of Revelation—the book most Pentecostals use to build their last-days timetable. As he did so, the emphasis on expecting a rapture, with which he had never felt fully comfortable, suddenly seemed a gross distortion. Now he saw Revelation as a message of Christians' victory—on earth as well as at the end of time—in the cosmic battle of good and evil.

Earl Paulk's unforeseen theological reorientation, contrary to his brother's fears, has magnified and uniquely distinguished the increasing influence of his ministry. Not only did Chapel Hill continue its rapid growth to megachurch proportions, but it became the center of a controversial movement that has upset many Pentecostal and charismatic applecarts.[1]

A PILGRIMAGE TOWARD RELEVANCE

Paulk's reinterpretation of Revelation accelerated his evolution away from the religious orientation in which he was raised. Earl Paulk, Jr., was born in 1927, the first son of a man who would rise to one of the top positions in the Church of God (Cleveland, Tennessee), a classical Pentecostal denomination. The elder Paulk unbendingly followed his denomination's strict rules, many of which reflected the influence of the Holiness Movement from which it had emerged in the late nineteenth century: no frivolous entertainments (including movies, drinking cola, or varsity athletics), no makeup or wedding rings, and (in an important addition to non-Pentecostal holiness codes) no doctors.

Earl, Jr., generally toed the line, receiving water baptism at age four and the Pentecostal Spirit-baptism (the emotional experience in which a Pentecostal traditionally receives the gift of tongues) as a teenager. At age seventeen, in another emotionally powerful experience, he perceived a call to full-time ministry. He stepped outside his subculture to attend Furman University, a Baptist school in South Carolina, but passed up a chance to play football there (though he did find a less obtrusive outlet for his athletic gifts with the track team). Nevertheless, especially as a youth minister, he became increasingly frustrated with what he perceived as legalism in the Church of God. When he began suggesting new approaches, he discovered, to his dismay, that his denomination "did not easily tolerate debate, radical changes or controversial ideas."[2]

Bucking the Church of God's antieducational leanings, Paulk earned a master's degree in divinity at Candler School of Theology (United Methodist) in Atlanta and accepted a call to that city's Hemphill Church of God in 1952. His ministry thrived but also aroused division, both among denominational traditionalists irked by Paulk's openness to innovation and among parishioners uncomfortable with his calls for racial equality and his support of the incipient civil-rights movement.[3]

Paulk's internal conflict between independence and loyalty to the denomination came to a head in 1960. According to his version of the story, he sought assistance from the denomination's state overseer for a situation in which he was counseling a woman with marital difficulties. The state overseer, however, warning Paulk that other church leaders would suspect him of impropriety if it became known that he had requested help in a relationship with a female parishioner, advised him to handle the mess quietly on his own. This rebuff unleashed Paulk's brewing disillusionment with a denomination that, as he saw it, insensitively branded troubled pastors as guilty without cause and failed to apply Christian principles of reconciliation and forgiveness. (His ministry since 1960 has been marked by a reaction against Holiness-style legalism and by a desire to restore wounded souls; the latter trait is so strong that some Chapel Hill staff find Paulk *too* tolerant of his associates' failings.) Paulk abruptly resigned his pastorate and headed west with his brother Don and brother-in-law Harry Mushegan.[4]

The three ministered briefly in Phoenix but returned east when Earl became convinced that God was calling them to start a new church in Atlanta. Beginning in the inner city, the church multiplied rapidly, moving in 1972 to the south suburbs and taking on its current name, Chapel Hill Harvester Church. Refusing to move again as blacks began to populate the vicinity, the church successfully became racially mixed and grew even faster. In 1984 it dedicated another new building, including a three-thousand-seat sanctuary, and in 1991 it moved into the magnificent seven-thousand-seat Cathedral of the Holy Spirit. Paulk has far outgrown his Church of God roots numerically as well as theologically.[5]

A MESSAGE OF SOCIAL RELEVANCE

The central theme of Paulk's theology is that God wants the church to "aggressively press toward Kingdom demonstration on earth,"[6] confronting oppressive ideologies and regaining its lost dominion. In fact, Paulk believes that rebellious angels had turned the earth into chaos even before the creation of Adam and Eve, so that the task of recovering lost dominion was intrinsic to God's initial purpose in creating the human race.[7] Although Satan remains active and powerful on earth, Christ decisively defeated him two thousand years ago. Ever since then God has been waiting for the church to get out of its "holding pattern"[8] by recognizing that kingdom power is available now (though it will not be fully consummated until the completion of history) and not just in some future state. The bolder Christians become in spreading dominion, the more they will face persecution; but God's "theocracy" will ultimately win.[9]

Before Jesus can return to earth in victory, "the Church must complete its assignment" of "becoming a standard by which world systems will be judged." This does not mean, as postmillennialists would say, that the world will get better and better; it does mean, however, that the *church* will improve, becoming a "mature, holy bride" and "worthy of the Bridegroom," Jesus Christ. The church must make an unmistakable witness in every area of life, including politics, education, business, and the arts, as well as its purely spiritual mission. It must become sufficiently discerning to know both how to avoid contamination by world systems and how to infiltrate them.[10]

Since the fully mature church "will usher in the ultimate Kingdom of God,"[11] it follows that no generation of believers has yet displayed adequate maturity. For example, the apostolic church was marred by Peter's prejudice toward Gentiles, internal mutiny by believers like Ananias and Sapphira (Ac 5), carnal behavior, and an otherworldly mentality.[12] The church must build on the true insights revealed to each generation, finally becoming complete in maturity before Christ returns.

Among the serious hindrances to the kingdom, otherworldliness has remained a widespread deception in modern Christianity. Believers have been content with "Salvation Church," which concentrates on saving people from hell through evangelism and waits for a heavenly escape from present circumstances. The rapture doctrine keeps Christians in spiritual infancy, "twiddling our thumbs waiting for the Kingdom to come" and unaware of the "Kingdom concept" that calls Christians to "subdue the world around them" and "take dominion over our circumstances through Jesus Christ."[13] Overly literal interpretations of biblical prophecy have also misled Christians into a preoccupation with the nation of Israel; the Jews will embrace the Gospel in large numbers at some future time, in accordance with Romans 11, but under Christ's new covenant the church, not the Jewish nation, is the true Israel.[14]

Although Paulk decries rapture theologies and believes the antichrist figure described in the New Testament represents evil world systems rather than any particular individual, he refuses to endorse any traditional millennial view. He considers most discussions of the last days "far more divisive than . . . edifying" and is concerned primarily that one's eschatology not induce spiritual pride, immaturity, or otherworldliness. "My calling is not relegated to discussions of eschatology. God has commanded me to prepare an army to do His will."[15]

WHAT PAULK BELIEVES THE CHURCH MUST DO

Interestingly, while Paulk calls believers to demonstrate the kingdom in every sphere of life, the three specific prescriptions he repeats most relentlessly all concern matters internal to the church, indicating that his vision of dominion is as much spiritual (that is, depending on special infusions of Holy Spirit power) as political in nature.

The first of those prescriptions is church unity. "Christ cannot return to earth until His Church is joined in spiritual unity of faith." Christians should settle their controversies privately and present a united front to the unbelieving world. "True born-again believers" should never be separated by matters of doctrine that are less important than "coming into a unity of faith."[16]

Second is the restoration of the "five-fold ministry," as dictated in Ephesians 4, which states that God gave apostles, prophets, evangelists, pastors, and teachers for the purpose of building up the church. These ministers are to lead the church into unity of faith, and their proper functioning is vital; they are "the only means by which God imparts His [continuing] revelation to us."[17] "Man has no right to private interpretation of the Word of God apart from those whom God sets in the Church as spiritual teachers and elders."[18] Paulk does not mean that church leaders are infallible; on the contrary, he explains in detail when their faults and errors should or should not be publicly exposed.[19] But he does believe that all Christians should submit to recognized spiritual leaders, receiving "protection, covering, and discernment" from their guidance.[20]

The importance Paulk places on modern-day prophecy embodies his third crucial prescription for kingdom churches: openness to discoveries of new spiritual truth. In line with standard charismatic theology, and in response to sharp criticisms of his earlier writings, Paulk agrees that modern prophecy does not equal the written Word of God and that "the Bible is the basis for all further revelation"; he now uses the term *insight* rather than *revelation* to describe these new discoveries, so as to allay fears that he believes the canon of inspired Scripture may not be complete or unique. But his principles of Bible interpretation include an insistence that Christians must "remain open to additional revelation [insight] and understanding."[21]

KINGDOM ON THE HORIZON

As one would expect from an evangelical, Paulk seeks to legitimate his basic ideas by claiming to restore biblical truth: "Kingdom teaching is not a new theology, new interpretation of Scripture, nor new revelation. It is as old as the Scriptures."[22] Nevertheless, Paulk also has expressed hope that the present generation will surpass all predecessors in fulfilling the requirements that must be met before God will restore his kingdom. Commenting on 1 Corinthians 15, where Paul writes that at the end of history some mortals would be transferred into immortality without experiencing death, Paulk has written, "I feel in my spirit that the generation now lives who will have this experience."[23] More often, though, he speaks with less certainty and greater caution, noting for instance that the Spirit told him in 1982 "that this is the generation who *can* be alive and remain until the coming of the Lord" (emphasis added). In a still less sanguine tone, he writes in the same chapter, "History will continue millennium after millennium until we do what God has said to do."[24]

Paulk never provides a systematic argument, comparable to Gary North's intricate scenario of Christian reconstruction, why he expects such great things from this generation; he simply appeals repeatedly to special revelation. "God will grant solutions through the Church to answer major social, medical, technological and political problems. . . . The true Church will be led by the Holy Spirit at a dimension never known before."[25] Although Chapel Hill's amazing effectiveness in implementing social ministries in the Atlanta area reflects Paulk's capacity for concrete world-transforming activity, his ventures into social theory are much more limited—partly because his eschatology requires Christians only to set up a *demonstration* of the kingdom, not to fully conquer society in postmillennial fashion. While calling on Christians to be involved in politics,[26] he is reluctant to promote specific public-policy action and reverts quickly from the ideological to the prophetic role: "I believe that God is beginning to work in the hearts of kings, rulers and leaders in governments around the world. We will soon see a great spiritual revival among political leaders."[27] Paulk predicts that Christians will soon rise to legislative offices and positions of influence,[28] yet, unlike most of his fellow religious conservatives, he stays aloof from partisan politics. He prefers "to edify all Democrats and Republicans in the gospel of the Kingdom and point to the authority of Jesus Christ as the solution in all the issues."[29]

In emphasizing humankind's potential to receive and release the power of God, Paulk tends toward the anthropocentric (i.e., human-centered) end of the traditional Christian paradox of divine sovereignty versus human ability. Paulk says the kingdom's progress is hindered because Christians fail to understand their status as the "ongoing incarnation of Christ." Paulk stresses the degree to which God, in granting humans free will, has made them personally sovereign over and responsible for their own sphere of influence. He even has described humans as "created with the potential for God-likeness," as "little gods."[30] In subsequent writings Paulk has sought to revise this highly controversial terminology, warning that a "like-God spirit" and human-centered theologies that reject God's direction and authority are evil.[31]

Among his Bible-based defenses of his kingdom expectations, Paulk parallels Reconstruction in interpreting the New Testament's

Great Commission mandate, which commands Christians to preach the Gospel and disciple all nations before the end of history (Mt 24:14; 28:19; Mk 16:15), as a call to full-scale kingdom demonstration and not only to personal evangelism and discipleship. However, he rests his case more heavily on his broader theological commitment to the cosmic good-versus-evil battle as the principle by which all Scripture should be interpreted.

A LIGHTNING BOLT FROM "LATTER RAIN"

The phenomenal growth and commitment level of Chapel Hill Harvester Church have given Paulk the resources by which to spread his message widely. The church has its own publications department and operates a television ministry that reaches not only the United States but also a dozen Latin American nations, broadcasting in both English and Spanish. Major conferences like the 1990 World Congress on the Kingdom of God have brought pastors and Christian leaders from all over the hemisphere to Atlanta to learn kingdom principles. None of these highly successful outreaches could have been launched without a multimillion-dollar budget. Furthermore, in a charismatic culture that views growth and big numbers as an important sign of success, the size of Paulk's congregation itself marks him as an unusually anointed man of God, one to be taken seriously.[32]

But these material resources would have had no distinctive message to promote if not for the *theological* freedom Paulk experienced twenty-three years after gaining his *denominational* freedom. His separation from the Church of God in 1960 enabled him to build an independent congregation in accord with his own preferences, but only after he abandoned the traditional view of the Rapture did he feel able to reshape his theology to match his burden for social activism, discarding classical Pentecostal thought forms in favor of more optimistic ones. This theological freedom also gave him the opportunity to incorporate ideas from an obscure branch of Pentecostal thought, one that Paulk says he had never heard of before 1983 but whose continuing reverberations have far exceeded its initially brief visible life: Latter Rain.[33]

The Latter Rain revival began in February 1948 at a tiny

Pentecostal outpost, Sharon Bible School in North Battleford, Saskatchewan. Distressed by a sense that Pentecostals were retreating from lively spirituality into dead denominationalism, the school's leader, George Hawtin (who had broken from Canada's main Pentecostal denomination, the Pentecostal Assemblies of Canada, the year before), and his seventy students embraced a fresh outbreak of the gift of prophecy in their midst. One of the prophetic messages they received promised that supernatural gifts could be imparted through laying on of hands by anointed spiritual leaders. Hawtin soon claimed preeminent authority, urging believers to join with what he predicted would be God's last and greatest revival by receiving instruction from him or from seven pastors, in Canada and the northern United States, whose "apostolic ministry" he had recognized. In July of that year the spreading news of a supernatural outpouring reportedly attracted a crowd of thousands for Sharon's summer camp meeting. Punctuated by typically Pentecostal claims of powerful and miraculous experiences, the message spread to large churches and teaching centers in Vancouver, British Columbia; Portland, Oregon; Detroit; and New York state.[34]

In a spiritually enthusiastic context marked by unusual openness to new ideas and by an overpowering expectation of imminent, unmistakable divine intervention, the Latter Rain revival quickly became associated with several doctrines that established Pentecostal groups found both unacceptable and threatening. Among these doctrines, Latter Rain's belief that this revival was restoring the five-fold ministry (headed by apostles and prophets) was probably the most divisive, since it implicitly denied the authority of denominational leaders. Latter Rain's widely reported claims of supernatural experiences as confirmation of the revival's genuineness further intensified the threat. Within just a few years the movement had been both expelled by the Pentecostal Assemblies of Canada and condemned by the Assemblies of God in the United States.[35]

Although Latter Rain soon faded from view, its ideas have survived and resurfaced repeatedly within North American Pentecostalism, exercising surprising influence on much later developments within the charismatic movement.[36] Kingdom Now is one of those resurfacings, exhibiting similarities with original Latter Rain ideas that are too noteworthy to be coincidental. These include restoration of the five-fold ministry; the continual, progressive unfolding of spiritual truth through new insights granted to apostles and prophets; the call for all Christians to recognize the inspired guidance of this identified apostolic leadership; the importance of unity within the restored church; and the expectation that the end is near and that mature believers will soon be able to conquer death.[37]

From its very beginning Latter Rain also discarded the prevailing Pentecostal hope for an any-moment rapture, instead viewing itself as the beginning of a global revival that would "transform the spiritual life and spiritual vision of the whole world." The former belief in the imminent return of Christ may have "served a useful purpose," said George Hawtin of the Sharon Bible School, but it is a "false hope," for "we have no right to expect His coming into the world with power and great glory until He is first manifest in us in power and glory." Only after the "restitution of all things" (Ac 3:21 KJV), including the establishment of a pure people of God (separate from "the wickedness, bondage and apostasy of the present denominational system") in whom God's power could be "demonstrated," could Christ return. Hawtin pulled no punches in estimating the impact this revival would have or in describing the havoc he expected it to play with accepted beliefs:

> We are entering into the Kingdom Age in a sense now, for the *Kingdom is being formed in us* and when it is completed . . . all judicial as well as religious authority will be vested in the church of Christ. . . . The farther we progress in this present revival the more we are discovering that almost all of our theology has to be enlarged or revised to accommodate the present measure of light.[38]

Unlike later charismatics, Latter Rain did not see social action as a way to produce this change; it retained the otherworldly emphasis of early Pentecostals. This separatist style lives on in Pentecostals like Bill Hamon, a descendant of Latter Rain and now a colleague of Paulk. Hamon, who was elevated to membership in the College of Bishops of the International Communion of Charis-

matic Churches (ICCC, an organization in which Paulk is
presiding bishop) in 1988, came into contact with Latter Rain at
least as early as 1954 and sees the whole history of the church since
Luther through Latter Rain eyes. His key interpretive tool is
Hebrews 6:1–2, which speaks of six doctrines its writer considered
"elementary": repentance, faith in God, baptisms, laying on of
hands, resurrection of the dead, and eternal judgment. Hamon,
following a frequent Latter Rain argument, says that to read
Hebrews 6:1–2 as a list of elementary doctrines is only one of "two
hermeneutically acceptable interpretations" of the passage. The
other interpretation, he says, is that the passage enumerates six
principles that the Holy Spirit has been restoring to the church, one
at a time and in chronological order, since the Protestant Reformation.[39]

This latter view is anything but "hermeneutically acceptable"
if one believes that the original writer's intent should determine the
interpretation of a text. But Hamon finds it sufficiently trustworthy
to guide him in correlating God's plan with modern church history.
The Protestant Reformation, he teaches, restored the doctrine of
repentance, while faith in God (for sanctification and healing) came
with the Methodist and Holiness movements. Then came the
doctrine of baptisms (including Spirit-baptism) with the Pentecostals and the laying on of hands with Latter Rain. Hamon departs
still further from the basic meaning of the Hebrews text to explain
how the last two doctrines will be restored before the end of this
century. "Resurrection of the dead," he writes, means that the last
generation of believers will attain a "translating faith" by which
they will conquer death and become immortalized. "Eternal
judgment" signifies the role the immortalized church as "Army of
the Lord" will play, along with Christ, in executing God's will and
wrath and inaugurating the Millennium.[40]

Hamon lacks the sociopolitical concern prevalent in Kingdom
Now, with the exception of a few warnings against humanism and
the World Council of Churches—the latter now a bit ironic in view
of his membership in the ICCC, which is affiliated with the World
Council. His answer to "What can Christians do now?" is purely
spiritual in nature.[41] But in many other ways Hamon's words,
published in 1981, set a clear pattern for what Paulk would say and

do. Hamon explicitly calls for a "full demonstration" of the "Gospel of the Kingdom" before the end can come; he apologizes for his previous belief in an imminent rapture (from 1954 to 1962, he admits, he preached that it would come in 1963); he predicts that the next stage of restoration will include the greatest outpouring of spiritual power in church history; he foresees that "new under-standing will come to the Church" on certain passages of Scripture; and he envisions the building of Christian communities, some of which "will evolve into small Christian cities which will be a prelude and prototype of the Kingdom to come."[42] He also repeats the familiar Latter Rain themes of unity among all believers and restoration of the five-fold ministry. Against this background, Paulk's theology begins to sound less original and more like the crystallization of earlier but unactualized Pentecostal ideas.

The sociopolitical gap between Paulk and Hamon, however, hints at a larger difference. Paulk has mainstreamed Latter Rain ideas, slicing off their rough spots for respectable presentation to a larger audience. Unlike Latter Rain he has acted out a genuine concern for social suffering, avoided potentially offensive language about the church ruling the world, changed his terminology (altering phrases like "little gods" and "new revelation" to mollify critics), and treated denominational Christians as equals.[43] Paulk's optimism and commitment to social change predisposed him to accept progressively inclined Latter Rain doctrines like openness to newly revealed insights, increase in spiritual power, and unity of faith. But his higher social standing tended to lead him away from those views that reflect the Latter Rain Pentecostals' disinherited, fringe status—their otherworldliness, disdain for all established denominations, and apocalyptic program of personally judging the unrighteous.

Hamon may have been one source by which Paulk came into contact with Latter Rain ideas while remaining unaware of their initial origins. Another intermediary between Latter Rain and Kingdom Now was John Meares, who has served since 1955 as the white pastor of a predominantly black congregation, Evangel Temple in Washington, D.C. Meares and Paulk have been friends since the 1950s, and their biographies have striking parallels. Meares too was raised in the Church of God (Cleveland, Tenn.)

and began his ministerial career in that denomination but chafed against its legalism and its racial insensitivity. Unlike Paulk, he did not have to resign from the denomination; by founding an integrated church, he was disfellowshipped. This expulsion freed him to develop new styles and new associations, including close contact with Bethesda Temple, the Latter Rain church in Detroit which Meares credits with having had an important influence on his ministry.[44] Meares later founded the ICCC, in which he also serves as bishop, and his niece Clariece is married to Don Paulk.

BUILDING A CONTEXT
FOR CHARISMATIC POLITICS:
JOHN GIMENEZ AND WASHINGTON FOR JESUS

In organizational terms Kingdom Now is an even less cohesive social movement than its fragmented dominionist cousin, Reconstruction. Paulk and Chapel Hill never set out to lead a movement at all, let alone an ideologically pure one. The protodenomination called the Network of Kingdom Churches that Chapel Hill has built around itself requires of affiliate congregations only basic Christian orthodoxy (as represented by the historic creeds) and a "Kingdom mentality"; there is no demand for conformity in worship style, church government, eschatology, or sociopolitical opinions. Even were he more interested in movement organization, Paulk alone could not replace the largely otherworldly mindset of the charismatic movement with the activism of Kingdom Now. But he has not been alone. Other key charismatics had preceded him in laying the groundwork for change.

The single most important date in the emergence of charismatic activism was April 29, 1980. On that day the seemingly implausible Latter Rain–Kingdom Now belief that the body of Christ will soon attain unprecedented unity of faith received a boost of plausibility as perhaps five hundred thousand Christians congregated at Washington for Jesus (WFJ), a day of repentance and prayer on the nation's behalf. To Bill Hamon this event, "the largest non-denominational Christian gathering ever recorded in history," signified a hope that the Holy Spirit was accomplishing "the greatest challenge of all," the task of unifying the church.[45]

Few of those present in the predominantly evangelical crowd knew that WFJ was the brainchild of a charismatic pastor with Latter Rain roots.

John Gimenez, a former drug addict and gang member and now Pentecostal evangelist, had settled in Virginia Beach in 1968 with his wife and fellow evangelist, Anne. Their small church with a fruitful ministry to addicts mushroomed when the Jesus Movement penetrated the Virginia Beach youth culture in 1971. By 1973 Rock Church had an extremely youthful congregation of twelve hundred. Divisiveness between Christian groups made a lasting impression on Gimenez during his early years as a believer; he says the battles among Christians "reminded me of my gang days, in which we'd fight over anything." He gravitated toward the Latter Rain or "restorationist" sector of Pentecostalism, adopting not only its stress on unity but also its views on the five-fold ministry and the role of personal prophecy. He also learned political realities the hard way, as his attempts to start a drug-rehabilitation center angered neighbors and were repeatedly blocked by city government.[46]

In 1978, while preaching at the restorationist Shiloh Temple in Oakland, California, Gimenez received a vision of a mass rally of Christians. After seeking and receiving endorsement of the vision from Pat Robertson, Gimenez bridged the often unbridgeable gap between Pentecostals and non-Pentecostal evangelicals mainly through the aid of Campus Crusade for Christ founder (and noncharismatic) Bill Bright, who himself had been a quiet participant in the Christian Right's birth pangs. Although Gimenez carefully kept WFJ 1980 (like its less massive successor in 1988) formally nonpartisan, there is little doubt that the arousal, in a presidential election year, of an evangelical throng whose primary social concerns were abortion, sexuality, and school prayer aided the Republican party. Bill Bright said that "the 1980 election wasn't won in November, it was won on April 29." Pat Robertson agreed: "The election of Ronald Reagan in 1980 was not the triumph of a very, very highly personable actor. . . . It was a sovereign act of God Almighty in answer to prayer."[47]

Regular attendance at Rock Church approached three thousand during the 1980s, giving Gimenez the resources and visibility with which to make an impact in other ways. In 1983 Rock Church announced plans to build a "City of Refuge"—with rehabilitation programs, agricultural facilities, a university, a retirement center, a television studio, and a five-thousand-seat sanctuary—on 802 acres of land it had purchased in an unpopulated section of Virginia Beach. The Gimenezes became more directly involved in politics in 1985, with Anne running unsuccessfully for city council. Although tied to Paulk only by personal friendship and by shared involvement in charismatic associations such as the Network of Christian Ministries, Gimenez was taking similar steps toward visible "Kingdom demonstration."[48]

A KUYPERIAN AMONG THE CHARISMATICS: TOMMY REID

While others have sought to avoid the label "Kingdom Now," a title as damning in some charismatic circles as "Reconstructionist" has been to many evangelicals, Tommy Reid has embraced it. Though frequently linked with Paulk,[49] Reid, whose affiliation with the Assemblies of God dates back to 1936 and who pastors a highly successful church south of Buffalo, New York, arrived at Kingdom theology by a path unlikely for a Pentecostal. Through his friendship with Crystal Cathedral pastor Robert Schuller, a rather atypical product of Dutch Calvinism but still a member of the Reformed Church in America, Reid began reading Reformed theology and was revolutionized by Kuyper's *Lectures on Calvinism.* He also, however, received a more typically Pentecostal style of reinforcement for his new ministry direction: around 1982 "God spoke to my heart about the future of the Church. He said to me, 'As the last move of the Holy Spirit affected the church, the next move of the Holy Spirit will affect society.' "[50]

With the same skillful diplomacy he has needed to survive in a denomination hostile to Paulk and Kingdom theology, Reid patiently reaffirms his classical Pentecostal heritage and continues to speak of a future "rapture." He expressly disavows any intent to establish a new "Kingdom theology."[51] But he echoes Paulk's interpretation of Genesis 1, stating that "man's very purpose is to take dominion" over a planet on which a rebellious Satan had built a stronghold even before the creation of the Garden of Eden.[52] Though he considers the idea of a Christian social takeover to be both incompatible with true Christian servanthood and unrealistic (like Paulk, he believes the church will only "be a powerful witness" and "raise up a standard," not take over society, before Christ returns), he calls the church to be an "aggressive occupying force" that will "penetrate the spheres of our society with the teachings and the demonstration of the Kingdom." His theology of social reformation is inseparable from charismatic supernaturalism; for example, he believes "the new emphasis on worship in the church is going to assist in enforcing the reign of Christ in the world as never before." Reid adds, "God is still placing dreams and visions into the hearts of His people to solve the problems of our society today."[53]

Reid has preached his central message, one of developing an all-encompassing Christian worldview and applying it to social change, repeatedly at large charismatic churches and conferences, winning strong approval from Gary North on one occasion. He has also founded the Association of Church-centered Bible Schools (ACBS), which enables churches to train their own leaders rather than needing to send them away to seminaries. As of 1989, according to its director, about one hundred churches had started affiliated schools and three hundred more were using parts of the curriculum.[54] Standing out among the theology courses is one entitled "A Biblical Theology of Dominion," the description of which states that the course will enable students to understand Kingdom theology and to "develop an attitude that the Church is responsible under God to further the rule and reign of Jesus Christ over every area of domain in the world."[55]

POLITICAL, THOUGH NOT RIGHT-WING

The seeds sown by the Latter Rain revival, though politically dormant for three decades, always carried the potential to reverse, at the right time, the previous apolitical behavior of charismatics and Pentecostals. By replacing the hope of an imminent rapture with expectations of great revival, Latter Rain introduced a vision that remained relatively insignificant when held by a handful of

Pentecostals but took on plausibility when joined, as was the case by the time of Washington for Jesus 1980, to the rising social concern of a broader, newly influential evangelical movement.

Latter Rain's (and, subsequently, the charismatic movement's) emphasis on the availability of supernatural gifts also reinforced the traditional Pentecostal belief that God's power is actively present on earth. From its inception the Pentecostal Movement accentuated the miraculous, treating tongue speaking as a sign of spiritual power and emphasizing divine healing so heavily that many Pentecostals rejected medicine. Latter Rain and the charismatic movement made these gifts even more accessible by replacing the established Pentecostal practice of "tarrying" (according to which seekers might expect to spend hours in agonizing prayer before receiving the gift of tongues) with the view that tongues and other gifts could be received instantly through laying on of hands by anointed leaders. Reid argues that the logical development of classical Pentecostal theology, with its emphasis on the Gospel's present-day power, would have had socially active implications from the beginning had the Pentecostals not been scared away by the fact that, in the early twentieth century, the "social gospel" was associated with theological liberalism.[56]

The Latter Rain-derived doctrine of modern-day apostles and prophets also contributed to the mobilization of charismatic and Pentecostal zeal. Established charismatic leaders' ability to claim apostolic or prophetic authority enables them to present themselves as messengers of God and predisposes church members to embrace their pastor's vision more readily and express less dissent. Furthermore, the attitude of overflowing charismatic enthusiasm creates an atmosphere in which members are more likely to participate actively in the church's activities. For example, when Chapel Hill Church "adopted" a violence-ridden housing project in northwest Atlanta, the whole worship and arts team agreed to make the sixty-mile round trips to provide artistic training for children and to put on performances.

Unlike the recognizably ideological goals of the Reconstructionists, however, this spontaneous charismatic zeal springs from a spiritual inspiration and is often politically undifferentiated. Rather than tying themselves to a particular organization, party, or political approach, charismatics tend to act in a more independent, prophetic manner or in response to pressing needs. Thus the temptation to link Kingdom Now with the Christian Right, let alone the Republican Right, proves misleading. Paulk's sensitivity to traumatized women has led him, despite his own prolife sentiments, to criticize Operation Rescue's confrontational blockades of abortion clinics, while his up-front concern for racial issues leads to an interest in civil-rights measures that also distances him from the Right.[57] Tommy Reid, who functions in an area "where most of the converts have been blue-collar rust-belt Democrats" and where a major steel-plant shutdown rocked the economy, says he has moved away from political conservatism toward a more middle-of-the-road position.[58] John Gimenez has dropped his Republican membership, having found the GOP "as full of error as the Democrats." Expressing a minority opinion among politically concerned evangelicals, Gimenez has said Christians should start a third party.[59] Even the charismatic group most associated with the Right, the one to which we will turn next, did not fully retain that association.

DOMINION ON CAMPUS: MARANATHA MINISTRIES

The boldest Christian outreach to hit American campuses since the Jesus Movement, Maranatha Ministries challenged students across the nation with open-air preaching, intensive discipleship for believers, and a hard-hitting, issues-oriented newspaper called *The Forerunner*. Maranatha's style derived directly from its founder, Bob Weiner, whose autobiography, misleadingly titled *Take Dominion*, is actually dominated not by any political agenda but by his unceasing burden for personal evangelism and discipleship. Nevertheless, Weiner, the only known postmillennialist among contemporary charismatic leaders,[60] does not neglect the sociopolitical aspect of world transformation. Taking Genesis 1:26 as "marching orders," Weiner says God's servants are called to bring every area of life "under His influence and under biblical principles." As part of Maranatha's contribution to this task, its Providence Foundation was "teaching Christian young people from all over America how to become governmental and political leaders."[61]

While the Providence Foundation, formed in 1983, "has existed to reform the world around them, not from a conservative or liberal platform, but from a worldview that is thoroughly biblical,"[62] the rest of Maranatha often appeared less bashful about partisanship. Maranatha members strongly supported several conservative Republicans, such as former Michigan congressman Mark Siljander, and the organization gained a reputation for supplying droves of dedicated volunteers to GOP campaigns.[63] Before the 1984 election *The Forerunner* printed David Balsiger's "Presidential Biblical Scorecard," which, though formally nonpartisan, presented the two candidates' stances in a fashion obviously skewed toward Reagan.[64]

Four years later *The Forerunner* had no similar bent. One reason may have been a relative lack of excitement about George Bush, as Weiner personally had energetically supported Pat Robertson and *The Forerunner* had named Robertson one of its 1987 "Reformers of the Year" for his pioneering of private initiatives.[65] But also, Maranatha was moving toward a view that being politically "prophetic" entailed standing apart from both conservative and liberal bonds. *Forerunner* editor Lee Grady warned that "in many cases [the biblical solution] will be completely different from what either side is proposing." While still expressing a strikingly strong faith in God's providential guidance of America, Maranatha was exercising greater caution not to give God an implicit party affiliation.[66] It appears that Weiner and Maranatha had resolved to impact the political sphere but, at the same time, to steer clear of political controversy that would hinder their primary calling of evangelism.

Maranatha disbanded as an organization at the end of 1989, but its legacy continues not only through the thousands of young, zealous Christians it has influenced but also through the generally campus-based fellowships it established that now function independently.[67]

PINNING DOWN PAT'S CHARISMATIC SIDE

Earl Paulk and Tommy Reid's expectation that God will sovereignly grant social and political solutions to the church would sound strange to most Americans. So would the widespread belief that the prayers offered at Washington for Jesus 1980 significantly altered the nation's course. So would Bob Weiner's 1979 prophecy that more people would be "saved" in the 1980s than in all of previous history combined.[68] So also—to take an example that received greater public notice—did Oral Roberts's prophecy that a cure for cancer would be discovered at his now-defunct City of Faith Hospital. But all these claims reflect and are typical of the openly supernatural ethos of charismatic Christianity. This ethos in part reasserts the traditional Christian belief that God answers prayer (after all, the noncharismatic Bill Bright was as convinced as anyone of the value of the WFJ prayers) but goes much farther in claiming access to God's supernatural powers and knowledge of the future.

In this context Pat Robertson's controversial claim to have diverted a hurricane away from Virginia Beach by prayer, a statement that struck much of America as somewhere between bizarre and megalomaniacal, is not at all out of place. On the contrary, Robertson could not have epitomized the evangelical move toward radical social transformation, nor could he have capitalized so successfully on that trend in mobilizing Christian support for his presidential candidacy, had he not shared the vibrant charismatic convictions present in a large portion of that constituency. Only a charismatic could satisfy those who envisioned a president "prophesying the word of the Lord over the country and over the world."[69]

Whereas Robertson the religious broadcaster was forced to revise his jargon for wider public consumption when he became Robertson the politician, he had been speaking the charismatics' language all along. In *The Secret Kingdom*, Robertson speaks of an "invisible world" whose kingdom-of-God principles can be tapped to cure the visible world's ills. As of 1982 he was expecting a "great revival of faith in Jesus Christ" that would enable the world to see kingdom truths more fully and thereby "transcend many of the limitations we are experiencing now." For example, Robertson proposed scientific advance through divine revelation: we face an energy crisis now, he said, but the oceans are full of hydrogen, and "sooner or later, God may give to one or more of His people a concept for running cars on such water."[70] By 1986, as he began to test the waters for a presidential candidacy, he was anticipating a similar revival in the political realm, inspired by God but actualized through Christians getting involved in government: "There is a new wave, . . . for the world is going to change in accordance with the plan of God."[71]

Robertson also interpreted history in ways unfamiliar to standard university textbooks. For instance, he said the American South has recently experienced economic prosperity because, in obedience to the law of reciprocity (which Robertson finds in Luke 6:38, "Give and it will be given to you"), it began taking steps to improve the living standards of the blacks it had trodden underfoot for so long.[72] Robertson understands socioeconomic processes, but in his supernaturalist worldview he sees them as subservient to and molded by God, the final cause.

We have suggested that by 1988 the sociopolitical concern of charismatics had risen significantly, with the dramatic impact of Paulk's ministry accentuating and providing a distinctive theology for an already bubbling movement. But how significantly? And how much of the charismatic world endorsed Pat Robertson? It is hard to tell. Certainly his candidacy attracted only lukewarm support among evangelicals in general, partly because even those who were politically active and Republican had other attractive choices in Vice President Bush and Jack Kemp. What is clear is that Robertson mobilized a group of believers who would not have become excited about any other candidate, and that many of them labored under a special sense of divine anointing, the product of their uniquely empowering charismatic spirituality. As one woman who worked at Robertson's national campaign headquarters summed it up: "I believed that Pat Robertson had a proven track record of hearing accurately from God, and was incapable of deception and illusions of grandeur. . . . I believed that this miracle [of Robertson winning the presidency], senseless by the world's standards, could easily happen."[73]

But the fact that Earl Paulk, the man at the center of the Kingdom Now "movement," is far from aligned with Robertson's policy views reminds us that the contemporary mobilization of charismatics is more diverse and powerful than one dark-horse presidential run. Far broader and more significant than Robertson alone, both as a religious movement and as a reflection of the status of conservative Christians in contemporary America, is the upsurge of kingdom-thinking charismatics who share Robertson's vision of social transformation and who, though by no means unified in their agenda, are all determined to become involved distinctively in society and politics in their own locale. Paulk's role, as the catalyst of Kingdom Now, has been to bring the dominionist style of thinking to such prominence within a charismatic context that other charismatics, whether in favor of or opposed to the new wave of social involvement, could no longer ignore it. In this regard he has lived up to his title of "provoker."

THE UNPREDICTABLES

As I studied Chapel Hill Harvester Church, I was perplexed by what seemed to be a paradox. Some sources criticized the church as overly authoritarian, while others viewed it as overly permissive. At first I was stumped, until I discovered the common thread: Chapel Hill—like all the charismatics described in this chapter— tends to have a high level of confidence in its ability to hear the Spirit of God. This same tendency, when misguided, can lead either to authoritarianism (when the person claiming a message from God is the congregation's leader) or to permissiveness (when the recipient of the message is a member of the congregation and is not restrained by those in leadership).

Believing themselves impelled by the Holy Spirit, charismatics have often shown a willingness to take risks and experiment with new ideas. This boldness has guided charismatics like Chapel Hill to many smashing successes in recent years. It has also led them, at times, into a myriad of abusive practices. Virtually every church or organization mentioned in this chapter has faced charges of serious theological error, gross mistreatment of its members, or both.

I feel unable to say much by way of either critique or

commendation of these charismatics, not only because of their diversity but also because their capacity for rapid evolution could leave my words outdated before my ink is dry. All who interact with these charismatics and their ideas, however, would be well advised to proceed with cautious discernment. A groundbreaking charismatic church like Chapel Hill or Rock Church may be blessed with particular insights, but it will also make its share of mistakes along the way. The real challenge—for them and for all of us—is to combine the zeal and energy characteristic of the charismatics with the personal stablility, moral reliability, and respect for other persons that they all too often have lacked.

• 5 •

Turning Visions
Into Tactics
Dominionist Offensives
in Contemporary America

Uncannily similar in many of their basic principles and
attitudes, the Reconstructionist and charismatic impulses of social
transformation nevertheless remain separated by central differences
that often surface when the two groups interact. Their on-again, off-
again relationship sheds light not only on the nature of these
movements but also on the dilemmas entailed in the attempt they
and other evangelicals are making to recapture and carry out a this-
worldly agenda.

BUILDING DOMINIONIST BRIDGES

While those who connect Reconstruction with Kingdom Now
as two branches of "dominion theology" tend to overlook the
substantial differences between them, the association does reflect
the fact that both groups rely on Genesis 1 for their dominion
mandate. This and other similarities can be easily illustrated by
comparing the main popularizers from each group, Gary North and
Earl Paulk.

Paulk insists that God's original plan, by which man was to
subdue the earth, has not changed and that Christians must live as
if God still rules this world. In doing so he uses terms similar to
North's constant ridicule of the defeatist mentality prevalent among
Christians.[1] In accord with this overriding concept of God's

ultimate rule, both Reconstructionists and Kingdom Now charismatics promote the necessity of a kingdom-centered worldview that relates Christianity to every sphere of life. Paulk's colleague Tommy Reid, as we have seen, even shares the Reconstructionists' debt to Kuyper.

Both North and Paulk also have prophesied impending world crisis and urged that Christians should be prepared to step into the breach when secular institutions crumble. This anticipation of unprecedented opportunity after a crisis is one of North's primary means of motivating readers of *Backward, Christian Soldiers?*, his most purely tactical book. Paulk, while lacking North's economic expertise, notes that no one needs prophetic gifts to perceive the fragile state of our economy. "I believe that world systems will collapse," he states forthrightly.[2]

North and Paulk also share a distinctly pragmatic streak, as seen in North's readiness to welcome as "operational" postmillennialists any Christians who share his practical goals (even if they do not share his eschatology) and Chapel Hill's assertion that "theology is almost secondary to ministry."[3] A frenetic worker, North dutifully devotes two hours a day to the continuing production of his *Economic Commentary on the Bible*; when he decided that a book on basic Christian truths from a Reconstructionist perspective was needed, he wrote it himself—in two weeks.[4] Paulk displays a similarly consuming passion for demonstration of the kingdom of God, in his lifestyle as well as his writing; fellow staff say they cannot convince him to take a vacation.

Additional similarities between the two lines of thought include their distaste, if not open ridicule, for rapture theology and otherworldly pietism; their belief that substantial improvement must take place in at least some portion of human society before Christ's return; and, in most cases, their view of the church as God's new Israel. Since the two groups developed their views separately, and largely before having contact with each other, the parallels reflect their shared sentiments regarding the need to push evangelicals toward theological constructs that foster social change.[5]

These similarities offered the potential for fruitful interaction between Kingdom Now and Reconstruction, with some observers and participants looking forward to a "marriage" between them.[6] The logical person to serve as a link between them was Dennis Peacocke. Charismatic in spirituality, yet friendly to Reconstructionist social theory; a student of Rushdoony and North and also a "spiritual son" to Earl Paulk;[7] radical in social activism yet theologically flexible—Peacocke was just the right person to connect the groups to each other and to a wider circle of conservative activists.

When Peacocke converted from Marxism to Christianity in 1967 while a graduate student at Berkeley, he did not give up his belief in the power of ideas to effect long-term social change. He was refreshed by his study of evangelical philosopher Francis Schaeffer and then of Rushdoony but became convinced that most of the evangelical church was mired in "intellectual stupidity." Determined to change that situation, Peacocke continued to study philosophical, social, and political issues while embarking in 1977 on a teaching ministry that extended beyond his home church in Santa Rosa, California. Peacocke's "Rebuilders" seminars are aimed at turning Christian leaders into "changers rather than escapists" and at encouraging them to seek and implement biblical solutions to society's problems.[8]

Functioning behind the scenes in the political sphere, Peacocke in 1984 formed the Anatole Fellowship as another means toward strategizing gradual, incremental change. Peacocke interacted with Christian Right leaders but felt their overtly political approach was dealing with secondary rather than foundational issues and falling into "the trap of expecting change via civil government." Desiring to develop Christians who will think "not electorally, but generationally," Peacocke replaced Anatole with the Christian Public Policy Council (CPPC), which functions more as a Christian think tank, discussing the long-term impact of social policy but not committing its participants to specific positions or concrete actions.[9]

Peacocke considers Rushdoony "one of the most seminal thinkers since the Protestant Reformation,"[10] but his public presentations avoid Reconstruction's most controversial aspects and thus are palatable to a broader audience. (His writings also show no trace of the vibrantly charismatic worship and preaching style that dominate his personal ministry in charismatic settings.) In his book, *Winning the Battle for the Minds of Men*, Peacocke urges Christians to put society back under biblical law but remains vague as to just how Old Testament civil laws should be applied today, cautioning that they "are to be interpreted by the Holy Spirit."[11] He decries the otherworldliness of rapture believers and expresses confidence that the kingdom will be progressively revealed on earth, yet he does not embrace postmillennialism or openly deny the Rapture.[12] When asked in an interview by a sympathetic Christian magazine whether he had a master blueprint guiding his social theory, he declined to comment.[13] His book names Rushdoony and North just once each (excluding the dedication to "Bob [Mumford, a well-known charismatic teacher] and Rush and Gary" and the Reconstructionist-dominated bibliography), but Peacocke's indebtedness to Reconstructionist concepts of sphere sovereignty, economics, and optimism is evident throughout. For example, he emphasizes that the family, not the state's printing of currency, is the source of wealth (though, diplomatically again, Peacocke stops short of the full-scale rejection of paper money) and echoes North's hope that humanism will soon collapse, giving Christians the chance to rule.[14]

Peacocke's bridge building received a boost from Bob Tilton, a bold charismatic megapastor from Dallas known for his pioneering development of Christian programming by satellite. Tilton's wife, impressed by Gary DeMar's *God and Government* books, convinced her husband to host a seminar in 1984 at which leading Reconstructionists spoke. An estimated one thousand charismatic pastors attended and responded positively, furthering North's hope that the charismatics would expand their faith in God's miracle-working power to include the healing of society as well as of individuals. DeMar subsequently taught principles of government on Tilton's satellite network.[15]

The interactions expanded as Peacocke arranged conferences in 1986 and 1987 and channeled members of both groups into his Anatole Fellowship and then the CPPC.[16] North, DeMar, and Joe Morecraft addressed conferences held by Paulk's church and by Maranatha Ministries, and Reconstructionist thinking began to permeate Maranatha's *Forerunner* magazine.[17]

The pattern of interaction, however, was peculiar, in that one group supplied the ideas while the other furnished the bodies and resources. The Reconstructionists acknowledged their need for the charismatics' media resources and mass appeal but not for any charismatic ideas. Thus the Reconstructionists appeared in charismatic churches and literature, but the reverse—for example, Tilton, Paulk, or Weiner writing for North or DeMar—never occurred. The only move resembling an ideological concession on the Reconstructionist side was nevertheless a significant one: North's departure from the Reformed doctrine that genuine charismatic gifts had ceased with the early church. North repudiated one paragraph of a 1974 Rushdoony article, "Power from Below," that attributed the charismatics' supernatural power to demonic sources, and he cited his wife's experience of physical healing as one factor motivating his change of heart. With uncharacteristic charity North excused Tilton's unorthodox theology, often judged deficient even by charismatic standards, as sloppiness rather than heresy.[18] (He subsequently decided Tilton was too far out theologically to justify such toleration.)

The signs of cooperation with charismatics provided useful ammunition for Wayne House and Tommy Ice, authors of the first book-length assessment of Reconstruction, *Dominion Theology: Blessing or Curse?* (1988). House and Ice, who firmly oppose the charismatic movement, used the Reconstructionist-charismatic relationship as evidence of the former group's lack of theological integrity. House and Ice supplied a list of parallels between Reconstructionist and Kingdom teaching, a collection Reconstructionists derided as superficial and inconclusive.[19]

DOMINION—BUT HOW?

House and Ice's tale of two cooperating groups is not the whole story. As Kingdom Now and Reconstruction leaders began to interact, they also became aware of the substantial differences between them.

First and foremost, on the central theological question of God's sovereignty and its relation to human ability, the two are light years apart. Paulk and Reid typify the charismatic tendency to endow Spirit-filled believers with semidivine power when they describe the church as "the ongoing incarnation of Christ";[20] in contrast, Rushdoony pronounces heretical any extension of Christ's incarnation into the church.[21] Kingdom Now, like most charismatics, emphasizes human ability to choose and do what is right, while Reconstructionists echo Calvin in their heavy stress on a sovereign God's predestination of human behavior. The immense gap between a holy God and human beings, a concept central to Gary North's theology, often seems to disappear as confident charismatics speak of human potential to be "like Jesus in the world."[22]

Concepts of law are another area of disagreement. Charismatics, who value so highly the importance of the supernatural gifts bestowed upon the New Testament church, are not prone to endorse a theonomic ethic based on the continuing preeminence of Old Testament directives. In contrast to Reconstruction, Paulk looks primarily to Jesus for his political ethic and to the Holy Spirit for modern-day direction. What he views as his attempts to apply biblical morality to today's society by the Spirit's guidance, Reconstructionists would reject as misguided wanderings that fail to honor God's law.

Predictably, the specific applications often differ as well. For example, Rushdoony rejects laws prohibiting racial discrimination as intrusions on personal freedom, while Paulk and his colleague John Meares say a godly civil government must promote equal opportunity.[23] Reconstruction consciously derives a concrete, extensive set of public-policy implications from Scripture, but for Paulk the connection is much less direct: "Christians make a mistake when they attempt to tie the gospel message to any national or political system."[24] Those charismatic leaders, like Paulk and John Meares, with substantial black followings have additional reason to avoid too close a connection to conservative political stances usually associated with white Republicans.

The issue of eschatology erects further barriers. While Reconstruction confidently plans for the establishment of a Christian majority and the complete reversal of world authority into Christian hands, Paulk and Reid are not postmillennial and require only that the kingdom be clearly "demonstrated"—a task that a committed Christian minority could achieve and that, in their view, "prototype" churches like their own are already implementing. The unacceptability of postmillennialism in Pentecostal circles also motivates Kingdom Now advocates to distance themselves firmly from this doctrine for public-relations purposes.

Furthermore, the Reconstructionists' adherence to Reformed tradition leaves them skeptical of charismatics' freewheeling, often independent, and authoritarian ministry styles. And, although North has softened his stance, other Reconstructionists continue to reject as theologically false the charismatics' claim to have rediscovered genuine supernatural power. The Kingdom Now leaders, for their part, wonder why the Reconstructionists, with their comparatively tiny churches, are unwilling to learn from the charismatics' successes in building large congregations full of spiritual enthusiasm and energy.

Kingdom Now and Reconstruction have come to know each other well enough that neither wants to be lumped with the other. Yet their agreement to disagree peacefully is more an aid than a hindrance in the early stages of dominionist movement building. Each group can continue to recruit—Reconstruction building its following among rigorously intellectual evangelicals, Kingdom Now among zealous charismatics—without having to explain or apologize for its cooperation with the other. Like any social movement in its expansion phase, dominion theology can spread most effectively if it remains decentralized and expresses itself in multiple, diverse forms rather than merging into a single platform based on a compromise that fully pleases no one.

Sociologically, the form of cooperation between Reconstructionist and charismatic dominionists that *would* have strategic value is not organizational unity but simply a network of loose ties by which to maintain personal contacts and share ideas. Peacocke's Christian Public Policy Council continues to supply this forum. Not until the time comes to assume public leadership and implement actual policies would tighter unity have substantial tactical value. That unity could take shape only under a recognized leader who could both articulate at least a somewhat dominionist ideology and exude a genuinely unbridled charismatic zeal. Amazingly this very combination—the one that makes Peacocke such a rare bird—

found its incarnation in a serious presidential candidate in the 1980s.

PAT ARRIVES

By 1980, as the New Christian Right was shifting into high gear, Pat Robertson's success in Christian television had made him one of American evangelicalism's most familiar names. As a Yale Law School graduate and son of a U.S. senator, Robertson knew politics much better than his colleagues in televangelism. He was also distinctly nonpartisan (surprisingly so, in retrospect), as can be demonstrated from his *Perspective* newsletter, which he began publishing in 1977 as "a special report to members of the 700 Club" on global and national developments. He initially described President Carter as "God's man" and criticized him only for not placing more evangelicals in leadership positions.[25] A year later Robertson, though sufficiently disillusioned to call Carter "honest and decent, but unsuited for his task,"[26] nevertheless avoided the open revulsion other right-wing evangelicals would heap upon the president. As late as April 1980 Robertson was praising Carter for his anti-inflation stance and his toughness in the Middle East. As the election neared and other prominent evangelicals cheered Reagan to victory, Robertson was soberly cautioning that "neither Democrats nor Republicans will usher in the millennium" and urging Christians to lead America "not through levers of political power, but through service to its people and godly example."[27]

Moreover, Robertson was personally committed to political aloofness. Bob Slosser, now Regent University's president, first came to the school as executive vice president in 1980. He recalls asking Robertson that fall about the possibility of a future in politics. According to Slosser, Robertson spoke of how valuable he considered the CBN ministry and said, "I'd have more impact here than in any political office but one." There was no indication then that he envisioned an eventual run for that office.[28]

Most fascinating of all, Pat Robertson in 1980 had anything but an optimistic long-term vision for changing America. Applying his literalistic, premillennial interpretations of Bible prophecy to current events, Robertson expected the Great Tribulation to begin in the 1980s. While he never clothed his predictions in absolute certainty, Robertson seemed fairly confident in asserting that "the present chaos in Iran [as the Shah's regime began to topple] was foretold by the prophet Ezekiel" or, more radically, in advocating survivalist behavior: "In a year or two there must be consideration given to the storage of food, fallout shelters, and primitive survival tools. We will survive the trouble, but life may be much different."[29]

By late 1985 Robertson was admitting that he might run for president.[30] What had changed? Some think the mass mobilization orchestrated by Washington for Jesus 1980 aroused Robertson's awareness of the potential a candidate with a large evangelical following could exploit.[31] Both his popularity in that religious sector and his clearly articulated policy stances led conservative Republicans to consider him seriously as a possible heir to the Reagan revolution. Slosser believes that some of these Republican regulars were encouraging Robertson to run by 1985; leading New Right strategist Paul Weyrich did not hesitate to make his affinity for Robertson public.[32]

Meanwhile Robertson's grass-roots organization, the Freedom Council, had become an ideal vehicle for galvanizing popular sentiment. By fall 1986, when he announced that he would run for president if three million signatures supporting his candidacy could be collected within a year, Robertson had already assembled the machinery that would produce several stunning political surprises, including victories in an Iowa Republican straw poll and in the early stages of Michigan's complex delegate-selection process.

Struck by Robertson's thorough preparation, sociologists Jeffrey Hadden and Anson Shupe predicted substantial success for his campaign, as well as for evangelical influence in American politics.[33] Their book appeared just in time for the more immediate of these predictions to be disproved by Robertson's disappointing showing in the southern primaries. The Republican party mechanism had proved too tough for an outsider, even an extremely well-organized one, to crack, and Robertson had hurt his own cause with a series of unwise statements and political blunders. Robertson accepted his chance to speak at the Republican National Convention, endorsed Bush, and then returned to CBN where his presidential candidacy and the televangelism scandals had left the ministry gasping for funds.[34]

If Robertson believed he could command broad evangelical support, his hopes were premature. Hadden and Shupe thought negative treatment of Robertson by Republican regulars and the media would cause evangelicals to rally behind "their own" candidate;[35] though the opposition materialized, the unified support did not. But this does not mean Robertson's campaign whimpered into oblivion and left no impact. On the contrary, not only did it continue the political awakening of evangelicals, but it also created a network of evangelicals determined to stand their ground in partisan politics. Instead of demanding that the two established parties pay heed to evangelical concerns, evangelicals now began to infiltrate, redirect, and even take over one of those parties. Formerly one among many special-interest groups in the GOP, the Christian Right now began to produce self-conscious agenda setters. The resulting legacy has been felt in several states where evangelicals have gained substantial control of the Republican party, including Georgia, Oregon, and Washington. In Arizona, the Christian Right led the state GOP to pass a resolution in February 1989 declaring America a "Christian nation."[36]

In 1989 Robertson's *Perspective*, discontinued when he left the "700 Club" to run for president, resumed publication. The man who nine years earlier had directed Christians away from an emphasis on "levers of political power" was now urging them to "learn the issues and then unite in concerted action . . . to insure that Evangelicals are elected to policy making positions" at every level of government.[37] He has also founded the Christian Coalition to fill the gap in evangelical activism left by the withdrawal of the Moral Majority.

Robertson's evolution epitomizes—but also has greatly influenced—the broadening evangelical commitment to social transformation. Those who wonder if he is a Reconstructionist (with a capital *R*) are asking the wrong question. More significant is the fact that he and a growing number of evangelicals, no longer satisfied with seeking legislative change on a handful of issues, are setting out to reconstruct America. They may not be theonomists, but many of them have moved beyond selective, periodic, issue-focused lobbying and adopted the patient, long-term, bottom-up, all-encompassing approach to change that the Reconstructionists have been advocating all along.

BROADENING THE EVANGELICAL BASE FOR DOMINION: COALITION ON REVIVAL

Another evangelical organization, the Coalition on Revival (COR), has diligently been seeking to unify as broad a spectrum of evangelicals as possible behind this dominionist approach to social change. COR is the brainchild of Jay Grimstead, who participated in the International Council on Biblical Inerrancy (ICBI, a ten-year program founded in 1977 to reaffirm a strict evangelical view of Scripture) but felt the affirmation of evangelical essentials should encompass social engagement as well as biblical inspiration. Grimstead, a convert from otherworldly pietism and a close friend of Dennis Peacocke, convened dozens of evangelical leaders for by-invitation-only conferences in the summer of 1984 and again in 1985. These meetings worked toward the creation of seventeen "Christian Worldview Documents" guiding believers' involvement in every sphere of life.[38]

When COR went public, unveiling the Worldview Documents and its "Manifesto for the Christian Church" in a solemn ceremony at Washington's Lincoln Memorial on July 4, 1986, its steering committee looked like a who's who of evangelicals. Among the big names were Josh McDowell of Campus Crusade, National Association of Evangelicals (NAE) public affairs director Bob Dugan, black social activist John Perkins, theologians J. I. Packer and Harold Lindsell, and Edith and Franky Schaeffer (Francis's wife and son). Also included were Reconstructionists DeMar, North, Rushdoony, and Chilton, along with fellow dominionists Peacocke and Weiner. Their presence illustrated the tenuous nature of evangelical unity, as others withdrew from COR rather than risk identification with dominion theology.[39]

In its effort to secure the broad evangelical unity that is both essential in maximizing sociopolitical impact and all but impossible to obtain, COR has attempted to define unmistakably what it expects of its adherents. Where it feels difference of opinion is legitimate, COR does not speak; but wherever it does speak, COR considers its words to be "fundamental and non-negotiable truths and mandates."[40] Its Christian Worldview Documents are designed to "declare where the *entire* Body of Christ *must stand* and what action it must take over the remaining years of this century if the Church is to fulfill its Biblical mandate."[41] The documents, COR claims, "focus on principles so fundamental that we are convinced no Bible-believing Christian who studied the major questions related to each sphere of life would come to a contradictory conclusion."[42]

COR has staked out a hard line on Christian disunity at all levels. Its manifesto calls for the creation of pastors' prayer fellowships, to help produce unity among congregations; within each congregation, the staff and board must be "deeply loyal and unified" around the pastor's leadership and vision. To emphasize the binding force these affirmations are intended to carry, COR has embodied them within its "Solemn Covenant," whose signers are expected to obey it continually "till the day you die or are caught up with [Christ] at His glorious return."[43] COR's interest in upgrading commitment and responsibility at the local-church level is evidenced by the recommendation that each church "develop a clear, concise, written policy on church discipline and excommunication" for all members to sign.[44]

COR's commitment to social change has by no means overridden its concern for theological purity. COR has intentionally narrowed its appeal by its strict definition of biblical inerrancy, a definition that explicitly includes science and history as areas where the Bible cannot err and, as part of its basic statement of faith, warns that "a liberal and neo-orthodox view of the Bible has subtly infiltrated much of evangelical Christianity." To ferret out this hidden liberalism, COR uses a set of twenty questions designed to determine whether one understands biblical inspiration correctly. The last three are particularly technical, and persons without sufficient theological background to grasp these technical questions are encouraged to "seek out a person who can explain why these are critical, watershed questions for evangelicals in the 1980s."[45] In view of COR founder Grimstead's prior involvement with the

ICBI, the acuteness of this concern for biblical inerrancy is not surprising.

In contrast, COR has tried to permit diversity of opinion and outlaw quarreling on two issues that may seem more directly relevant to maintenance of a Christian political coalition: law and eschatology. Grimstead stated in 1989 that the question of how Old Testament civil law applies to modern society remains "absolutely unsettled,"[46] and two sentences from COR's document on law put the ambiguity in stark relief:

> (Affirmation 25): We affirm that standards and principles set forth in the Old Testament apply to civil law today, provided that they are repeated in the New Testament in such a way as to be applicable to civil law today.

> (Affirmation 26): We affirm that principles expressed in the Old Testament, whether or not repeated in the New Testament, apply to civil law today unless those principles are limited by their immediate context or by other scriptures to circumstances not existing today, or unless those principles are abrogated by subsequent scripture. . . .

These two affirmations, one stating that Old Testament principles apply to civil law today unless abrogated and the other implying that they do not apply unless repeated in the New Testament, are at least in tension, though not quite in absolute logical contradiction, with each other. This may be a diplomatically strategic ambiguity, intended to satisfy the breadth of COR signers' views on biblical law. Hard-line Reconstructionists in COR, however, have perhaps conveniently overlooked affirmation 26, as it goes on to state that laws "designed for Old Testament theocratic Israel . . . are therefore not applicable to the nontheocratic civil law of today."[47]

COR's attempt to unite evangelicals of varying eschatologies on a platform of social transformation has required additional tightrope walking. COR can justifiably claim that no eschatology necessarily precludes social concern, but lack of eschatological agreement does preclude consensus regarding feasible goals or criteria for success. The COR *Manifesto* bridges this gap rather clumsily by declaring that Christians should work "to see God's will done, on earth as it is in heaven, insofar as that is possible" before Christ's return.[48]

COR consistently parallels the Reconstructionist version of sphere sovereignty in distinguishing four governmental jurisdictions: self, family, church, and state.[49] However, it stipulates an important loophole, permitting civil law to expand its concerns when other spheres neglect the needy.

> We deny . . . that civil law properly respects human dignity when it . . . neglects the truly helpless or needy when others fail to care for them as God requires. [While rejecting "massive government welfare programs," COR does appear to endorse some state concern for the needy, albeit as a last resort.]
>
> We affirm . . . that God may from time to time grant civil law secondary or "back-up" jurisdiction when other human agents fail to perform as God intends. [The text goes on to place this secondary jurisdiction within God's "permissive" will and to deny that it should ever be "permanent or extensive."]
>
> We deny that civil government has a duty to care financially for . . . the truly needy through a coercive tax system, unless the primary providers totally fail to fulfill their responsibility to do so. [Again the loophole exists, though the word *totally* declares COR's distaste for such means.][50]

These halting statements seem to signify a limited tolerance for government social programs, but, if so, COR's Economics Committee did not receive the message. Transferral of responsibility for the poor from family and church to state, the economics document warns, "invariably results in threats to liberty and property." Firmly rejecting all "coerced redistribution of wealth" as "contrary to justice and love," it affirms the free market without qualification or exception and advocates evangelism and discipleship as the primary response to poverty. While the Economics Committee urges the publication of "sound, irenic answers" to erroneous Christian economic views, Grimstead has not hesitated to recommend as essential reading David Chilton's *Productive Christians in an Age of Guilt-Manipulators*, in which the attack on welfare and other social programs is anything but gentle.[51]

COR is not as inflexibly presuppositionalist as Reconstruction, affirming the role of "human reason" in the development of law and the ability of non-Christians to have a positive influence on civil law. But it also eschews the religious neutrality of conventional

American political action, affirming that "civil law should reflect Christian values."[52]

To those who deem it wiser to make immediate use of the influence one has than to plot a total reshaping of society that would take generations (if it can ever be achieved at all), COR's ultimate vision may sound grandiose and irrelevant. As one evangelical at a Washington think tank put it, "They come to town, blow their trumpets, and then go home and are never heard from again."[53] And Grimstead's bold personal style has made it even harder to hold this evangelical coalition together. In late 1990 the NAE's Dugan was among those rapidly distancing themselves from COR after Grimstead circulated a wide-ranging list of tentative goals that included eliminating the Internal Revenue Service and the Federal Reserve Bank by the year 2000.[54]

COR and Grimstead are right in their conviction that the only way to change a society fundamentally and radically—to really penetrate and transform the collective mind of a culture—is to reshape it gradually over multiple generations. After all, it was only by a gradual evolution over generations that Christianity lost its former position of cultural leadership in America. But COR's experience shows how difficult it is to unite even a small core of reasonably like-minded believers in such a project. In the next chapter we will take a closer look at some of the disagreements that make dominion theology a divisive topic even among evangelicals.

• 6 •

"Go Away, You're Embarrassing Me"

Dominion Theology and American Evangelicalism

Though it hopes to change the way American evangelicals relate to society, dominion theology has no quibble with the basic tenets of evangelical theology. All the dominionists we have discussed in the previous chapters desire to reform evangelicalism from within, not to contest its role as protector of orthodox Christianity in the modern world. They unhesitantly endorse the two beliefs required for acceptance within the American evangelical community: (1) personal faith in Jesus Christ as the only means of salvation, and (2) the complete inspiration of the Bible as free from error.[1]

Displaying these two ideological "badges," usually confirmed by formal affirmation of the historic creeds of the church, is generally sufficient to gain recognition as an evangelical. Once recognized as such, one can permissibly present within the evangelical community differing views as to what implications personal faith in Christ entails for one's life, or as to what the wholly inspired Bible teaches. Thus the dominionists, precisely because of their apparent adherence to evangelical essentials, pose a difficult problem for several groups of fellow evangelicals who wish the dominionists would disappear. These critics cannot easily justify exclusion of Reconstruction and Kingdom Now believers from the evangelical camp, but neither are they anxious to welcome dominion theology as an acceptable evangelical option.

Dominion theology's tenuous relationship with mainline

American evangelicalism has arisen because it *is* meeting the two basic criteria for evangelical membership while also promoting other views that clash boldly with the evangelical consensus. In this chapter we will see how other evangelicals have sought to counter the perceived threat from the dominionists. Before we do that, however, let us look more closely at how Reconstruction and Kingdom Now have redefined those two essential badges of evangelicalism.

BADGE 1: PERSONAL COMMITMENT

Ask an evangelical what the lordship of Christ means, and the answer will typically begin with lofty generalities about the need to glorify God in everything you do. If you probe for more specifics, though, you will usually hear about personal (or interpersonal) rather than society-oriented requirements: prayer, Bible study, active participation in a local church, fellowship with other Christians, spreading the Gospel through personal evangelism, and holy living.

Ask a Reconstruction or Kingdom Now adherent about the lordship of Christ and you will get a markedly different answer, usually reflecting allegiance to the dominionist motto that Christ's lordship is to be extended into every sphere of society. Dominionists do not ignore the individual-centered requirements other evangelicals stress, but they raise the Christian cultural mandate to the same plane.

The nondominionist definition of Christian commitment has predominated so universally in some sectors of evangelicalism that believers are often shocked to discover how much of American evangelical history stands opposed to them. The seventeenth-century Puritans came to America to build a holy society, not just holy individual lives. When the U.S. Constitution, followed by the repeal of religious-establishment clauses in state constitutions, solidified the separation of church and state, the impulse to establish God's kingdom in America as it is in heaven was transferred from the governmental structure to voluntary societies. Leading evangelicals divided their energies between personal and social forms of Christian action; in fact, it would not have occurred to them to separate the two categories. The "benevolent empire" of Christian societies that sprang up in the early 1800s unified the nation's evangelicals in both types of pursuits—through Bible, tract, Sunday school, education, and mission organizations on the one hand, and temperance, peace, antislavery, and Sabbatarian (i.e., keeping the Sabbath holy) endeavors on the other. Efforts at social reform generally began with large-scale persuasion and then turned to political hardball when persuasion proved inadequate.[2]

Only after the Civil War did evangelical attitudes change. Numerous factors combined, especially in the North where the mandate to Christianize society had been strongest, to defeat the evangelicals and push them toward an increasingly marginal status in American culture. These factors included Catholic immigration, urbanization (which created teeming ghettos of impoverished souls largely untouched by religion), modern scholarship that questioned traditional views of the Bible, Darwin's theory of evolution, and liberal theology.

Both intellectually and socially, evangelicals saw the world slipping out of their control rather than progressing toward the Millennium. They tried to fight back, but by 1925, the year of the famous Scopes trial in which evolution won out over biblicist fundamentalism in the court of public opinion, it was clear that they had lost. The evangelicals then, in a "great reversal," withdrew from public life; either forming their own separatist denominations or becoming quiet dissidents in the mainline Protestant churches, they focused on the personal side of Christianity and left social action in the hands of the liberals. Their only— albeit temporary—social victory during these years was Prohibition, in which they succeeded largely because liberal Protestants agreed with them. Not until after World War II did murmurings of substantial evangelical resurgence first arise, and not until the 1970s did the movement reemerge significantly onto the public stage.[3]

In linking the lordship of Christ with sweeping social transformation, then, dominion theology is hardly an innovator. It finds ample precedent in American evangelical history, not to mention earlier Protestants like Calvin, the Swiss Reformation, and English Puritanism. In the contemporary context, however, dominion theology remains a minority opinion—and in view of its social implications, an unavoidably explosive one.

BADGE 2: BIBLICAL INSPIRATION

The often-quoted line, "God has still more light to break forth from his holy word," was first attributed to a deeply biblical evangelical, the Puritan leader John Robinson. Ironically, the quotation has proved useful to Protestant liberals, like the Presbyterian group that took the name "More Light" for its crusade to convince its denomination that Christianity and homosexual behavior are now compatible. One does not hear many evangelicals speak of "more light to break forth" any more, now that they have become the guardians of traditional orthodoxy against the inroads of liberal theology and higher criticism. Though a few reinterpretations of tradition—most notably regarding women in ministerial leadership—have gained a strong foothold within the ranks, evangelicalism can usually be found upholding traditional views and resisting change, on fronts ranging from the sinfulness of homosexual practice to the veracity of biblical miracles.

Evangelicals by no means discourage biblical scholarship, but they expect their scholarship to reinforce traditionally held views. Those who question the traditional paradigm of biblical inspiration may lose their membership in the evangelical community, as did theologian Robert Gundry when he described Matthew as creating rather than simply recording the words of Jesus in the First Gospel.[4] But that was a relatively easy one. More perplexing to evangelicalism are those innovators who, unlike the liberals who are easily identifiable as opponents, derive new ideas from the Bible while still affirming its infallibility.

Both dominionist groups have done exactly that. Reconstruction holds a very strong view of biblical inspiration, as shown by its insistence on the absolute historicity of Genesis and its vociferous denunciation of neo-orthodox theology;[5] but its Tyler faction, at least, is quick to proclaim groundbreaking new discoveries. One must take Gary North's rhetoric with numerous grains of salt, of course, as he regularly uses inflated language to emphasize the achievements of Reconstructionist writers. But North outdoes himself in lavishing endless praise on colleague Ray Sutton's five-part model of the pattern of biblical covenants, as described in Sutton's book *That You May Prosper*. North regards Sutton's covenant model as providing "an integrating theological framework" for Reconstruction, one "that will at last unshackle Christianity as an intellectual force for total, worldwide social transformation."[6] North's other books repeatedly refer readers to Sutton. He even reorganized both Gary DeMar's treatise on biblical principles of government and George Grant's book on principles of political action into two sets of five chapters, each set paralleling Sutton's model.[7]

The claim to newly discovered truth becomes tactically valuable as Reconstruction seeks to make its gallant visions plausible. Against those who say a re-Christianization of society can never happen, North can point to these new truths as evidence that Christians' current opportunity surpasses that of all previous ages. And when critics scoff at his claims, North can retort that they have to read Sutton first, along with Chilton's commentary on Revelation and Rushdoony's *Institutes*. Since these three books add up to eighteen hundred pages of text, that diversion will keep the critics busy for a while.[8]

Whereas intellectually oriented Christians expect that major, new theological breakthroughs (if any more are needed at all) will come only from mature, extensively trained Christian scholars, charismatics are more likely to expect them by divine intervention. This is the means adopted by Earl Paulk, for example, who believes that "in these last days God, by His Spirit, is bringing us revelations we did not have previously."[9] Paulk generally seeks to defend his insights from Scripture, but his emphasis on receiving guidance directly from the Holy Spirit grants him a confident openness to new ideas.

Whether it originates in scholarly research or a charismatic vision, a new idea is very hard to expel from evangelicalism once it gains a following. This is because of the lack of consensus in evangelical opinion beyond the two badges we have identified. Decentralized in structure and individualistic in attitude, evangelicalism has no recognized authority that can pass official judgment on new teachings. Denominations, parachurch groups, theology schools, research centers, and prophetically inclined charismatics all seek that authority, and their multiple claims cancel each other out.

REFORM 1: ESCHATOLOGY AND SOCIAL HOPE

We have seen that the dominionists wear, with a few important quirks, the two badges of evangelicalism. What about the areas in which they function intentionally as agents of reform? In the Reconstructionists' case, the controversy over their desire to reinvigorate evangelicals with a confident vision for social reform often comes to a head in eschatology. Although postmillennialism is technically a lawful view within the evangelical boundaries, since it is compatible with the two badges discussed above, it is so much a minority opinion today as to bring forth forceful rebuttals, and occasionally even unbridled cries of heresy, from Reconstruction's irate critics.

Again, a long historical tale lies behind this conflict, and again, the farther one goes back in American history, the better the Reconstructionist case looks. Jonathan Edwards, the eighteenth-century Puritan theologian unmatched in scope as an American religious thinker, was an ardent postmillennialist. Edwards inherited an eschatological hopefulness that had been born in the previous century, when Puritan exegesis began to take seriously the apparent prediction in Romans 11 of a mass conversion of Jews.[10] Although his carefully calculated one-to-one connections between episodes from the book of Revelation and historical events led him to guess that the world would continue for a few more centuries, the great spiritual awakening over which he presided in the 1740s tantalized him with the thought that the victorious completion of history might be much closer.[11]

Charles Finney, the most influential revivalist in America between Edwards and the Civil War, also dared to hope that his evangelistic successes presaged a soon-coming millennium.[12] Post-millennial ideology spurred Christian enthusiasm for the American Revolution and for nineteenth-century evangelicals' ambitious social-reform undertakings.[13] Until the Civil War, postmillennialism, intensified by confidence that the anticipated Christianization of the world would begin with America, was the standard evangelical eschatology.

But the post-Civil War events that dimmed evangelicals' faith in social progress turned them toward premillennialism, which taught that no lasting social improvement could occur until after Christ returned to earth. Especially attractive was the new, "dispensational" version of premillennialism. Dispensationalism, popularized on both sides of the Atlantic by British sectarian evangelist John Nelson Darby, taught that the Christian era of history (the age or "dispensation" of the church) would end with all living believers being suddenly taken from the earth ("raptured") to join Christ in the heavens. Seven years of great tribulation would ensue for those unfortunate enough to be left behind; then Christ would return to earth to inaugurate the millennium. This escapist dispensational outlook flourished in late nineteenth-century America largely because it provided an effective rationalization for defeated evangelicals: having failed to transform society, they discovered that God had never intended them to do so anyhow.[14] (Explaining the historical reasons for dispensationalism's popularity does not, of course, prove the theory to be theologically false.)

The old vision of progressive social change was thus abandoned largely to liberal exponents of the social gospel. As American evangelicals uncharacteristically withdrew from the public arena, premillennialism took hold as the practically unquestioned eschatological paradigm. By the 1970s millions of Americans were so wedded to the dispensational interpretation popularized by Hal Lindsey in *The Late Great Planet Earth* that they were unaware of alternative possibilities. It was taken for granted that the Bible prophesied the literal restoration of the modern state of Israel; that this historic event meant the world's final events would begin to unfold within a generation; that the nations outlined in Ezekiel, Daniel, and Revelation could be equated specifically with countries on the twentieth-century world stage; and that end-times disasters would ensue in a fashion somewhat resembling the pattern Lindsey had deciphered, with the Christians being raptured before the worst of the Tribulation could materialize.

Until the 1980s, defenders of postmillennialism were all but invisible in American evangelicalism.[15] Moreover, the rise of secular humanism has led the conservative Christian subculture to associate conceptions of human progress with godlessness. This completed the turnabout: now the once-prevalent postmillennial hope of social improvement strikes many evangelicals not simply as theological error but as secularist heresy.

Lindsey the dispensationalist has not remained quiet while Reconstruction revived postmillennialism. In a book undiplomatically entitled *The Road to Holocaust*, he repeated the common charge that, by transferring the Old Testament's promises regarding Israel to the Christian church rather than applying them to the modern Jewish nation, dominion theology opens the door to anti-Semitism. (Both Reconstruction and Kingdom Now have been dealing with this attack for some time.)[16] Lindsey considers both Reconstruction's postmillennialism and its view of Israel to be dual results of "a [symbolic] method of interpretation that has not only been proven to be false in history, but the cause of terrible, inexcusable suffering for 'the lost sheep of the house of Israel.' "[17] Lindsey's ire was such that he rebuffed Reconstructionist Gary DeMar's request for dialogue before publication of *The Road to Holocaust*.[18]

Ironically, the free-market economic system Reconstructionists so lavishly praise works against them in their current squabbles. Publishers of Christian books, like televangelists, often evaluate their products by whether they generate income more than by their theological integrity. Therefore, guaranteed best-sellers by big names like Lindsey are rushed into print with little theological quality control.[19]

In dispensationalism's war on dominion theology, Dave Hunt has carried a higher profile than Lindsey. Hunt, after earning a reputation as an evangelical cultwatcher, turned his attention to error *inside* the church in *The Seduction of Christianity*, criticizing almost anyone who hoped for human progress or questioned the doctrine of the pretribulation rapture. *Seduction* sold over seven hundred thousand copies and propelled Hunt into a best-seller-a-year pace, his most direct attacks against dominion theology appearing in *Whatever Happened to Heaven?*[20]

We will look more closely at Hunt in chapter 8. At this point it is important to observe that Hunt joins Lindsey in rejecting both the Reconstructionists' eschatology and their social hope. (In fact, with regard to social action his stance is more hard-line than that of Lindsey, who expresses limited agreement with Reconstructionist political goals.) Insisting that Christians should concentrate on their heavenly goal, Hunt laments the resurgence of "the unbiblical hope that, by exerting godly influence upon government, society could be transformed."[21]

The third major dispensational counterattack, *Dominion Theology: Blessing or Curse?*,[22] veils an internal conflict between its two authors. Both Wayne House and Tommy Ice, in line with the dispensational Dallas Seminary tradition in which they have worked, affirm rapture eschatology, but the book's criticisms of social action apparently derive primarily from Ice, as House has debated *against* Dave Hunt in favor of Christian social activism.

House's position embodies the spiritual schizophrenia that has characterized American evangelical social theory for the past century. When evangelical postmillennialism and the goal of worldwide renewal faded, the urge for moral reform persisted. Many evangelicals were split between the "lifeboat theology" of late nineteenth-century evangelist D. L. Moody, who said Christians could aspire only to rescue individual souls until Christ returned, and residual motivation for social change, which led to strong support for Prohibition and antievolution legislation in the early twentieth century. The internal contradiction was largely resolved in favor of lifeboat theology as the Scopes evolution trial, the victory of liberal and social-gospel ideas in major northern denominations, and the repeal of Prohibition pushed premillennialists further into social apathy. However, the same contradiction plagued the "new evangelicals" who sought to make conservative Christianity socially relevant again after World War II.[23] And the revival of evangelical activism since 1975 has also revived the schizophrenia, as Christians strive to improve a world their theology has marked as ultimately unimprovable.

If people seem to have trouble discerning where Pat Robertson stands on issues of eschatology and social reform, it is because he too is caught in the middle of this schizophrenia. In *The Secret Kingdom* he repeatedly expressed hope for great world improvements, even suggesting that the implementation of biblical principles would advance Christianity "perhaps to the point of winning the world."[24] Yet Robertson placed alongside his sanguine hopes a futuristic exegesis of Ezekiel, claiming this ancient prophecy speaks of the Soviet Union, Ethiopia, and perhaps even America. He suggested that the mark of the Beast (Rev 13) might be literally embedded in our foreheads at some point—perhaps via microchips—and that the catastrophic violence of Armageddon was coming soon. At the very same time, nevertheless, "the kingdom of God will move forward, its future never in doubt"; and even after Christ returns to inaugurate the Millennium, God's people will be expected to know how to run a just government. This last claim, that principles learned before the Millennium will still be applicable during the Millennium, helps Robertson maintain both an expansive sociopolitical agenda and a premillennial eschatology.[25]

Aware of postmillennialism's overwhelming unpopularity in the contemporary evangelical world, Reconstructionists soften their stance when seeking to broaden their support. North has said he does not care whether or not Christians actually hold a postmillennial eschatology as long as they adopt an "operational" postmillennialism.[26] He still believes that as Christians get more involved in working to change society they will see the contradictions between social optimism and premillennialism and will turn to an optimistic eschatology. But here, as elsewhere, North is willing to settle temporarily for a partial ideological conquest of the evangelical community whose previous withdrawal from society he and his colleagues have so consistently decried.

Paulk and Kingdom Now, while more original in their eschatological thinking, also have more limited options. Whereas the Reconstructionists work primarily in nondispensationalist sectors of evangelicalism, Kingdom Now must interact with classical Pentecostal denominations for whom the Rapture is a cardinal point of doctrine. Paulk and Tommy Reid have diligently sought to disassociate themselves from the view that the world will get better and better until Christ's return. Their avoidance of postmillennialism, however, has not satisfied the Assemblies of God, who officially condemned Paulk's error of rejecting the Rapture.[27]

Like skilled diplomats, the dominionist leaders know when to play their hand and when to back down. Despite Paulk's reputation as a "provoker," he and Chapel Hill insist dogmatically on none of their most controversial doctrines, with the exception of a commitment to impacting society through application of a "Kingdom mentality." Paulk frequently expresses his openness to dialogue with all Christian groups.[28] Similarly, in intraevangelical discussion the Reconstructionists offer latitude on theonomy and eschatology (in their cooperation with the Coalition on Revival, for instance) while saving their fiercest criticism for the vulnerable target of dispensationalism and its antisocial theory.

In this regard Hunt and Lindsey may have unwittingly contributed to the Reconstructionist cause. Sociologists have described the phenomenon of "movement-countermovement symbiosis," in which each of two opposing groups benefits from the other's existence; in this case the controversy has granted each side an excuse to write more books, but the Reconstructionists have gained far greater profit by leapfrogging on their adversaries' already-established popularity. They find Hunt especially useful, because he is unhesitant to enter public debate and is relatively unschooled on fine points of church history and theology.

The Reconstructionist Hunt-ing party began with Gary DeMar and Peter Leithart's *The Reduction of Christianity: Dave Hunt's Theology of Cultural Surrender*, a parroting of *The Seduction of Christianity* that caused Hunt's publisher, Harvest House, to drop all pretensions of evangelical camaraderie and threaten a lawsuit for violation of copyright. Harvest House's lawyers claimed the confusion was so great that one major bookstore buyer had requested a shipment of "Hunt's new book, *The Reduction of Christianity*." The two sides agreed to Christian mediation, after which Gary North's Dominion Press (publisher of *Reduction*) changed the subtitle to *A Biblical Response to Dave Hunt*.[29]

In April 1988, after North and DeMar held a much-ballyhooed debate with Hunt and former Reconstructionist Tommy Ice, DeMar rushed into print a book that further defended Reconstruction and described the clash with dispensationalist social pessimism as comparable to the Protestant Reformation in significance. Reconstructionists have since produced a ponderous response to House and Ice and briefer dissections of Lindsey's book.[30]

Paulk too climbed on Hunt's name recognition by heavily

marketing his 1987 book *That the World May Know*, the cover of which announced the book's intent of "clearing the air after *The Seduction of Christianity*." In this volume Paulk set aside Hunt's criticisms by pointing out that, since Hunt is not a recognized elder or pastor or even a trained theologian, his claim to authority contradicts the biblical doctrine of the five-fold ministry as Paulk understands it. Paulk also stated that Hunt's theological presuppositions run counter to those of the charismatic movement. He then went on to portray Hunt's broadsides as exactly the kind of persecution bold kingdom proclaimers should expect as spiritual warfare intensifies in these last days.[31]

REFORM 2: KINGDOM NOW VERSUS THE EVANGELICAL POWERS THAT BE

While partners in promoting a socially relevant gospel and an eschatology to match it, Reconstruction and Kingdom Now also have waged separate battles on their own particular fronts. Kingdom Now, largely due to its bold and innovative openness to new ideas, has locked horns with organizations that see themselves as guardians of theological orthodoxy. Among these guardians of orthodoxy none has had a higher reputation within contemporary evangelicalism than the California-based Christian Research Institute (CRI), which since its founding by premier cult researcher Walter Martin in 1960 has specialized in defining the true faith and defending it against aberrant religious movements.

One sign of CRI's recognized preeminence in this field was that when Bob Weiner's Maranatha Ministries began receiving complaints, mostly from concerned parents of young members, about both its theology and its zealous recruiting and discipling practices, it turned to CRI for support. The interaction, however, also showed the limits of CRI's ability to enforce its rulings. At Maranatha's request, CRI put together a team of six experts who spent a year examining evidence and concluded, in May 1984, that they could not recommend Maranatha to anyone. Shocked by this rejection, Maranatha saved face by circulating a written refutation of the committee's report, declaring the matter closed, and going on as if nothing had happened. A few glaring theological gaffes, such as a teaching that God has only limited knowledge of future events, were corrected,[32] but Maranatha basically was able to shrug off the attack for two major reasons: resources (it and other large charismatic ministries have had more money, popular support, personal charisma, and media access than do the watchdog groups) and the general trend toward intracharismatic unity, which predisposes all charismatic leaders to welcome and endorse each other except in very extreme cases.

Four years later CRI, this time without invitation, took issue with Paulk, as its staff analyzed his books and found them suspect on several points. CRI was suspicious of Paulk's concept of "little gods," the limitations he placed on God's sovereignty, and his heavy insistence on the authority of apostles and prophets (which CRI accused of creating a "Pentecostal papacy").[33] Based on Paulk's published works, the concerns were justifiable. However, Paulk's books, hastily produced (usually from tapes of his extemporaneously preached sermons) by a publications department whose staff have no formal theological background, do not convey his theological convictions in a careful form. Given Paulk's freewheeling style, it is not surprising that his books should contain statements that appear to verge on heresy.[34]

During my visit to Chapel Hill Harvester Church, I was able to reconstruct the process by which one of these controversies developed. At his Wednesday evening services Paulk fields questions from the congregation on pastoral concerns. One evening a woman raised in a Mormon home asked how she should relate to her family and whether she should cut off ties with them now that she was a Christian. Paulk answered by urging her to stay in contact, noting the value of dialogue and pointing out that Christians can often learn from other groups, even ones not professing an orthodox gospel. A portion of that answer, edited by ghostwriter Tricia Weeks, ended up in Paulk's book *Unity of Faith*:

> What would a meeting be like which brought together liberal evangelicals, such as we are, conservative theologians, represented by Holiness groups and Southern Baptists, and Catholics, Seventh-Day Adventists, and members of the Church of Jesus Christ of Latter-Day Saints [i.e., Mormons]? Many of

these groups have become so different that we almost regard
them as enemies, rather than as brothers and sisters in the faith.

This passage has led critics to accuse Paulk of heretically accepting
Mormons, despite their deviant doctrines of God and salvation, as
fellow believers with whom Paulk could have unity of faith. Paulk
told me he does not consider the Mormons fellow believers and
never intended that meaning, but the lack of internal critique or
sufficiently careful copyediting has caused this and other dangerous
ambiguities to go unnoticed before publication.[35] In some cases the
controversial statements have appeared in more than one book,
leading researchers to conclude that Paulk is not simply careless but
seriously deficient in his theology.

Had Paulk and CRI been able to discuss these matters in an
atmosphere of mutual trust, they might have been resolved. But
CRI never had the opportunity for such face-to-face clarification,
because when two CRI researchers phoned Chapel Hill and were
referred to Tricia Weeks, the church's public relations specialist as
well as ghostwriter, she felt they were confrontational in tone.
Believing that CRI had already made up its mind and that nothing
would be gained through discussion, Paulk decided not to speak
personally with the researchers.

CRI then published a two-part article in its journal, blasting
Paulk for reversing his publicly expressed openness to dialogue and
bluntly terming him a heretic. The authors unintentionally widened
the chasm between the two sides further by claiming that Paulk had
adopted a "new posture" of refusal to dialogue. They contrasted the
openness to dialogue Paulk had expressed in a 1987 Chapel Hill
newsletter article with the following sentence from a 1988 Paulk
publication: "I prefer pouring my life into ministry to people rather
than gearing my thoughts toward answering challenges from those
who enjoy theological debate." CRI overlooked the fact that this
very sentence had originally appeared in the same article in which
Paulk had affirmed his willingness to dialogue! Paulk was expressing a preference for active ministry, not a refusal to interact with
critics.[36]

Paulk and CRI thus arrived at a stalemate similar to that in
the Maranatha incident, although in this case CRI was, unfortu-

nately, able to interact only with Paulk's books and not with his person. The stalemate embodies a deeper conflict between two widely differing approaches to Christian faith and ministry. On one hand, Paulk wants Christians primarily to *do* right. As we noted in chapter 4, Chapel Hill affirms the historical creeds of the Christian church and considers that commitment sufficient to establish its orthodoxy; beyond that, as Don Paulk repeatedly told me during my visit to Atlanta, "theology is almost secondary." The emphasis is on reaching and changing lives through active ministry—and their work in this regard has gained national recognition. On the other hand, CRI also expects Christians to *think* right. Acting as theological inspector, and unable to gain clarification from Paulk personally, CRI judged the existence or nonexistence of hands-on ministry to be irrelevant and assessed Paulk's Christianity solely from his books.

The Scriptures leave room for tension as to whether true Christianity should be judged by orthodoxy (right believing) or orthopraxy (right acting). Although in theory both Paulk and CRI would call for both orthodoxy *and* orthopraxy, in practice their emphases are far apart. This is a key reason why their rift may be unresolvable. The two sides differ just as fundamentally over what a Christian book is supposed to do and against what standards it should be judged; thus Paulk has felt comfortable transferring sermon material into print with minimal theological control and apologizing later for "poorly stated" passages,[37] while CRI tends to treat published books as definitive theological statements and shows less willingness to distinguish heresy from carelessness.

The situation is not likely to change (with regard either to Paulk specifically or such theologian-versus-charismatic conflicts in general), because the watchdogs and the independent charismatics represent nearly distinct subsets within the diverse, disjointed world of evangelicalism. The two groups have largely separate clienteles, one of them highly esteeming theological sophistication, the other valuing charismatic inspiration. Each side affirms its key figures' disdain for the other; each side can scream "heresy" or "blasphe-my," but neither has any power of enforcement; so each gives the other a wide berth and accepts in practice the inevitability of their peaceful coexistence.

Well, more or less peaceful. In his first major book after the tussle with CRI, *Spiritual Megatrends* (1988), Paulk continued firing back. Three specific passages in that book, though naming no names, appeared to be thinly veiled references to his three main foes—Dave Hunt, CRI, and Jimmy Swaggart, respectively.

> Some self-proclaimed inspectors took out a magnifying glass and began accusing spiritual leaders of seduction. They called true visions of God *visualization* [a practice some critics have termed occultic]. They attacked Christian counseling as being grounded in sorcery—though some of the attackers needed counseling desperately themselves.[38] [Hunt has lodged all of these charges against Christian leaders and has used the word *seduction* in two of his book titles.]
>
> I fear for those who are calling men of God *heretics*. They are opening themselves to spiritual death.[39] [CRI had declared Paulk a heretic earlier that year.]
>
> One of the most blatant examples of deception in the Church today is the work of people who believe that they are called *to purify* the Church. We have seen this deception manifested in top positions of major ministries who have recently fallen.[40] [Jimmy Swaggart had led the way in exposing Jim Bakker and had loudly attacked Paulk and other charismatic leaders before his own sexual improprieties were uncovered in early 1988.]

Not content to defend against past criticisms, though, Paulk also took steps to delegitimate all future theological attacks in advance. Such criticisms, he wrote, create "a verbal war of debate among the theological elite, an open-ended book war that slows down those following the direction of the Holy Spirit." Paulk predicted that his "new reformation will face critical dissection by theologians and scholars, while the move of God continues among common people who are open to God's voice."[41] It is admirable that, despite holding such views, Paulk continues to enter graciously into dialogue with "theologians" such as this author and to express openness to the views of those who examine his ministry critically.

The second battle surrounding Kingdom Now has presented greater challenges and risks to the combatants. Kingdom Now has had a tense relationship with established (or "classical") Pentecostals, and especially with the largest American Pentecostal denomination, the Assemblies of God (AG).

The Assemblies, of course, have a history of their own, one that illustrates how precarious a position they are in as they try to make a case against Paulk credible to charismatics or even to their own churches. The earliest AG leaders were supernaturally oriented Pentecostals for whom forming a denomination (as they did in 1914) was a reluctant step taken only when they saw the dangers inherent in total lack of structure, licensing control, or theological accountability. This was part of the inevitable process of "routinization," by which the need for order and structure gradually places limits on the spontaneity and freedom of an enthusiastic new religious group. The process of routinization was hastened in this case by the AG's need to defend itself against schismatic movements, most notably the Jesus Only schism of 1913–16 and Latter Rain in 1948–52.[42]

By the 1980s the Assemblies had developed their own distinctive but solidified form of evangelical orthodoxy, against which Kingdom Now's view of the Rapture and of this world's future rubbed the wrong way. But Paulk's openness to charismatic inspiration posed a particular threat to the AG because most AG churches have experienced routinization of their original charisma, to a degree that sometimes leaves many charismatics unsure whether the Spirit's activity is still welcome in that denomination. The Assemblies still affirm the reality of charismatic expressions, such as prophecies or speaking in tongues, but in many local churches worship has become tame and predictable over the years and these spectacular gifts seldom occur in practice. The denomination continues to grow, but much of the most impressive growth is taking place in churches that have disregarded the warnings of denominational leadership and remained open to fresh and discrepant ideas from other charismatic streams, such as Kenneth Hagin and the "faith movement," John Wimber with his stress on personal appropriation of spiritual gifts, and Earl Paulk.[43]

The Assemblies–Kingdom Now conflict has another dimension as well. Not only do Paulk and his cohorts speak critically of denominationalism[44] and work largely outside previously established denominations, but their endowment of anointed apostles and prophets with primary spiritual authority directly collides with the authority structure of the AG and other Pentecostal denominations, which do not conform directly to the five-fold ministry pattern. No denominational leader could endorse Kingdom Now's view of spiritual leadership without denying the legitimacy of his own office![45]

In seeking to clamp down on the Kingdom Now threat, however, the denominations face a dilemma: should they choose unity or purity? They can maintain unity by tolerating theological deviance, but such toleration of internal dissent could encourage still further dissent and thereby weaken the denomination's foundations. On the other hand, efforts at tight enforcement may simply cause strong leaders or congregations to withdraw, as televangelist Jimmy Swaggart did when faced with AG ecclesiastical discipline in 1988. The AG's loose structure and the wide-open market for charismatic religion leave the denomination nearly powerless to hold large, successful congregations in line.[46]

Nevertheless, the Assemblies have tried to bar the door to Kingdom Now. In 1987 its Commission on Doctrinal Purity denounced Paulk's work as "a revival of some of the teachings of the Latter Rain movement," arguing that Kingdom Now's open-ended approach to interpreting Scripture and to the role of modern-day prophets "makes it possible for them to defend any position they may want to adopt." The committee found Paulk at odds with AG positions on eschatology and Israel; it also criticized his reference to "little gods" and his hope that believers will conquer death. The underlying suspicion of unchecked charismatic authority, however, was the main concern and regained prominence in the concluding warning: "It is understandable that with the belief that pronouncements of prophets are equal to Scripture, other variations can occur at any time."[47]

Tommy Reid, who produces his books more carefully than Paulk, has been forced into exquisite diplomacy as he seeks to express Kingdom theology in language acceptable to his denomination. In *Kingdom Now . . . But Not Yet* Reid affirmed his allegiance to classical Pentecostalism and to premillennialism. He emphasized that "the fullness of the Kingdom of God . . . awaits [Jesus'] physical return to this planet."[48] He even solicited a testimonial from a veteran Assemblies leader for the back cover. And he disavowed any intent to develop a new theology.[49]

Kingdom Now's interaction with the Pentecostal Assemblies of Canada (PAOC) offers an interesting contrast with these simmering conflicts in the United States. When this denomination, Canada's main Pentecostal body with approximately two hundred thousand members, saw Latter Rain ideology creeping back into its native land after thirty-five years of exile, it responded more gently than did its sister denomination south of the border. PAOC administrator William Griffin paid Paulk and Chapel Hill a cordial visit and wrote an incisive but balanced critique of his theology. While some Canadian Pentecostals continued to rail against Paulk and all forms of "restoration theology," the PAOC officially took a more diplomatic approach, reminding congregations of their denomination's stability and solid tradition and encouraging them to stay within the fold. This wooing apparently stemmed the small wave of defections that had occasioned Griffin's involvement. The smaller size and less complete bureaucratization of the PAOC, as compared to that of the AG, may have also been partly responsible for its less rigid reaction.[50]

REFORM 3: RECONSTRUCTION VERSUS PLURALISM

While strict dispensationalism retains a large popular following, it carries less weight within the evangelical intelligentsia. For this reason Reconstructionists profit tactically when they are able to portray the central debate as between themselves and the socially uninvolved dispensationalists and to overlook the existence of alternatives less radical than Reconstruction yet still socially relevant. The main such alternative, and the most challenging evangelical opposition, comes from another set of intellectual Protestants, generally referred to as pluralists, who have done their homework as painstakingly as the Reconstructionists but have arrived at different conclusions.

Like the Reconstructionists, the pluralists come in different types. In fact, an analysis and comparison of the most sophisticated pluralists and their imposing political philosophies would be worth a book in itself. What the pluralists share, however, is a belief that, while Christians should inject biblical principles into public life, they should not seek to cause civil government to favor Christianity in any way. The pluralists argue that all faiths, including secularism, should be granted equal status, and they accept all persons, whatever their religious commitment, as equal participants in the democratic process. This stance pits the pluralists against the dominionists in important, hotly debated areas.

One key stream of pluralist thinking, usually called "principled pluralism," predominates within the more progressive branch of Reformed evangelical scholarship and is best represented by the Association for Public Justice (APJ), a public-issues think tank and advocacy organization in Washington. These pluralists admire Kuyper's idea of sphere sovereignty, which recognizes a plurality of social spheres each of which "has above itself nothing but God."[51] This they refer to as *structural* pluralism. But they also, drawing more from Kuyper's political practice than from his presuppositionalist philosophy, cite him as model of a *confessional* pluralism in which each faith community enjoys equal freedom to exercise its religious principles. Leading Reformed pluralists point especially to Kuyper's work in guiding the Netherlands toward a policy of aiding equally both government-run and private schools.[52] APJ and its executive director, James Skillen, stand out as persistent advocates for this policy in the United States. They argue that since public schools are unavoidably "religious," government's practice of funding only these schools constitutes de facto establishment of secular humanist or civil religion. To fulfill the constitutional requirement that the government establish no religion, they claim, requires tuition tax credits, vouchers, or other forms of nondiscriminatory funding for all schools.[53]

Sociologist Os Guinness, a Britisher living near Washington, D.C., champions a second important version of evangelical pluralism. Guinness calls his theory "chartered pluralism" because it rests upon the concept of a written charter that lays a foundation upon which all members of society can interact peaceably for the common good despite their deep differences over ultimate values. From 1987 to 1990 Guinness directed the Williamsburg Charter Foundation, a high-profile project designed to reaffirm the genius of the First Amendment's approach to religious freedom. To bring national attention to the protection of religious liberty in an increasingly pluralistic society, the foundation conducted the largest survey ever on the relationship between religion and American public life, held a symposium at the University of Virginia and a series of forums in major cities, and released well-received public school curricula on religious liberty. On top of those efforts it staged a gala celebration in June 1988 to mark the two hundredth anniversary of the meeting at which the Commonwealth of Virginia "changed the course of human history by demanding a written declaration of human rights as a condition for ratifying the U.S. Constitution."[54] (That demand, of course, led to the amendment of the Constitution by the Bill of Rights.)

During that June 1988 commemoration the Williamsburg Charter, a carefully worded seventeen-page document, was unveiled. Among its signers were dozens of recognized leaders, covering practically the whole ideological spectrum, from the realms of politics (Chief Justices Warren Burger and William Rehnquist, then-presidential candidate Michael Dukakis, Senators Robert Dole and Ted Kennedy, ten other members of Congress, and the heads of both political parties' national committees), religion (representatives of the National Council of Churches, the National Association of Evangelicals, and the Jewish, Muslim, Mormon, Christian Science, and Buddhist faiths), education, and business. Though conceived by evangelicals, the project welcomed liberal columnist Nat Hentoff and National Council of Churches civil-liberties specialist Dean Kelley on the committee that drafted the document. As a symbol of how far the foundation had stretched beyond its evangelical roots, which were neither concealed nor emphasized, John Buchanan (chairman of the liberal group People for the American Way) signed the charter while Jerry Falwell declined. At the extreme ends of the spectrum, dominionists (including Pat Robertson) and the American Civil Liberties Union also stayed away.[55]

One can hardly blame the dominionists for keeping their distance, for the charter explicitly criticizes them. Though it recognizes expanding government power as the chief threat to religious liberty today, the document deems the "de facto semi-establishment of . . . a generalized Protestantism" in earlier America just as regrettable as the favoritism granted to secular worldviews today. It continues: "Justifiable fears are raised by those who advocate theocracy or the coercive power of law to establish a 'Christian America.' While this advocacy is and should be legally protected, such proposals contradict freedom of conscience and the genius of the Religious Liberty provisions."[56]

The pluralists stand at odds with all three foundational points of the Reconstructionist tripod. First, they disagree firmly with theonomy. George Weigel, a conservative Catholic public-policy thinker, and Lutheran-turned-Catholic scholar Richard John Neuhaus, author of *The Naked Public Square* (in which he forcefully presents the dangers inherent in the banishment of religion from public life), allude to the "theonomist temptation" to which those who "call for a 'Christian America' ruled by 'Bible law'" have succumbed. Weigel expresses relief that Pat Robertson's failed candidacy has shown the narrowness of support for even soft-core versions of theonomy.[57] Both Weigel and Neuhaus were members of the Williamsburg Charter's drafting committee.

Linked to but more pervasive than their disdain of theonomy is the rejection by the Williamsburg Charter pluralists of the Reconstructionists' hard-line presuppositionalism. Weigel urges evangelicals to avoid appealing directly to biblical revelation and instead to affirm common grace working within all persons so that moral argument can be conducted in a "genuinely *public*" way that cuts across confessional lines. He believes in the "possibility of a moral discourse which is rigorously normative without being confessionally sectarian."[58] Such common ground between believers and unbelievers would be an impossibility for a strict presuppositionalist. (Guinness and APJ's Skillen consider themselves presuppositionalist, but their versions are much less extreme than that of Reconstruction and leave much more room for shared public discourse.)

The charter appears to rest religious liberty not on the nature, or even the existence, of God (which, to presuppositionalists, is the only adequate base for liberty) but "upon the inviolable dignity of the human person."[59] This was highly unsatisfactory to Regent University's Herb Titus, who successfully advised his boss, Pat Robertson, not to sign the charter. Titus believes the charter accepts "reasoned consensus" as a sufficient base for law and thereby concedes too much ground to the unbeliever.[60]

Guinness vehemently denies this charge. He notes that the paragraph in the charter that speaks of the "inviolable dignity of the human person" concludes, "This basic liberty is clearly acknowledged in the Declaration of Independence and is ineradicable from the long tradition of rights and liberties from which the Revolution sprang." This recognition of a "long tradition," Guinness says, is a veiled reference to the Judeo-Christian tradition. He thus believes that the charter fully upholds a biblical base for law, but in language acceptable to unbelievers.[61]

It could be argued that Guinness is doing exactly what the writers of the Declaration of Independence did two centuries earlier. Titus himself has written that the Declaration, in asserting the right of a people to rebel against unjust authorities, "retained the essence of the Biblical claim [that the people indeed have this right] in language which unified all Christians and satisfied even deists and unbelievers."[62] If Titus permits the Declaration to put Christian ideas in the language of public discourse, why should he not permit the charter to do the same?

To the charter's drafters, the broad endorsement elicited for their statement represents a victory for inalienable rights over the evolutionary approach to law, an approach that eradicates religious-based absolute values and is epitomized by prominent Harvard law professor Laurence Tribe.[63] But Titus can justifiably reply that, on his terms, the Williamsburg formulation embodies an unacceptable concession because, unlike the Declaration of Independence, it fails to invoke a Creator as source of human rights.

William Bentley Ball, a constitutional lawyer noted for his defense of religious liberties and another drafter of the charter, approached this subtle distinction in much the same way as Guinness when he defended what he called "the Charter's emphatic reliance on a 'higher law.' " The charter, Ball wrote, "stated that the Founding Fathers envisioned a 'higher law without whose substance and spirit even the Constitution itself would soon be only paper.' "[64] Actually, however, this statement appears nowhere in the charter, nor does any other direct reference to "higher law." The charter's text would pose no barrier to an atheist who acknowledges no higher law but is willing to grant the right of religious liberty to all faiths. Rather, the charter settles for a noticeably less explicit claim that the American system "depends upon *ultimate beliefs*."[65]

Titus and Guinness have also clashed over the role of public education. Guinness and his charter colleagues see public schools as an essential way, not to teach a civil religion or a least-common-denominator belief system, but to articulate a widely shared vision of the common good, a mutual understanding upon which our deepest differences (including religious differences) can be aired openly and discussed peacefully. Thus his foundation has developed and promoted a curriculum that would help schools teach *about* religion. On the other hand, Titus has no use for public schools. When invited to present a paper at the Williamsburg Charter symposium, Titus put aside the skillful diplomacy he had displayed before the American Bar Association. Instead he forthrightly asserted the inadequacy of anything other than a biblical base for law and proclaimed that, to restore educational justice, the public schools must be dismantled.[66]

In no way should Guinness or Skillen or Neuhaus be seen as compromisers: these are men of great intellectual substance, deeply concerned for applying Christian thought to public life with the utmost integrity. The differences between them and Herb Titus represent an honest disagreement of principles. But between them and the Reconstructionists there is also a recognizable difference in tactics, and it is here that the third Reconstructionist tenet, postmillennialism, comes into play. Whereas their eschatology gives the Reconstructionists confidence that they will ultimately win the battle, the pluralists have no similar certainty. Thus, while Reconstructionists certain of eventual victory fearlessly advocate such unpopular principles as the return of religious establishment, pluralists, keenly aware of the dangers of further encroachment on religious freedom (and less disposed to distrust the motivations of all unbelievers), are ready to engage in constructive negotiation.

The pluralists agree that Christians should strive "to reclaim every sphere of life for the King." Thus there arises an apparent contradiction between bringing all of life under God's authority and granting legal respect to all religions. However, as one pluralist has stated, "Structural pluralism is normative, but . . . confessional diversity or religious heterogeneity is a historical reality." The implication is that, though we might prefer that all were Christians, non-Christians are here to stay, and we must treat them as equals in the civil sphere.[67]

The pluralist formulation has a clear tactical strength over theonomy in clarifying much more convincingly that Christians would not engage in religious coercion even if they could. But since theonomists also eschew coercion, at least in theory, much of the difference between the two positions seems to hinge (perhaps subconsciously) on one's negotiation stance—on whether one is aiming for the best available common ground with one's opponents or for unconditional surrender. Principled pluralist Will Barker, in his response to a paper presented by Greg Bahnsen, warned that if Christians have a right to legislate prejudicially to their own faith, then so would other religions if they rise to power.[68] Bahnsen would have to agree, presumably, that he would have no basis on which to appeal for clemency from the non-Christian. He and his fellow Reconstructionists are pursuing an all-or-nothing approach that ultimately offers no mutual tolerance to false, nontheonomic perspectives.

All-or-nothing methodology makes good sense to a postmillennialist who believes that God will eventually unseat ungodly rulers and lead his followers to victory. But if one does not expect total victory and if one does share substantial common ground with other groups, as the pluralists do, then negotiation is no longer a "zero-sum" game, in which each side can gain only by taking from the other; rather, it offers the path to mutually beneficial agreement. The pluralists therefore offer a truce to other ideologies in the public square, in effect promising, "We won't try to exterminate you if you don't try to exterminate us."

Since the pluralists' diplomacy forces them to convince nonevangelicals to count on evangelical collegiality and goodwill, the appearance of theonomic evangelicals on the public scene poses an embarrassing threat to their agenda. How can they win the world's trust if they are in any way linked to Gary North, who long ago gave up on being accepted by the world and who bluntly terms pluralism "a political cease-fire until one side is ready to resume the fight to the death—which the Bible teaches is humanism's death"?[69] Thus the pluralists, especially in their public presentations, can be expected to distance themselves vigorously from Reconstruction. Ed Dobson and Ed Hindson, who were then associates of beleaguered, often-misunderstood nontheocrat Jerry Falwell, made the distinction with particular energy in an article designed primarily to show that fundamentalists have no plans to hasten the arrival of Armageddon. "Our religious beliefs are entirely compatible with democratic pluralism," they proclaimed. Dobson and Hindson briefly, and rather inadequately, described Rushdoony's ideas but assured their readers that that lone California postmillennialist was both very wrong and ridiculously utopian. "No doubt [Rushdoony's vision] is a frightening prospect for many secularists and members of [non-Christian] faiths. But they are not alone. It is a scary vision for the majority of evangelicals and fundamentalists as well—the two of us included. . . . Fortunately, we can say with confidence that he represents a very small group with absolutely no chance of achieving their agenda."[70] Though with less inflammatory rhetoric, Carl Henry has joined Neuhaus and Weigel of the Williamsburg Charter project in directly contrasting theonomic ethics with what he considers responsible Christian political philosophy.[71]

SUMMARY: DON'T ROCK THE BOAT

We have seen that the dominion theology twins, Kingdom Now and Reconstruction, have had to battle their evangelical brethren on several fronts, both together (regarding social concern) and separately (regarding points such as theonomy, eschatology, and spiritual authority, on which the two groups themselves do not share common views). One all-important thread runs through all these intraevangelical debates, however: the dominionists are trying to rock the evangelical boat, and those evangelicals who find the boat relatively comfortable do not want it to be rocked.

As we will see more extensively in chapter 7, evangelicals have many reasons for dissatisfaction with their current status in American society; but they also have many causes for rejoicing, more (on the surface, at least) than most evangelicals have known at any point in their lifetimes. This is especially true for the classical Pentecostals. Eighty years ago they were scorned; forty years ago they were still marginal, though the fledgling National Association of Evangelicals cautiously admitted them to membership; twenty-five years ago the emerging charismatics within mainline denominations were willing to learn from them but not to adopt the stigmatizing label "Pentecostal." But today the Assemblies of God have achieved mainstream respectability as America's fastest-growing denomination, with two million members. They have a highly successful product and feel understandably averse to new theologies or social ideas that might tamper with it, especially in such a way as to risk a new round of confrontations with society. Kingdom Now represents just such a threat.

Much the same scenario applies to other evangelicals. Forty years ago, the brand-new Fuller Seminary in California could not get its graduates into mainline denominations; now it is the nation's second-largest seminary, feeding more ministers into the Presbyterian Church (U.S.A.) than any Presbyterian-related school. Forty years ago Carl Henry seemed a lone voice calling evangelicals to social involvement; now conservative Christians loom as one of the most significant political blocs in America. Forty years ago the tiny National Association of Evangelicals harshly reviled the ogre of ecumenism and related to its mainline Protestant foe, the National Council of Churches, as a mosquito to a grizzly bear; now a flourishing evangelical movement is forcing redefinition of the term "mainline Protestant." Once shut out from leadership positions, evangelicals have now penetrated every sphere of important social influence; so why rock the boat?

The Assemblies of God leaders, the dispensationalists, and the pluralists, though they share little else in common, all agree on the inadvisability of adversarial, open confrontation with the status quo. They either affirm, as the successful Pentecostals and the Williamsburg Charter sponsors do, that the currently prevailing system is a fairly good one or—in the dispensationalist case—figure that attempts to improve things substantially are futile this side of the Second Coming. The dominionists, in contrast, believe the system should be overhauled. To defend their call for head-on confrontation with the world, they point to signs that American society is becoming an increasingly hostile climate for true Christianity. Dominionists, however, have not been the only evangelicals sounding this alarm; others, even in what has seemed the heyday of American evangelical renewal, have spoken forthrightly of ominously threatening social developments. In the next chapter we will examine these aspects of contemporary society that have tended to reinforce the dominionist impulse in American evangelical thinking.

Dominion Theology and American Politics

When Herb Titus, then of the University of Oregon Law School, became a Christian in 1975, he immediately began looking for intelligent evangelical works that related Christian thought to the modern world. He didn't find many. Titus's conservative Presbyterian pastor had little to recommend beyond Francis Schaeffer and the relatively unknown R. J. Rushdoony, with whom that pastor happened to be familiar because one of the church's elders was Gary North's father.

How things have changed over fifteen years. The proliferation of books promoting a "Christian worldview," and of evangelical organizations concerned with public issues, marks a major shift in consciousness. Many others have noted that, after a half century of uncharacteristic apathy regarding public life, American evangelicals since 1975 have been "reversing the great reversal" and returning to social engagement in significant numbers.[1]

But the growth of dominion theology represents a further stage of development, in which Christians are not simply emerging from their cocoons but generating their own bold, sweeping conceptions of a transformed society radically different from the one we now know. And these dominionists are resolutely digging in for a long-term battle against a culture they perceive as increasingly hostile.

It would be far off the mark to suggest that any more than a small minority of evangelicals has consciously espoused dominion theology. On the contrary, dominionist ideologies remain radical, not mainstream, within the broader evangelical impulse toward social and political involvement. But conservative Christians in America are becoming increasingly skeptical of their prior assumption that if they approach society in a cooperative spirit they will receive tolerance in return. To the degree that they are exchanging their former posture of cultural accommodation for one of resistance, one can say that there is a dominionist trend within evangelical thought.

It is impossible to trace a pattern of causes and effects, or to measure the impact of any particular Reconstructionist or Kingdom Now-style thinker, but it is clear that the profusion of dominionist writing and preaching has dovetailed with a number of social factors that have tended to encourage this dominionist trend. As evangelicals grew in numbers and visibility from 1960 on, a series of adverse legislative and judicial decisions motivated an increase in political concern and spawned the Christian-school movement, which became both an instigator of and a vehicle for renewal of Christian worldview thinking. Then, during the 1980s, evangelicals became more sophisticated and extensive in their political thinking; American political developments, most notably regarding abortion, turned the focus of evangelical concern from Washington to state and local arenas; and while continuing to grow in numbers and expanse of vision, evangelicals confronted the limitations of conventional politics and the realities of the Republican party. These factors, while turning very few Christians into pure Reconstructionists, have all increased the plausibility of the dominionist style of public engagement.

TO RUN A SCHOOL, YOU HAVE TO THINK

The story of the conservative Christian political awakening needs little retelling. Evangelicals shuddered quietly as social change during the 1960s threatened to obliterate traditional morality, especially in the sacred area of sexuality. Feminists promoted an Equal Rights Amendment to the Constitution and cheered when the Supreme Court's historic *Roe v. Wade* decision in 1973 guaranteed a woman's right to abortion. The shock of *Roe v. Wade* aroused conservative Protestant concern over what previously had been a Catholic issue.[2] Gay-rights initiatives followed not far behind. The fiascoes of Vietnam and Watergate further convinced many evangelicals that, as America approached its two hundredth birthday, its disintegrating moral fiber desperately needed restoration. In the hands of a few skillful political strategists, this pervasive evangelical anxiety coalesced during the late 1970s and mobilized in the form of the New Christian Right, receiving legitimacy from Ronald Reagan and providing substantial support for the conservative "revolution" over which he presided.[3]

With regard to the arousal of evangelicals, however, the most important single issue is education, because conservative Christians see education as the battleground where families and government will tussle over the minds of the next generation. Back in the nineteenth century, many American evangelicals themselves saw the public schools as an ideal means to inculcate their religious views into society. But since the early 1960s, when the Supreme Court banned prayer and Bible reading in public schools, the tables have been turned and evangelicals have complained that "secular humanism" has gained control of the educational system. Various groups of Christians have charged that school curricula systematically ignore the impact of Christianity on history; that sex-education programs encourage students to think relativistically and to disrespect parental authority; that science courses are biased in favor of unproved theories of evolution and against biblical views of the universe; and that an anti-God religion of humanism has subtly supplanted traditional theism as the faith of the public schools.

While evangelicals have found broader sympathy for their claim that religion is, and should not be, understressed in public-school curricula, they have lost nearly all their other public-school battles. As a result, increasing numbers of evangelicals have quit trying to rescue public education and are operating their own schools instead. More recently, home schooling has gained popularity as well. Although accurate numbers are hard to obtain, the Christian-school movement appears to have seen its greatest growth in the late 1970s and 1980s.[4]

Already angry that they must pay twice (school tax plus private-school fees) in order to give their children what they consider an acceptable education, evangelical parents became further incensed when the government refused to leave them alone. On the federal level, during the Carter administration the Internal Revenue Service threatened revocation of tax exemptions for schools that failed to meet guidelines for racial integration.[5] At the state level, Christian schools resisted various regulatory demands, arguing that the state's attempt to impose its standards upon private schools represented an infringement of parents' religious freedom and of their right to educate their children as they see fit. Home schoolers, meanwhile, often found the legislative environment even more restrictive.

Strongly committed to maintaining the nuclear family, evangelicals doggedly pursued the school conflicts because they believed their children's morality and values were at stake. Especially poignant was the 1983 case of Faith Baptist School in Louisville, Nebraska, which refused to supply the required records on its students. State officials padlocked the school and sent seven fathers—including the principal, Reconstructionist Everett Sileven—to jail while the mothers fled the state to avoid prosecution. Nebraska eventually gave up on trying to enforce its restrictive regulations, but in the meantime, Christian-school activist and Reconstructionist Robert Thoburn compared the state's attempt to tell the church how to behave with Soviet totalitarianism.[6]

From a Reconstructionist perspective, the Christian-school movement has had several important consequences. First, it has pushed more Christians toward viewing their government as an ungodly enemy to be opposed and ultimately replaced, rather than as an ally in keeping the peace. Second, it opened many doors for Rushdoony, who had long ago dissected the public schools' messianic pretensions and who became an expert witness on behalf of beleaguered Christian schools.[7] Third, and most broadly, the process of developing their own schools and curricula forced evangelicals to begin thinking in a Christian manner about *all* topics. It is in this sense that education is far more than a "single issue." Parents will not shell out extra money and turn down the public schools' superior facilities just so that their children can have a few prayers and a daily Bible class; rather, Christian schools, especially if fueled by active, self-conscious resistance to state-sponsored education, will tend to seek distinctly Christian approaches to all areas of study, from literature to history to government. Reconstructionists, of course, specialize in providing the tools and ideas for just such an enterprise.

THE MESSIAH'S INITIALS ARE NOT GOP

The evangelicals' association with Ronald Reagan gave them an enormous opportunity to establish a solid base for political influence during his eight years in office but did not translate into enactment of their legislative agenda. By 1988, forecasts of the conservative Christians' future impact varied widely. At one end of the spectrum, Jeffrey Hadden and Anson Shupe were predicting that evangelicals could become the nation's strongest political bloc by the end of the century, since many of their traditionalist themes still carried broad appeal; on the other hand, Steve Bruce, in a fashion representative of those social scientists who believe the secularization of American society has doomed the moral conservatives to permanent marginality, was already chronicling *The Rise and Fall of the New Christian Right*.[8]

Actually, the evangelicals' situation combines aspects of both analyses in an uneasy ambivalence. As evangelicals have gained political maturity and experience, they have solidified themselves as a recognizable power bloc, closely linked with, yet not sheepishly beholden to, the Republican party.[9] Yet they remain dissatisfied with the results. This pair of factors is precisely the combination needed to motivate a large social movement: people must be dissatisfied with the current situation but must also believe that, by acting, they can change it.

Some evangelicals, of whom Jerry Falwell may be one, appear to believe that they cannot expect much more progress beyond the niche they have already achieved on the American cultural and political scene. With the loss of such hope, a key ingredient necessary to maintaining the social movement disappears. Among many evangelicals who remain active, the hope persists but the impatience has been redirected. No longer just angry at liberals, they are in many cases also frustrated with the political situation in general or with the Republican party, the political vehicle through which the great majority of them have worked.

While the Republicans' sociomoral platform has represented the obvious choice for most evangelicals, observers have consistently noted the presence of discrepant elements within the party. The main group counterbalancing the Christian Right is comprised of libertarians who support the GOP's call for free-market economics and limited government but are indifferent to its moral conservatism.[10] With even the Christian Right's darling, President Reagan, needing to please both groups within the party, policy efforts did not always match the Republican platform's solidly conservative rhetoric on abortion, school prayer, and tuition tax credits for private schools.

Evangelical frustrations came to a head, however, after the Supreme Court's 1989 *Webster* decision opened the doors for states to begin passing laws restricting abortion. Prolifers expected to begin posting legislative victories, but instead they watched prolife candidates change their tune. The sudden disruption of the abortion debate had an immediate impact in Virginia, where Marshall Coleman had voiced a clear prolife, profamily agenda in upending former senator Paul Trible for the Republican nomination for governor. Following the *Webster* decision, Coleman suddenly turned quiet, afraid to position himself too visibly as prolife, while his opponent, prochoice Democrat Doug Wilder, exploited the abortion issue to put Coleman on the defensive. When Wilder narrowly won the election, some commentators noted that it was not Coleman's prolife position but his abandonment of it that likely had cost him victory.[11] But National Republican Committee chairman Lee Atwater immediately sought to redefine the party's stance as more broadly tolerant of varying views on abortion.[12]

Atwater's comments were not the only sign that both the administration and Republican leadership were seeking to downplay abortion and stress that the party had room for diverse views on the issue. Christian Right alarm had risen early in President Bush's tenure when he assured evangelicals that they would like his appointments but then nominated as Health and Human Services secretary a man whose statements on abortion were inconsistent.[13] By late 1989 evangelicals were charging the Bush administration with excluding them from power. An irate Pat Robertson reported that "the head of the Republican Party" had responded to evangelical objections by stating, "That's tough. The evangelicals have nowhere else to go."[14] Their fears intensified when Bush omitted abortion from his 1990 State of the Union address and when Doug Wead, the President's religious liaison, resigned, reportedly after complaining that the White House had invited representatives of the homosexual community to two bill-signing ceremonies.[15]

HERE COME THE NEW DARK AGES

The sharpening of evangelical dissatisfaction with Republicans would tend to lend credence to the dominionist preference for working through distinctly Christian channels. Meanwhile, other cultural developments were leading a number of well-respected nondominionists to sound more like dominionists in their predictions for American society and their prescriptions for Christian response.

A relatively early example of a thundering, thoroughgoing critique of all prevailing ideologies was Herbert Schlossberg's *Idols for Destruction* (1983). Faulting the political right (largely for its captivity to banking and business interests) as much as the left, Schlossberg called on the Christian church to become a "deviant subculture," rigorously devoted to building a distinctive worldview. Schlossberg promised no earthly victories to those who faithfully undertook the "Great Adventure" of Christian discipleship in a society he viewed as increasingly hostile to Christianity, but his lack of optimism did not reduce his insistence that the adventure must be energetically pursued.[16]

While not overtly political in focus, Schlossberg's message communicated a clear skepticism regarding the fruitfulness of ordinary political methods. Particularly significant is Schlossberg's willingness, unlike most of his evangelical colleagues, to attack the political right and left with equal vigor. This attitude is reminiscent of the Reconstructionists' frequent statements that the Christian Right's program was inadequate.

For many evangelicals, Schlossberg's social pessimism would

ring true by the late 1980s. As drug wars escalated and moral standards continued to erode, two of evangelicalism's most honored spokesmen declared grimly that Western society was entering the "New Dark Ages."

The first was Carl Henry, long acclaimed as the dean of American evangelical theologians, who pronounced Western culture near death in his 1988 book *Twilight of a Great Civilization*. This collection of essays and speeches opens with his 1969 address "The Barbarians Are Coming," but the other sixteen pieces all date from 1986 to 1988. Reflecting on the uncomfortable accuracy of the title of his 1969 speech, Henry observed that since then "both the pagan forces and the Christian forces have accelerated their initiative and seem increasingly locked into a life-and-death struggle."[17] Repeatedly deploring society's departure from an absolute basis for law and ethics, Henry predicted the further expansion of "raw paganism" and underscored with ominous language the further import of this trend: "American culture seems to me to be sinking toward sunset." "More and more the wicked subculture comes to open cultural manifestation." "We may even now live in the half-generation before hell breaks loose." This was not the automatic social pessimism of a dispensationalist but a frightening lament from the man whose early works had done so much to restore a vision of social involvement among evangelicals in the late 1940s.[18]

Against this bleak backdrop, Henry urged repeatedly that evangelicals recognize that "the Christian world and life view is staggeringly comprehensive" and learn to articulate it more fully and convincingly. This was nothing new for him, nor was his concern that evangelicals develop and act out of a "comprehensive political philosophy." The new ingredients were the sense of urgency and the heavy emphasis on the level of cultural antagonism he saw facing Christian thought in America. Henry's exposition of the sharp antitheses between Christian and modern philosophies overshadowed his less firmly expressed hope that believers could successfully defend their proposals even on the secular world's premises.[19]

Henry's erudite pessimism found confirmation on a more popular level from Charles Colson, who since his post-Watergate conversion has risen to the highest echelon of prominence as a spokesman both to and for evangelicals. Dedicating his 1989 book *Against the Night* to Henry, and quoting his "The Barbarians Are Coming" lecture in the preface, Colson declared, "I believe that we do face a crisis in Western culture, and that it presents the greatest threat to civilization since the barbarians invaded Rome." Enlightenment individualism and relativism have dissolved our society's moral standards, Colson stated, and it is not clear whether these new barbarians can be resisted. While urging Christians not to abdicate their role in contemporary moral debates, he also endorsed the monastic strategy of holy withdrawal from a hostile culture: "Out of tiny monastic outposts come education, moral endurance, and artistic excellence that can save a civilization."[20]

These grim prescriptions, coming from two of evangelicalism's most respected, experienced, and widely read figures, cannot be dismissed as if they were angry, uncontrolled outbursts from frustrated unknowns. Further proof of the pervasiveness of new-dark-ages thinking among evangelicals can be found in the phenomenal success of Frank Peretti's novels *This Present Darkness* and *Piercing the Darkness*, which have sold a combined total of three million copies. In his books, Peretti paints scenes of spiritual warfare between angels and demons, and the results of this extraterrestrial war directly affect events in a modern American culture in which Christianity is unwelcome. *Piercing the Darkness*, whose back cover calls the book "a penetrating portrayal of our times," pits intrusive secularists against a Christian elementary school, and its secularist-turned-heroine has the suggestive surname Roe.

Peretti's works may be fictional, but their import is all too clear to less confrontational Christians, like those of the Williamsburg Charter project, who remain committed to maintaining cordial relations between religious groups and American society. As one Charter staff member observed with regret, *Piercing the Darkness* "satanizes" opponents like the American Civil Liberties Union, whose real-life identity is hardly concealed by Peretti's creation of an "American Citizens' Freedom Association . . . all-for-freedom on the exterior but viciously liberal and anti-Christian in its motives and agenda. Nowadays it was getting hard to find any legal action taken against Christians, churches, or parachurch organizations that did not have the ACFA and its numerous, nationwide affiliates behind it." Peretti depicts the government's "Child Protection Department" as no friendlier toward believers than the privately funded ACFA.[21]

Both Henry and Colson have publicly distanced themselves from dominion theology,[22] yet their current social diagnosis makes dominionist approaches to society more attractive, as can be shown by a comparison with their main predecessor in mobilizing sophisticated evangelicals, Francis Schaeffer. In *A Christian Manifesto* (1981), Schaeffer fervently insisted that Christians must wake up and roll back the contemporary tide of humanism, but he also affirmed America's democratic system and expressed confidence that, if decision-making power were removed from humanistic elites like the Supreme Court and returned to the people, the nation's moral demise would be reversed. The problem with Schaeffer's approach is that it works only if backed by adequate popular support; it would be defenseless in a culture that had become so post-Christian that, even if decisions were returned to the people, the people would vote in the same "humanist" way.[23]

Such a post-Christian culture is precisely what Henry and Colson saw as they described the America of the late 1980s as a society that had turned away from the timeless standards of absolute law and instead was following the dictates of current consensus and convenience. "Western culture itself," Henry stated, ". . . is becoming more impervious to Christian influences than are African and Asian cultures. Post-theistic atheism stands guard against any tatters of transcendence."[24]

If evangelicals come to view American society as tumbling toward a moral disarray in which not even basic liberties are solidly guaranteed and in which Christian thought is specially marked for exclusion, then they will feel that they have little to gain by cooperating with that society and little to lose if they diverge into radical ideologies like Reconstruction.

THE DOMINIONIST ALTERNATIVE

When we add up the developing elements in this new evangelical consciousness—a desire to see God's kingdom make a concrete impact on social structures; skepticism regarding the potential for working through established political parties; growing antagonism toward the state and its prevailing ideologies; rejection of quick remedies in favor of patient, grass-roots, long-term, gradual efforts—we have precisely the mindset of dominion theology. The expectations of ultimate success characteristic of dominion theology are lacking,[25] but the method of engagement with contemporary society is the same. The new-dark-ages thinkers are joining the dominionists in announcing that now is a time for evangelical resistance, not friendly accommodation.

What would this development mean on the political scene? The best way to answer would begin with an analysis of Reconstructionist political thought, as this is the purest and most developed form of dominion theology.

It is not surprising that Reconstruction's social theory should yield a distinctive approach to politics. Its theonomic view of law calls for a total revamping of the current system; its eschatology anticipates total victory; its presuppositionalist philosophy leads Reconstructionists to consider the unbeliever's worldview as, if not totally wrong, at least totally suspect. Thus they are less likely than other evangelicals to seek broad-based coalitions and more likely to work independently in carrying out their program.

This independence is reflected in the Reconstructionist commitment to working from the bottom up, revitalizing individuals, families, and churches before they plot their large-scale transformation of the political system. This does not mean that Reconstructionists act single-handedly, or even only with Christians, when they enter the political arena; but their use of alliances is governed by their vision of total transformation. To borrow the title of the political-action book in Gary North's Biblical Blueprints Series, their goal is *The Changing of the Guard*.

In that book, George Grant writes that "the goal of Christian political action . . . is . . . to *acknowledge* the theocracy that *already exists*" and to place civil government, like all of life, under the rule of God.[26] Grant by no means ignores the potential for working within the system, and he encourages Christians to use conventional means of influence like writing to representatives and volunteering within a political party. But his tips on working within the system reveal a desire for Christians to take control, not just become cooperative participants. Here is his recommendation on how to approach a local precinct meeting: "Get neighbors, friends, and church members in your precinct together for a pre-caucus strategy session. Decide on a convention and an agenda that you all can vote for en masse. Then go expecting to win."[27]

Dominionists, with their confidence in ultimate substantial victory, can be expected to approach political involvement along the lines illustrated by Grant, tending to seek comprehensive implementation of their agenda rather than to collaborate with other groups who share some of the same concerns. The more power they believe they have, the more likely they are to abandon pragmatic coalition building and go for victory on their own terms.

This dominionist style of politics was often present in the Robertson presidential campaign's combative tactics and has motivated evangelical efforts to take over the Republican party apparatus at state or local levels. Sometimes, at least in practical terms, the style is singularly counterproductive, arousing intraparty hostility strong enough to hamstring the chances of all nominees. In many cases Republican strategists' fears about their party moving too far to the right have been confirmed, as the Christian Right's ability to commandeer the party has helped the Democrats win in general elections.[28]

One closely analyzed 1990 congressional race in central Florida provides a typical illustration. In the Republican primary, a candidate closely associated with the Christian Right depended on the zealous activism of that sector of the population to defeat a better-known politician who held virtually identical views on social issues and who would have been a stronger candidate in the general election. The net result of Christian Right involvement, in this case, was the eventual election to Congress of a Democrat far less receptive to Christian Right concerns than either of the Republicans.[29]

MODERATING THE DOMINIONISTS' RADICALISM

Usually, however, the practical activity of evangelicals indicates that they continue to prefer conventional participation in the system rather than resistance, believing that there remain enough upright and moral people in America, or in the Republican party, to make conventional means of public engagement effective. Most observers and participants have confirmed my own experience that politically active evangelicals are generally becoming more cooperative with other groups as they recognize that they have gained influence roughly proportionate to their numbers. These evangelicals, especially those active in Republican circles, are committed to staying involved for the long haul, but they seldom behave in a confrontational way except when placed on the defensive by a frontal attack (e.g., by an attempt to implement an abortion-rights agenda at a party caucus). Many of these evangelicals have been inspired by dominionist thought, but few expect or seek to carry out the whole dominionist program. As one evangelical activist in Texas put it: "Reconstructionist writers have encouraged me, but I'm not sure we will see the victory of which these people speak." The work of such organizations as the Christian Coalition, Concerned Women for America, and the Family Research Council suggests that evangelicals, both leaders and followers, still believe they can produce the most fruit by playing harder at the game of standard American politics, not by abandoning it.

Looking at the specific areas in which Reconstructionists have influenced other Christian leaders further reinforces this analysis. Herbert Schlossberg, Francis Schaeffer, Herb Titus, John Whitehead of the Rutherford Institute, and even Doug Bandow (an evangelical who does policy analysis at a major secular think tank in Washington) are all what Gary North calls "negative Reconstructionists." They all endorse, and are in varying degrees indebted to, Reconstruction's negative side—its critique of secular society—but none of them endorses Reconstruction's proposal for replacing it.

This pattern is exactly what we should expect if, as we have noted earlier, Reconstruction has functioned as the provocative, radical side of a broader evangelical recovery of sociopolitical activism. The radicals in a social movement are the members least willing to compromise for immediate, partial gains and the ones most extreme in their visions of change. As such, they are generally the most distant from sources of social power but also the most able to articulate the movement's ideology in pure, bold form without having to worry about diplomatic niceties.

In this case the undiplomatic Reconstructionists' contribution is their dissection, from an evangelical perspective, of the failings of the secular American state. Their vehemence and absolutism make them unwelcome in the realm of practical, short-term political change, with even some sympathetic evangelicals carefully disavowing them. But their ideas help to form the intellectual framework for the more practical actors who seek to achieve those concrete goals that are indeed within evangelicals' grasp at this time.

Even though dominion theology, as its leading exponents repeatedly insist, is not primarily a political movement, its future impact will depend in large part on the relationship between the Republican party and conservative Christians. People who believe the GOP is representing their social concerns effectively will have no reason to devote substantial energy to furthering a seemingly unachievable vision of social transformation that is taken seriously only within the evangelical subculture. But if they perceive the Republican party to be a black hole that absorbs their support and offers little in return, more of them may look for more radical alternatives, such as the ideas presented by dominion theology.

Two centuries ago, the original American revolution began because a sufficient number of colonial leaders concluded that they had no better option than to openly declare their independence. Thus far, only a small portion of evangelicals has decided that the outlook is so bleak as to call for confrontation such as that in which Nebraska Baptist school principal Everett Sileven and, more recently, the antiabortion radicals of Operation Rescue have engaged. It still appears that evangelicals can win more victories through the political system than through civil disobedience. However, it is reasonable to posit that, if the evangelicals should lose their foothold within the Republican party or if the abortion battle should swing against them with an aura of irreversible finality, a larger number of conservative Christians will begin to think more seriously about overt forms of social protest and resistance. If that should occur, the Reconstructionists will be waiting for them with open arms.

As far as broader influence is concerned, dominion theology in

all its forms is likely to remain politically marginal unless, as North patiently hopes, a major social or economic crisis overturns American attitudes. As long as Americans enjoy social stability and economic prosperity, they will ignore calls for major restructuring. A severe financial crisis could create enough desperation, though, to send the electorate looking for an articulate, authoritarian economic whiz who exudes confidence in his blunt, concrete, cut-and-dried solutions. Should such a scenario arise, one could image the Republican presidential nomination being up for grabs between Pat Robertson and Gary North. Without that assistance from history, dominion theology will have to settle for making a major impact only within its own subculture, where it is forcing evangelicals to decide whether to come to terms with a society their political efforts have altered only slightly or to gravitate toward more radical forms of dissent.

• 8 •

Biblical Politics in the Modern World

In mid-1989, as an intense legislative battle loomed in the U.S. Congress between supporters and opponents of gun-ownership restrictions, *Christianity Today* magazine sought out a prominent evangelical spokesman for each side. By comparing the views of Larry Pratt, executive director of Gun Owners of America, and Ron Sider of Evangelicals for Social Action, the article showed that the divergence of opinion among biblically oriented Christians on this issue was as broad as that among the general public.

Both Pratt and Sider cited the Bible in their defense, but not in the same style. Pratt gave specific texts, including two from the Old Testament, that described the use of weapons in self-defense and that, in his opinion, justified the same practice today. Sider, on the other hand, based his advocacy of gun-control measures on what he considered foundational biblical principles, such as the sacredness of life. Rejecting reliance on particular proof texts, Sider said that "there is no simple biblical answer which says that it is appropriate or right in 1989 in American democracy for citizens to own guns or not to."[1]

It is not coincidental that Larry Pratt has close ties to Christian Reconstruction while Ron Sider is one of its best-known foes, for the conflicts between Reconstruction and other evangelicals often take the same form as this one over gun control. Reconstructionists like Pratt tend to move more directly from biblical texts to contemporary situations than do others, like Sider, who place greater weight on cultural differences between biblical times and the present and who thus frequently contend that "there is no simple biblical answer" to modern questions.[2]

The wide disagreement between these two evangelicals on gun control illustrates a pervasive problem: evangelicals agree that the Bible is authoritative, but they disagree on how to use it. Robert Johnston, in his often-quoted book *Evangelicals at an Impasse*, summed up the problem as "how the evangelical is going to *do* theology while holding to biblical authority."[3] Not all evangelicals use the same hermeneutical (i.e., interpretive) principles in determining how to apply biblical texts to questions the biblical writers never had to ask. This easily overlooked but crucial conflict between hermeneutical principles lies at the root of the stalemates that plague the evangelical debate over dominion theology.

In this chapter we will uncover some of the key interpretive presuppositions underlying the intellectual frameworks of dominion theology and its evangelical opponents (using Dave Hunt as the clearest example of antidominion theology). In doing so, we will gain a deeper understanding of how each side develops its positions, as well as whether and how the differences can be resolved.

SOCIOPOLITICAL INVOLVEMENT

The New Testament lacks a direct mandate for social transformation for an obvious reason: the early Christians, as a small minority within the Roman Empire, never dreamed of attaining direct social influence. This does not mean that they failed to consider their Gospel to be one that would ultimately transform the world (see, e.g., 1Co 15:25–28; 2Co 5:18–19), or that they were indifferent to what others thought of them (Mt 5:13–16; Col 4:5–6; 1Pe 3:15–16), or that they were not prepared to resist political powers (Ac 4:19–20). It does mean, however, that the first Christian writers did not teach social or political action as a means of spreading the Gospel. Only an incurably idealistic zealot could have hoped that the handful of Christians spread throughout the centralized, undemocratic Roman Empire would ever have that type of influence. Instead the early Christians shared their faith by preaching and healing, and their acts of mercy were directed primarily, though not solely, toward fellow believers, their "brothers" (see Mt 25:40; Jn 13:34–35; 15:12–13 on the believers' love for one another; 1Pe 4:9; 1Jn 3:16–17; Jas 2:15–17).

How does one apply the New Testament, then, to a participatory democracy in which Christians do have considerable opportunity for public involvement? In general, the dominionists tend to find sociopolitical implications in texts not originally written with that purpose in mind. In contrast, antidominionists like Dave Hunt take the New Testament believers' cultural situation as normative; since the early church did not enter the sociopolitical battlefield, Hunt says, neither should Christians today. Hunt calls the belief that godly influence could transform society an "unbiblical hope" that diverts attention from the heavenly kingdom toward which Christians should look.[4]

Hunt implicitly assumes that the early Christians abstained from politics by conviction and not simply by necessity. Dominionists dispute this assumption by finding a social mandate in embryo in the call to "let your light shine before men" (Mt 5:16) and "make disciples of all nations" (Mt 28:19).

Are these contemporary combatants doing exegesis (i.e., deriving their social views from their biblical interpretation) or eisegesis (misreading the biblical text through the lens of preconceived notions)? Like all evangelicals, both groups assert that theirs is the biblical position. But they also, like any reader, approach the text with a particular set of previously formed values and assumptions. These preconceptions occasionally appear to emerge through exegetical oversights or idiosyncracies that suggest that the interpreter may be arriving at predetermined conclusions.

One such idiosyncracy involves an archaic wording from the King James Version. In one of Jesus' parables, a nobleman gives money to ten of his servants and tells them, "Put this money to work until I come back" (Lk 19:13 NIV). The King James renders his words, "Occupy till I come." The word *occupy* (Greek *pragmateuomai*) means "do business," not "take possession" as it might in modern English. Dominionists almost certainly know this, yet they frequently rely on this verse (always, for obvious reasons, in the

King James translation) as evidence of a Christian mandate of social takeover. Dennis Peacocke writes:

> Jesus left the Church as His representative, occupying until He returns. If the Church abandons its care and responsibility for the nations, the world becomes like a rental property abandoned by the rental agent, subject to vandalism and destruction. That is exactly our present situation. . . . The vandals are those anti-God leaders who have infected the nations with political and social programs totally at odds with the laws of God's universe.[5]

What about the Great Commission of Matthew 28:18–20, probably the dominionists' most quoted New Testament text? When they say "making disciples of the nations" means teaching biblical principles to political entities,[6] they are on dubious ground. The New Testament uses "nations" (Greek *ethnē*) to refer to political entities (cf. Mk 13:8, Ac 2:5) but also, more generally, to people-groups, especially Gentiles (e.g., Mt 6:32; Gal 2:9; Eph 2:11). The latter meaning seems to have been intended in Matthew 28:19–20, which commands the believers to baptize and teach the *ethnē*; after all, one baptizes individual persons, not civil institutions. Therefore, to find a mandate for national discipleship in this passage seems unwarranted.

Finally, turning back to the dominionists' foundational passage, we find further unstated assumptions. Reconstructionist and Kingdom Now writers connect Genesis 1:26–28, their "dominion mandate," with transformation of political structures so readily that one could suspect that they have forgotten that the original command gave humanity dominion over the environment, not over fellow human beings. It may seem that the dominionists are playing flippantly with Scripture—until one grasps the assumptions from which their interpretation is a logical deduction.

For Reconstructionists, the dominion mandate sets forth God's never-revoked intent to set humanity as regents over a harmonious planet. Ever since Adam's fall into sin, disobedient humans have been among the obstacles preventing the planet from being harmonious. Thus, even though Genesis 1 does not speak of dominion in the political realm, the degeneration of human society requires redefinition of the dominion assignment to include political dominion.

This is the line of logic by which Rushdoony hears a summons to total sociopolitical transformation in Genesis 1. Humanity's fall into an unregenerate state, he says, meant that "more than a garden was now to be subdued; the nations and empires of the world were to be brought under the dominion of Christ and His members."[7] Elsewhere he details in order the three steps of the process by which, as he sees it, God gave a mandate, humanity rejected it, and God therefore redefined the assignment without canceling the mandate.

> God, in creating man, ordered him to subdue the earth and to exercise dominion over the earth (Gen. 1:28). Man, in attempting to establish separate dominion and autonomous jurisdiction over the earth (Gen. 3:5), fell into sin and death. God, in order to re-establish the Kingdom of God, called Abraham, and then Israel, to be His people, to subdue the earth, and to exercise dominion under God.[8]

This definition of humanity's purpose under God leads to the succinct conclusion, "All enemies of Christ in this fallen world must be conquered."[9]

Reconstruction's tenacious commitment to postmillennialism and to God's absolute sovereignty implicitly buttresses this interpretation of the dominion mandate as well. If God gives the human race a task, Reconstructionists assume, it *will* be carried out, sooner or later. No adversity or human rebellion can ultimately stop God from exercising dominion through humanity as he intended. Premillennialists, lacking this conviction that God's final victory will be achieved through worldwide social transformation, are unlikely to define the dominion mandate in such sweeping terms and may feel that their role in subduing the earth is simply to live productively and reduce pollution.[10] In still sharper contrast to Reconstructionist assumptions, dispensationalists do not hesitate to attribute to God a thoroughgoing change of plans; for example, they have usually held that Jesus came to earth to inaugurate the kingdom of God but, when rejected by the Jews, narrowed his agenda and called forth the church instead.[11] If human disobedience can cause God to make considerable midcourse adjustments, as the dispensationalists assume, then it is no longer certain that a dominion mandate pronounced before the Fall bears any relevance to the post-Fall human condition.

Kingdom Now advocates Earl Paulk and Tommy Reid represent an interesting variation on the Reconstructionist theme of dominion. In their view, the description of the earth as "formless and empty" in Genesis 1:2 "reveals that some disruptive events had already taken place in the universe." Lucifer's rebellion had turned this planet into "a wilderness ravaged by satanic forces."[12] Therefore, in Kingdom Now theology, even Adam and Eve were created for the express purpose of defeating the powers of evil and restoring godly dominion to earth. The train of thought differs from that of Reconstruction, but the conclusion is the same: the task of dominion requires believers to confront and overturn ungodly forces.

While the dominionists face trouble in building an airtight case for social action from the relatively apolitical New Testament, Hunt faces a different problem: how to remain logically consistent while not seeming indifferent to political threats against Christians' basic religious freedoms. To Hunt, Jesus' silence about the dominion mandate and about political action proves that Jesus was not interested in these topics; since Jesus was not involved in politics, Christians today should not be involved in politics either. Yet Hunt is unwilling to proceed to the absolutist conclusion that one must totally abstain from politics as a matter of principle whatever the consequences of that decision may be. Instead he concedes that political action "tempered by wisdom" is acceptable when needed to protect basic Christian rights. This concession is a serious weakness in his argument, because once Hunt has granted that minimal political action represents "wisdom," he has no clear grounds for concluding that further political action does not represent more wisdom. This ambivalence on whether social action is justifiable leads Hunt to the unlikely statement that, due to the compromises entailed in large-scale politics, a Christian can have greater social impact on a local school board than in the President's cabinet.[13] (To grasp the implications of that statement, imagine Pat Robertson turning down the post of secretary of state in order to run for Virginia Beach school board.) Hunt fails to note that

compromise is an equally inevitable facet of decision making at any level of politics. Presumably he has never served on a local school board.

Whereas Scripture is infallible to evangelicals, church history is not. Therefore, whereas both sides of the debate are obligated to claim Jesus and Paul for their side, they can pick and choose their heroes from then on. To Reconstructionists the early church took over the world; to Hunt the early church became worldly and polluted. Calvin can be seen as either a great visionary reformer or the terroristic enforcer of endless laws. Pietists can be praised for recovering the centrality of the heavenly hope or criticized for their social irrelevance. Abraham Kuyper is a hero to dominionists, but to Hunt the current secularized condition of Holland proves that Kuyper wasted his energy. And Charles Colson, who diagnoses modern society's ills but stops short of offering much in the way of political solutions, can be either praised for his reticence or criticized for failing to progress to advocating theonomy as God's answer to contemporary evils.

ESCHATOLOGY

We have seen a few examples of how the dominionist mission of social involvement depends upon theological positions not shared with other evangelicals. For this reason the dominionists' arguments are frequently inconclusive even within evangelical circles, due to the uncertainty of the essential theological foundations that underlie the practical dominionist agenda. Nowhere does this uncertainty protrude more clearly than in the heated debates over eschatology.

Evangelicals remain deeply divided over how to interpret the inspired words of first-century Christians who appear to have expected that the world would end fairly soon (Ro 13:11–12; 1Co 7:29–31; 1Th 4:16–17; Jas 5:8). Now that another two thousand years have passed, can any reliable doctrine of the world's future be derived from the Scriptures?

Dave Hunt, again treating the early church as strictly normative, follows this logic to the conclusion that, since the first-century Christians lived in imminent expectation of Christ's return, so should we. In fact, he goes a step further. Jesus, Hunt notes, told the disciples to "keep watch, because you do not know on what day your Lord will come" (Mt 24:42; cf. Mk 13:35–37) even though he certainly did not (being free from error) hold the false belief that the end was definitely coming soon. Therefore, Jesus must have believed there is intrinsic benefit in maintaining an *attitude* of expectancy whether or not we are destined to see Christ's return in our lifetime. That benefit, according to Hunt, lies in keeping Christians consistently focused on their heavenly hope and immunized against the misconception "that the Christian's primary responsibility is to improve this present world."[14]

To legitimize their worldly agenda, the dominionists must dispel the traditional dispensationalist fixation, here represented by Hunt, on the possibility of being raptured into the heavens at any moment. One way to do so is to claim that the Rapture cannot happen at any moment because there remain biblical predictions, not yet fulfilled, whose fulfillment must precede the end. Paulk, for example, relies on Matthew 24:14: "And this gospel of the kingdom will be preached in the whole world as a testimony to all nations, and then the end will come." Since the "gospel of the kingdom" includes, for Paulk, church unity and social transformation as well as the message of individual salvation, this promise remains unfulfilled: "The next move of God [i.e., Christ's return] cannot occur until Christ in us takes dominion. I have not seen a full demonstration. I have seen only bits and pieces of Kingdom authority and dominion."[15]

Paulk's argument here remains inconclusive, because his definition of "gospel of the kingdom" assumes the necessity of social transformation, the very point many of his critics contest.[16] Ironically, his argument also contains an assumption held *in common with* his dispensationalist opponents, one that would strike most nonevangelicals as improbable: that Jesus, in the midst of alerting his disciples to imminent catastrophes, would have also told them to watch for signs that would go unfulfilled for centuries. On the other hand, Reconstructionists readily agree that this assumption is improbable, since they believe these passages referred to an event well within the disciples' lifetimes—the destruction of Jerusalem in A.D. 70. David Chilton argues that all the signs of Matthew 24:5–14, including worldwide evangelization, were fulfilled before that date.[17] All the predictions of Revelation 1–19 also referred to the Roman invasion of Jerusalem, say the Reconstructionists. By denying the end-times relevance of virtually all the New Testament passages other evangelicals use to foresee the last days, they open up a gaping interpretive hole regarding just what *will* happen in the last days. They then fill that gap by declaring the continuing applicability of Old Testament promises (e.g., Isa 2:2–4; 11:6–9; 65:17–25) that God will restore peace and harmony to the whole earth.[18]

Strangely, Chilton does not hesitate to interpret Jesus' parables of growth (Mt 13:31–33) as long-term prophecies of total victory. The parable of the leaven hardly seems, at first glance, an unequivocal postmillennial statement: "The kingdom of heaven is like yeast [leaven] that a woman took and mixed into a large amount of flour until it worked all through the dough" (Mt 13:33). But Chilton assumes that the parable applies not just to individual lives or to the immediate impact of Jesus' own life, but to worldwide renewal. "Like leaven in bread," he says, "[the kingdom] will transform the world, as surely as it transforms individual lives. . . . After looking at this parable, you might wonder how in the world anyone could deny a dominion eschatology."[19]

Similarly, while relegating Revelation 1–19 to first-century application, the Reconstructionists do not hesitate to apply Revelation 20 to "the very last days of this world."[20] Their method sometimes seems exegetically inconsistent in that they nullify (by linking them to first-century history) the predictive force of passages that suggest the world could end suddenly, while they retain last-days relevance for those passages that promise victory to Christians. Dispensationalists do just the reverse; in their scheme, biblical texts forecasting an imminent end of the world remain in force, while promises of godly transformation of society are postponed until after the Second Coming, or (in the case of the Gospels) canceled because Jesus later shifted his mission from the world to the church. Despite good intentions, each side's exegesis seems to depend on prior theological commitments.

Similar suspicions arise regarding what we called (in chapter 2) the theological and logical arguments Reconstruction joins to its exegetical case for postmillennialism. In the theological category, Reconstructionists repeatedly delineate three parts of salvation—definitive, progressive, and final—but never show convincingly that the progressive aspect applies to improvement of social institutions as well as to individual salvation.[21] Gary North leaps from the concept that God judges nations as well as individuals to a faith that nations, like individuals, can attain gradual sanctification.[22] But this analogy does not prove that any nation ever *will* be sanctified.

North's logical deduction that if Christians do not subdue the whole earth, God is "a loser in history" is also problematic, especially because he concedes that Revelation 20 promises Satan one last fling. "When all men have before their eyes the testimony of God to the success of His law and the success of His ambassadors in bringing peace and justice to the world, *then* the rebels will have something to rebel against in that last desperate act of Satan and his host (Rev. 20:7–10)," North says.[23] But if humanity requires heavenly intervention to fend off that last rebellion, is God not still a loser in history? On the other hand, if this near-complete transformation suffices to make God a "winner," just how much improvement must take place? Why is Earl Paulk's forecast of kingdom demonstration by a smaller number of believers not adequate? North and his fellow Reconstructionists seem to be groping unsuccessfully for decisive biblical evidence that Christians are destined to transform society.[24]

How heavily does dominion theology rest on its eschatology? Reconstructionists, as we have seen, offer different answers to this question, ranging from North, who calls postmillennialism indispensable to his program, to Greg Bahnsen, who presents theonomy as not dependent on postmillennialism. Gary DeMar and Peter Leithart split the difference by pointing out that nonpostmillennialists may actively seek social change but are not likely to adopt the Reconstructionist program of slow building toward sweeping cultural renewal: "Only a long-term effort to change all facets of society will bring about significant and lasting transformation. This means changing the hearts and minds of millions of people. All this takes time, time that is not on the side of the pretribulational premillennialist." Or, in fact, anyone who is not postmillennial.

They will not consider such a methodical, all-encompassing strategy of change to be worth the effort, for they do not share the Reconstructionist conviction that "all facets of life will come under the sway of the gospel and biblical law."[25]

This eschatological difference explains much of the dispute between Ronald Sider and David Chilton. Sider, like Reconstruction, is wary of big government and agrees that justice must begin through the voluntary action of Christians.[26] But Sider welcomes government participation in economic redistribution in ways that Reconstructionists find intolerable, because he sees no other way to reach the needy. Chilton, who envisions thoroughly Christianizing society from the bottom up, rejects Sider's proposals of government intervention on behalf of the poor as unbiblical stopgap measures that would perpetuate injustice; Sider, who aims only to "erect small imperfect signs of the shalom which God will finally bring," wants to address dire human need and does not expect the church ever to become numerous or powerful enough to do the whole job itself. Sider explicitly denies the Reconstructionist tenet of inevitable progress: "There will be fundamental disjuncture between fallen history as we know it and the shalom of heaven."[27]

Certainly, even if eschatological differences were removed, Sider and Chilton would still disagree on what justice means and on what economic measures help the poor most effectively. But, in general, those who anticipate a bright future for the church will tend to restrict governmental interventions more than those who believe that only the state will have the resources to respond to pressing social needs. Keenly aware of Third World poverty, Sider is not about to wait while Chilton, who fulminates that Sider "has called for dozens of interventionist and socialist programs which Scripture specifically forbids," promises that poverty will be reversed "only as men are converted and nations discipled to the obedience of the Christian faith."[28]

APPLICATION OF OLD TESTAMENT CIVIL LAW

The question of whether Old Testament law "specifically forbids" government actions like welfare and foreign aid brings us to the third key controversy in which the New Testament offers only indirect assistance. Does Old Testament civil law remain valid in the Christian era? Christians recognize the continuing relevance of the Old Testament, since the New Testament writers quote it so frequently and since it is the canon to which Paul referred when he said, "All Scripture is God-breathed and is useful" (2Ti 3:16). But Paul proclaimed the expiration of Old Testament ceremonial law. Does the Mosaic civil code retain binding authority for Christians or not? Since the politically powerless apostles had no reason to set forth New Testament principles of civil law, their silence opens the gates to another unresolved debate.

Most evangelicals look to Old Testament law only for general principles that might be transferable in altered fashion to contemporary society. Sider writes, "I do not believe God wants American, German or Indian governments today to legislate these specific provisions [of Old Testament law]. Rather, God wants us to apply the biblical material as one applies a paradigm."[29] In urging that Jesus came not to abolish but to "confirm" the law of Moses (Mt 5:17 in Greg Bahnsen's translation), Reconstructionists argue that only the ceremonial law has been abrogated. But the distinction between ceremonial, moral, and civil law is not always clear in the Old Testament, leaving uncertainty as to which prescriptions apply to nations other than Old Testament Israel.[30]

Reconstruction's attempt to make civil law a Christian concern leads once again to some idiosyncratic exegesis. For example, in the following passage from his *Institutes*, Rushdoony strains to turn a brief Pauline greeting into a hint of the early Christian agenda of infiltrating civil government:

> Because the saints were called to *manage* or *govern* the world, very quickly it became their purpose to move into positions of authority and power. The letters of St. Paul show clearly that prominent Romans were converted. The salutations include those "that are of Caesar's household" (Phil. 4:22).[31]

Actually, the word *household* (*oikia*) refers most likely to Caesar's servants (or conceivably to family members). The most plausible exegesis is that some of the emperor's servants had become Christians; presumably the persons indicated were in Caesar's entourage before their conversion, and certainly no Christian would be carrying out a "purpose to move into positions of authority and power" by becoming a servant of Caesar.

Reconstructionists seldom make such recognizably eisegetical use of biblical texts, but they do lean heavily on the Old Testament as a basis for abiding norms. This practice extends beyond Mosaic law to narrative sections also. Rushdoony, for instance, describes the decree of the Persian king Artaxerxes, who granted the Jewish priests and officials freedom from taxation (Ezr 7), as "the first clear recognition of the immunity of God's house and work from state control."[32] Many Christians would join Rushdoony in working to protect religious freedom, but few would cite Artaxerxes' decree as a normative precedent for church-state relations today. In a similar example, Greg Bahnsen interprets Psalm 2:10–12, which instructs kings to "kiss the Son," as a requirement that *all* civil governments should "be prejudiced toward Christianity."[33]

Since most evangelicals acknowledge the continuing moral authority of the Old Testament in some form, and since they believe in an unchanging God who does not revise moral absolutes, Reconstructionists can find strong support for their claim that the Old Testament must be applied to Christian ethics.[34] Their version of *how* to apply it, however, remains less widely accepted. Those (like this author) who do not fully share their view of the relation between the Testaments will not end up with a Reconstructionist social policy.

THE SOURCE OF CONFLICT RESOLUTION

We have seen that an evangelical approach to Scripture does not necessarily lead to a strictly defined set of policy prescriptions. This discovery reminds us that Scripture, while important to any Christian policymaker, is not by itself a sufficient guide to contemporary Christian social action.

This conclusion should not be surprising, for Christians supplement the Bible with other sources of guidance throughout their lives. The Bible warns against marrying unbelievers but does not dictate which believer to marry; it prohibits dishonest business practices but does not tell individuals what honest employment to select; it teaches generosity and responsible stewardship of resources but leaves each family with the task of preparing its own budget. Throughout life we find that Scripture does not dictate daily activities but sets parameters within which tradition, reason, experience, conscience, God's still small voice, and factors specific to the particular situation all interrelate in guiding our decisions. Similarly, our proposals for modern society must be governed by biblical truth, but they cannot be fully defined by biblical truth.[35]

This potential for variance between individual Christians, as they each pursue their particular callings and emphases, means that we cannot move from biblical principles to concrete policies as dogmatically and confidently as many do. We must recognize that even uniting Christians in agreement on principles will not produce a united policy agenda.[36]

In conceding the permanence of diversity among Christians, however, we need not resign ourselves to the paralysis of uncertainty. We cannot expect unanimous Christian adherence to our political agenda (or even a unanimous Christian commitment to becoming politically active), but we can teach principles of justice, righteousness, and ministry that enable every Christian to be prepared should God call him or her to public service. The ambiguities of eschatology preclude widespread agreement on any theory that rests on eschatological assumptions, but the improbability of Christ's immediate return means that responsible Christian theory and policy must take future generations into account. We will not reach full-fledged consensus on what the Old Testament requires of twentieth-century civil governments, but we can sensitively inject its divine inspiration into our culture—as, for example, Chuck Colson has done in applying Mosaic principles of restitution to his influential prison-reform efforts.[37]

Now that we have looked at dominion theology from historical, sociological, political, and biblical perspectives, we are ready to conclude with an overall response to the dominionist impulse. This will be the focus of the final chapter.

The Pinnacle of Overconfidence

An Evaluation and Response to Dominion Theology

One who seeks to evaluate dominion theology must avoid falling into the same trap of overconfidence that, I believe, sometimes snares the dominionists. I do not anticipate unprecedented improvement in either the world (as Reconstruction expects) or the church (as in Kingdom Now), but I freely acknowledge that I could be wrong. If I am wrong, then some day the glory of the Lord will put to shame the skepticism of this author toward those Christians who, as I see it, derive their patterns of social engagement from imperfect theologies. But until that time, the following observations remain valid.

First, the full-scale spiritual and moral renewal of a society simply does not happen. A renewal movement cannot avoid infection by the culture around it unless it self-consciously separates itself from that culture. The separation can be physical (as with the Puritans, who crossed the ocean to America, or the Amish, whose unique dress and lifestyle set clear group boundaries), or simply ideological (as with strictly sectarian groups who, while living within a larger culture, emphasize the dangers of interacting with it). But unless a movement clearly defines and maintains this sectarian distance from society in some way, its initial impulses will lose their distinctive sharpness over time.

Maintenance of sectarian norms requires firm discipline and expulsion of those who deviate even slightly from those norms,[1] and this firmness inevitably inhibits numerical growth. The more a movement succeeds numerically, the more certain it is to accommodate to the norms of the surrounding culture as its leaders become unable to inspect the ideological purity of every member.[2] Dominionists can reasonably hope for the wide dissemination of a few key ideas, but not for the reproduction of the whole matrix of attitudes and beliefs that would be needed to stimulate large-scale social reform of a dominionist sort. And the harder they work to convert people, the more diluted the message becomes.

The Puritan experience in America illustrates further that, even if a group does detach itself so as to become a holy nation, it cannot transfer its values en masse into succeeding generations.[3] Those born into the community cannot adequately internalize the group's core values except by their own voluntary decision—a choice that is impossible unless they also have the freedom to dissent. Inevitably, given that choice, some *will* dissent; and whether the dissenters leave the community or remain within it, the exclusive authority of the group's original values is ruptured. One can obtain outward allegiance by coercion, as totalitarian rulers of all stripes have demonstrated; but, as the Old Testament record graphically and repeatedly shows, not even the Hebrews, the first benefactors of theonomy, could sustain a unanimous, heartfelt commitment to the community's guidelines across successive generations.

Second, dominion theology presumes an all-encompassing Christian competence that does not exist. Christians can make distinctive and desperately needed contributions to countless areas of public life, but to call on Christians to transform every area of life may be the pride that precedes a fall, as it encourages Christians to speak where they lack competence.[4] The many differences of opinion that persist even between groups who share substantial theological agreement, such as between evangelical pluralists and theonomists, remind us that Christians, whatever spiritual redemption they may have experienced, are demonstrably imperfect in social and political wisdom. Furthermore, many areas of modern life require technical skills unrelated to questions of spiritual regeneration or ethical judgment. Christians have no clear edge over unbelievers in determining the nation's defense needs or in assessing the dangers of global warming.

The Reconstructionists have perhaps not applied adequately to themselves Reformed theology's emphasis on the fallenness of all humans, including those who have received spiritual salvation. Ironically, it is this very doctrine of depravity that drives their insightful critique of the modern Western state's messianic pretensions. As Rushdoony has shown in great detail, laws proliferate uncontrollably when government futilely tries to achieve social harmony through regulation. Soon the main effect is not increased social justice but the ballooning of an equally uncontrollable government bureaucracy, as legislators, judges, staff assistants, policy analysts, and police try to write, interpret, enforce, evaluate, and rewrite law in a never-ending circle. The Reconstructionists may go overboard in their calls for a sharply restricted state, but they have accurately spotted the misguided utopianism implicit in our culture's effort to constantly improve the system. This quest to right every perceived injustice may in fact both reduce economic productivity (by increasing the size of the bureaucracy) and hamper the cultivation of public virtue (by assuming that social progress depends more on technical policy-making expertise than on personal integrity and moral responsibility). What is the value of a society characterized by absolute equality, exquisitely planned formal justice, and moral degradation?[5]

Third, the dominionists do not fully consider the tension between their social and spiritual agendas. Their movement could not have gained a following within American evangelicalism until the coming of a generation that knew not Walter Rauschenbusch, Lyman Abbott, Washington Gladden, and Shailer Mathews. These four men were leading proponents, between 1885 and 1925, of a social gospel that made spiritual conversion secondary to social improvement. When dominionists speak of the coming of God's kingdom as the central theme of Christianity; when North and Chilton describe Constantine's conversion as the capstone of the early church's success, overlooking the ensuing spiritual contamination and decline; when Earl Paulk or John Gimenez or Bill Hamon prophesies unprecedented spiritual unity without specifying the limits or doctrinal prerequisites for such unity—in all these messages the echoes of the social gospel movement's themes of the kingdom, practical unity, the brotherhood of man, and social justice as the mark of a Christianized culture are surprisingly precise.[6] The dominionists' calls for structural change have not yet overshadowed their evangelical insistence on every individual's need for personal salvation through Christ; but it is worth remembering that the social gospel movement of a century ago was more evangelical at its inception than in its later years. Emphasizing social concern tends to lead toward doctrinal tolerance, both because there is less time and energy left to attend to doctrinal matters and because doctrinal disputes increasingly become seen as divisive distractions from the central task of redeeming society. The credally precise hard-line theonomists will doubtless resist this pressure, but their followers may not, and the charismatic dominionists have already displayed plenty of doctrinal vagueness.

That is not to imply that even the charismatic activists have subordinated religious principles to political pragmatism. The fact that Kingdom Now and Reconstruction have yet to merge reflects both groups' continuing, if not always clearly articulated, commitment to the retention of theological distinctives. This commitment will help them resist the temptation to give central priority to the political implications of their religious system and thereby to tacitly endorse modern culture's assumption (which is furthered by the media's skewed coverage of religious activities) that religion is significant if and only if it functions politically. But the often-inflated rhetoric dominionists use in motivating evangelicals to pursue social transformation tends to transfer ultimate meaning from the next world to this one.[7]

This problem of inflated rhetoric leads us to a fourth point of critique: the potential for dominionist disillusionment. Dominionist leaders have often suggested that tremendous opportunities await Christians who become active now. North, Rushdoony, and Peacocke suggest that humanism's impending collapse could give Christians their turn to lead if they are prepared; Hamon says the believers will soon become the "army of the Lord"; Paulk says this could be the generation whose "Kingdom demonstration" is sufficiently pervasive so that Christ can return. Bob Weiner matched these rosy political and eschatological proposals with equally unchecked evangelistic optimism when he said in 1979 that God had told him "that more people are going to be saved in the 1980s than all those who have ever been saved in the history of the world"—a prediction that could hardly have carried credibility even in charismatic circles had it not come from a major charismatic leader.[8] One could say that, now that the Christian Right has lessened by frequent use the value of the *stick* (i.e., warnings that "we may lose our religious freedoms if we don't act now") as a motivating tool, dominionists are turning to the *carrot*: "We can really transform society if we do act now."

In the short term, the masses often need to sense either a serious threat or a major opportunity before they will be aroused to action. But these inflated expectations set such high standards that eventual disillusionment seems all the more certain. The approach may excite initial enthusiasm but may make long-term activism harder to sustain.

We can sum up all four points of critique by suggesting that dominion theology errs in thinking it can do everything. It aims to redirect, if not take over, modern society; to bring healing to every area of culture; to foment not just outward changes but widespread spiritual revival as well; and, in those cases where dominionist rhetoric gets carried away, to do all this very soon. The healthiest medicine for the problem may be Herbert Schlossberg's book *Idols for Destruction*, which emphasizes Christians' imperative to change society and their potential to do so but just as forcefully argues that Christian social involvement should not be related to any hope of worldly success. If the church does its job in public witness, he says, it will incur increased persecution. He has no interest in formulating a theology of victory like David Chilton's, but rather a "theology of disaster," firmly rooted in God's faithfulness, that can survive any misfortunes that might rock this world.[9]

We desperately need social and political leaders who will be public servants in spirit, not just in name. Christians should be especially qualified for this role, because if they take Jesus' words seriously they will be the persons least bound by self-interest. The dominionist surge within American evangelicalism has within it the insights, the moral backbone, the dedication, and the human compassion to produce such servantlike leaders. If its overconfident triumphalism can be tempered with humility and a greater submissiveness to insights from other streams, its ideas may yet emerge from the evangelical subculture to win broader approval and bring genuine revival and revitalization to the American democratic experiment.

DO WE FIRE A SLINGSHOT AT BUREAUCRATIC GOLIATH? DOING CHRISTIAN POLITICS IN CONTEMPORARY AMERICA

While the Bible (especially in the book of Revelation) warns about the danger of a state with unlimited power, it does not set absolute limits on what government should do. It does entrust to government the task of maintaining peace and order (Ro 13:1–7; 1Ti 2:1–2)—a task that is far more complex now than in biblical times due to the arrival of instantaneous communications, highly developed international relations, global environmental concerns, public utilities and transportation, and high-technology warfare. All these concerns need to be addressed collectively, at the state, national, and even global levels.

As a result there arises an inevitable tension between the virtue of decentralized social order and the necessary expansion of justifiable government action. The key to resolving this tension is the parable of the good Samaritan (Lk 10:25–37). When asked "Who is my neighbor?"—that is, whom are we responsible to love?—Jesus answered with a story illustrating that we are responsible to *anyone* who crosses our path, whatever his or her nationality or background. For Jesus' initial Jewish listeners, this meant neighbors of any culture, including the detested Samaritans; for us today, in a global society in which we become aware instantly of earthquakes in Asia or famines in Africa, it means potentially everyone who is living or will live on this planet.

We can show the practical implications of this truth for government's role in society by reference to concerns for the health and safety of children. Clearly, both Scripture and good policy analysis teach that parents should have primary responsibility for raising children. However, no one would stand by idly while a father physically maimed his child; all would agree that the state can intrude into the family relationship to protect the innocent victim. Beyond this obvious case of physical danger, we are all too aware of the economic deprivation and parental irresponsibility that leave children seriously at risk if they have only their parents to depend on. Not only does compassion dictate the need for programs that make it more possible to reach such children, but it is justifiable for government to address this concern since it poses a direct threat to social order: neglected children become drug abusers, criminals, and unproductive members of society.

This argument for a modern state not as minimal as Reconstructionists advocate, though not nearly as maximal as urged by many social planners, should propel Christians into sensitive participation in government as one appropriate means, albeit not the primary one, of addressing issues of concern to all persons.

There are two main reasons why evangelical Christians tend not to see government as the main solution to society's problems. First, the biblical doctrine of sin leads Christians to be "pessimistic about human beings"[10] and thereby about humanly devised programs and social orders. Second, from a Christian standpoint the most important questions of life lie outside the purview of any political order. The state can maintain public peace, but it cannot lead anyone to salvation or create Christian love.

For these reasons, most Christians are more likely to pray for government's stability, as directed in 1 Timothy 2, than to aspire to positions of political leadership. They appreciate good government but would rather not be the ones charged with operating it; they have more important things to do. Even postmillennialists like Jonathan Edwards, Charles Finney, or today's Reconstructionists have expected the ideal society to arise primarily through the sweeping success of revival and evangelism, not government action.

This prevailing attitude of peaceful coexistence with government changes, however, when Christians perceive government as an intrusive threat, so large and out of control as to *cause* problems. This is why Christian Right politics so often seem reactionary: its spokespersons, for the most part, would have preferred not to have to enter politics at all, and the purpose of their involvement is primarily to get government off their back. The agendas of both

Falwell and Rushdoony reflect this central concern; the reason why Falwell became active twenty years later than Rushdoony is that he holds a far less restrictive view of the state's legitimate role. Falwell needed several severe aggravations (particularly the infringements upon Christian schools' tax exemptions and on the sacredness of preborn life) to push him toward action, while mere licensing of state schools, along with welfarism and progressive taxation, were sufficient to arouse Rushdoony much earlier.

For the last fifteen years conservative Christians have been playing political catch-up, mobilizing and organizing to reverse the measures passed while they sat placidly on the sidelines. (A similar development has occurred in most mainline Protestant denominations, where reawakened evangelicals have sought to end liberal dominance of denominational structures and committees, a dominance made possible largely because the evangelicals long ignored the church bureaucracy as irrelevant.) By the late 1980s they appeared to have caught up, achieving political influence roughly commensurate with their numbers; thus Falwell could declare his political work complete and return to his pulpit. On the other hand, dominionists, with their far broader vision of social transformation, see the task as barely begun.

But if they hope to capture the allegiance of many Americans outside their own ideological circle, dominionists must address the actual American situation with greater sensitivity. They cannot simply deplore welfare, Medicare, the minimum wage, unions, and antidiscrimination laws. Nearly every member of our society knows someone whom these laws have protected from abject poverty or injustice.

As we have already noted, my objection does not negate the positive value of dominion theology's critique of the state-as-savior myth that has pervaded the modern West. On the contrary, this critique should be broadcast all the more clearly, for even many Christians have been seduced by the promises of big government. Indoctrinated by information sources that speak instinctively of government as the answer to social problems, Christians have unwittingly compromised the superior claims of their spiritual gospel, behaving as if salvation came through law—that is, law of the supposedly enlightened American type, not the Old Testament.

In depending so heavily on the state, Christians and all other members of society are gradually putting their own freedom at risk. Not only is the state an inadequate source of social righteousness, but its capacity to coerce obedience and conformity makes it the greatest potential threat to personal freedom. Thus dominion theology offers an essential corrective to dangerously complacent views of the state as "society acting as a whole, with the ultimate power to compel compliance within its own jurisdiction."[11] Society encompasses too many diverse interests for it ever to act as a whole without infringing upon someone's rights. This fact and the inevitable threat concentration of power poses to individual liberty make the best arguments for limited central government.

Our nation's economic time bomb, the escalating federal budget deficit, will eventually force a large-scale reexamination of government's role in American society. But we cannot simply turn back the clock two hundred or four thousand years, yearning for earlier social systems from which we can learn much but which we cannot fully restore. Instead, the best solutions will address the contemporary scene with creativity and relevance. Here is where dominion theology often fails, both because it tends to lack adequate mechanisms by which to move from ideal theory to balanced real-world political practice and because it frequently assumes an unnecessarily adversarial stance toward the state. This adversarial tendency, visible at times in the defiant rhetoric of angry charismatic dominionists, also appears in the more concrete area of policy formulation when the Reconstructionists' overly rigid conception of "sphere sovereignty" causes them to treat many areas of modern government activity as absolutely, nonnegotiably unjustifiable. When Reconstructionists declare public education and welfare categorically unbiblical, rather than just a less-than-ideal option, they approach social problems in an unbalanced fashion. They are right to warn about the dangers inherent in an expanding state, but they ignore the fact that economic and social deprivation are just as dangerous to social order.[12]

In an ideal situation, private charity is far preferable to impersonal, inefficient, tax-financed state bureaucracy programs; but we do not live in an ideal situation. To eliminate the state totally from social welfare would, barring uncharacteristic mushrooming of private-sector generosity, leave the underprivileged with no assistance in overcoming conditions (ghetto upbringing, mental or physical handicaps, lack of educational opportunity) they face by no fault of their own; their alienation from the means of improving their plight might push them into socially disruptive behavior.

In our distinctly unideal world, democratic governments are usually forced to distribute the injustices as equally as possible between the libertarian and socialistic extremes—for instance, through moderately progressive taxation and ameliorative but not overly generous social programs—so that no economic group feels so consistently mistreated as to contemplate revolution. Thus the most stable democracies have tended to inch toward various forms of "welfare capitalism," tempering the rough edges of the free market with various forms of social assistance. The United States, whose prosperity has resulted partly from its hesitancy to embrace democratic socialism and from its emphasis on individual initiative, nevertheless has also committed itself to developing a "safety net" of basic food, shelter, and health-care support through which no member of society should slip.

We should always recognize that such state actions represent forced redistribution of goods, thereby reducing personal freedom, and also tend to reduce total economic productivity by diminishing incentives for production. For these reasons, in addition to their impersonal nature, government social programs should be treated as a fallback mechanism to be activated only when private initiatives are recognizably insufficient. But they cannot be eliminated across the board unless it is clear that private sources are ready and able to meet the basic needs of those whose mental or physical condition precludes them from caring for themselves. Until that time, clamoring for the abolition of government assistance is not a posture designed to help the "orphans and widows in their distress" whom "true religion" is called to help (Jas 1:27).

Called to live at peace with all persons, insofar as that is possible (Ro 12:18), Christians should treat cooperative interaction with the state as the norm (Ro 13:1–7) and adversarial postures as an undesirable necessity, to be taken only under duress (Rev 13).[13] The contrast between Romans and Revelation reminds us that Christians should not expect to adopt the same attitude toward the state in all contexts. In a context of friendly pluralism, believers might safely endorse a public school system that permits "released time" during the day for each child to attend religious instruction conducted and funded by the church of the parents' choice (or to attend none at all). On the other hand, Christians in a hostile, secularist society may be obligated to build their own tight, separated communities for solidarity and protection, teaching their children at home while considering whether to resist oppression or flee the country. Reconstructionist principles provide wise guidance for situations in which the state forces a confrontation upon the church, but, by treating Old Testament Israel too directly as a normative paradigm for all cultures, they lack flexibility to deal with other situations where a broader role for the state may be both biblically permissible and practically advisable. Reconstructionists tend to be not just perennially critical of the state (as any independent voice should be) but perennially adversarial until such time as they can take charge and reshape it.

The variable but always imperfect nature of human society also has bearing on how we define and advocate religious liberty. All Christians yearn for a society fully imbued by true religion, but the name for that society is heaven. Since true faith cannot be coerced, Christians should avoid social arrangements that exert coercive pressure on unbelievers. No Christian should desire to discriminate against law-abiding non-Christians in such areas as employment, educational opportunity, or eligibility for public office. On the other hand, since all law is based on some conception of morality, it would be seriously unjust to deny Christians or any other group the right to seek legislation in accord with their moral values. The question of how much to legislate must, again, depend on the specific context, but in general Christians will have to balance opposition to socially harmful behavior with protection of religious and personal liberty. Thus, for example, they may seek to criminalize homosexual acts but not to invade private bedrooms; they may argue that advocating religiously motivated violence should be a civil offense but that public expressions of blasphemy should not.[14]

A MODEST MODEL OF PRINCIPLED POLITICS

Although Reconstructionists show little concern for practical politics, they offer a refreshingly clear model of political principle, a model much needed in an age when so many politicians appear to follow only the principle of "How should I vote in order to get reelected?" Since the Reconstructionists argue in deductive, logical fashion, from Bible to principles to precepts, one can see clearly how and why they have arrived at their positions. It is not acceptable to criticize Reconstruction simply because it sounds inconvenient or unattractive. If we do not like its principles, we must offer alternative ones.

I have argued that Reconstruction overstates the degree to which the civil laws of Old Testament Israel should be transferred directly into a Christian context. However, many timeless principles do emerge. For example, capital punishment is clearly justifiable in God's eyes, although proper application of the death penalty depends on cultural circumstances as well. Restitution, rather than imprisonment, remains an eminently wise and socially beneficial treatment for nonviolent criminals. And we can presume that, if God considered forced redistribution the preferred remedy for social inequities, he would have given this command to Moses, as it could easily have been implemented. (The law of Jubilee, which canceled debts every seven years, would have reduced extremes of rich and poor but would not have eradicated social disparities.)

In addition to the specific civil prescriptions that remain applicable, one can derive a set of premises, which I believe are both biblically and rationally defensible, that lay the foundation for a principled politics. Here are some of what I would consider essential principles, of which the biblical citations are illustrative:

> *Safety net*: A Christian should use whatever means are available to help meet the basic needs of every person, except those who are unwilling to work. (Jas 2:14–17; Php 4:12; 2Th 3:10)
>
> *Materialism*: Government should in no way promote the falsehood that material items carry ultimate value. (Lk 12:13–21; Isa 31:1)

Personal responsibility: Since each person must ultimately stand before God, government should encourage people to take responsibility for their own lives, not rob that responsibility from them. (Eze 18; Ro 1:18–20; Gal 6:4–5; 2Co 5:10)

Limited government: Government should do only those things that need to be done and cannot be done more effectively in any other way. This can be deduced from a number of premises: government is responsible primarily to maintain order and restrain evil (Ro 13:1–7); neither government nor any human source can provide ultimate meaning (Mt 4:4); many areas of society should be directed not by the state but by the church, family, and other institutions (Eph 5:22–6:4; 1Co 6:1–8); unchecked, centralized power is inevitably dangerous, due to the pervasiveness of human sin (Ro 3:23; Ge 11:1–9; Rev 13).

Justice as reciprocity: Government must not treat any individual, group, or nation in a way that it would consider unjust if it were on the receiving end of that treatment. (Lk 6:31)

Of course, these premises cannot determine how a congressman should vote on every bill, since so many policy decisions pit valid claims against each other. The budgeting process is the most obvious example: even if we can agree on which government programs are justifiable, who could possibly deliver the perfect formula that decides how much money to give to each? Similarly, issues related to children (e.g., educational or child-care regulations) repeatedly weigh parents' rights to build meaningful relationships with their offspring, free from government interference in matters that parents feel they can handle, versus government's concern to help each child become productive and protect each child from neglect.

Nevertheless, neither are these premises just empty platitudes. Here are some ways in which one might move from this foundation to constructive policy making:

Trade. While the U.S. trade deficit has many causes, one key factor is an unhealthy proliferation of material desire. To tell Asian nations that they should become more insatiably acquisitive in order to offset their trade imbalance with America is an unconscionable exporting of false values. Incentives to save and disincentives to purchase luxury items would be more justifiable. In view of the degree to which the "boob tube" has created a culture of couch potatoes and hampered the development of meaningful family relationships and cultural literacy, a surtax on televisions might not be a bad idea either.

Resource consumption. To consume environmental and natural resources that cannot be replenished perpetrates an injustice not only against vague "future generations" but potentially even against our own children. Since environmental control requires regulation of every sector of society, government must unavoidably be involved but should seek to address these issues as much as possible by incentives (e.g., tax credits for energy-saving improvements) rather than costly bureaucratic supervision.

Education. Compulsory-education laws make sense in a society in which the illiterate and uneducated struggle to survive. Government must provide public schools in order to make education available to all children. But families, churches, and private organizations are often more able than government to provide education that reinforces family relationships, parental freedom, and moral values. Government should, in general, seek to encourage private schools (e.g., through evenhanded funding of all schools, both public and private) and should regulate private schools only with regard to basic essentials such as core curriculum and health standards.

Abortion. In a culture where reverence for the sacredness of life has declined, the use of tax dollars to help pregnant women feel they have feasible options other than abortion is eminently desirable. Government could help meet the material, counseling, and educational needs of women with unwanted pregnancies. The added tax burden, though not ideal, is far better than permitting the social conditions that encourage women to extinguish human lives through abortion. It would also be necessary to support the extreme, highly visible social services that would have to accompany any reversal of abortion rights.

Social spending. It should be privatized as much as possible to decrease bureaucratic inefficiency and because private groups can provide charity more sensitively and compassionately than impersonal government programs. Government must meet the basic needs of all persons if the private sector is unable or unwilling to do so. However, to decrease taxes and stimulate private charity is preferable. The federal government might be able to encourage the replacement of public by private social-service programs by offering tax deductions for charitable contributions to all citizens (not only those who itemize). It could even offer a bonus by permitting taxpayers to deduct *more* than their actual contribution (say, 125 percent of the amount donated) from their taxable income. This step would actively encourage generosity, in contrast to the current system that discourages generosity by causing Americans to feel they already support the needy more than enough through involuntary taxation.

I make no claim for the absolute superiority of these or any other specific policy proposals. But I believe they illustrate the real possibility of political action that is both morally responsible and practically feasible, even amidst the almost undecipherable complexities of modern American society.

POLITICS AS SERVANTHOOD

The question of whether Christians should be politically active dissolves when one recognizes that, for the Christian, politics should be a means of servanthood—a way in which we care for others by seeking to improve the world in which we all live. To ignore this vehicle of Christian compassion would be as irresponsible as to ignore the neighbor whose house has burned down.[15] And to reject politics as a "dirty" pursuit sullied by compromise is inconsistent, for servanthood in every area of life—the business world, civic organizations, even church leadership—requires practical compromise.

Defining politics as servanthood may help to chase away a few of those who envision politics as an opportunity for self-aggrandizement or for the protection of self-interest. It may also correct the attitudinal imbalance present in many well-meaning Christians who see political action as primarily a way to muster a voting majority and defeat the enemies of what they consider the "Christian" position.

This unservantlike attitude is especially misguided when it begins to ostracize fellow Christians for holding deviant political views. It is understandable, in view of the rising tide of humanism, that conservative Christians have upped the urgency of their calls to unified political action. But the noblest of political goals does not justify spiritual bullying. Because political success in a democratic republic requires numerical strength, Christians with particular political agendas inevitably face the temptation to urge that others conform not only to Christ's spiritual authority but to their own ideological platform as well. We must constantly seek to maintain the distance between God's nonnegotiable requirements for salvation and the political views we have derived from Scripture. To do otherwise politicizes the Gospel and thereby hamstrings its spiritual power.[16]

This approach by no means solves all the practical questions, since the spiritual and political spheres inextricably overlap. If a professional thief came to my church wanting to accept Christ as Lord, I would insist that he change his profession, and I would not be swayed if he retorted that my prohibition of thievery represented an unbiblical attachment of conservative social views to the Gospel! Premeditated stealing, I would assert, is a conscious, direct affront to Christ's lordship and not a negotiable "political view." Of course, free-market economics is just as evidently Christian to some persons as intolerance of robbery is to me. Nevertheless, the existence of opposing economic views within the evangelical community reinforces the fact that Christians can dogmatically assert only basic principles while entering patient, open dialogue as to concrete applications of those principles.

Different groups of Christians, then, will bring differing emphases into the public square. In accord with Paul's instruction on the value of each individual Christian's gifts (1Co 12:7; 14:26), and since no one person can give special priority to all issues at the same time, many of these differing emphases may be simultaneously valid—even if they lead fellow Christians to competing political stances or into opposing parties. Only the combined voices of all legitimate Christian views can bring a complete Christian influence into public life.

This means, first, that we must remain open to fellow believers of other perspectives, listening for any godly, justifiable concerns that may be motivating their stance. It also suggests that efforts to unite the saints into a single voting bloc are not only utopian but misguided. In learning to exercise greater gentleness toward fellow believers, Christians may also find themselves more successfully modeling Christ's compassion toward the rest of the world. Dennis Peacocke's declaration that Christian activism flows from "our love for people"[17] is all too often drowned out by unrestrained expressions of anger toward those whom we perceive as enemies— be they abortionists, gays, humanists, or the whole collection of unenlightened Democrats. If we truly share Christ's love for every human being, we can both seek to bring a biblical influence to society *and* sincerely proclaim that we are concerned for the best interests of all persons, not just our ideological compatriots. We can both advocate the prolife cause with every ounce of energy and sit down to dialogue with prochoice leaders, listening to their legitimate concerns and identifying areas of common ground. Obviously, some of our most radical political opponents will refuse to acknowledge our overriding sense of compassion no matter how clearly we state it. But if they fail to discern the spirit of Christ in our political action, let it not be because we did not bother to communicate it.

This principle of compassion should also guide our coalition-building efforts across religious lines. It would never occur to us that banding with non-Christian neighbors to fight crime in our town might compromise our Christian witness; why should we apply a stricter standard to political coalitions? We should be able to affirm our areas of agreement with unbelievers without implying that we therefore think everything they believe is true. Even Reconstructionists do this, acknowledging the contributions of secular theorists of free-market economics while cautioning that capitalism's success also depends on the internal motivations provided by Christianity. In fact, Christians (especially the many evangelicals whose social lives are largely limited to the evangelical subculture) need to establish areas of common ground and mutual interest on which to interact with unbelievers if they expect the Gospel to gain a wider hearing. Refusing to praise Jews or Mormons for their social or political insights makes as much sense as refusing to praise Mom's cooking because she is not saved. (At the same time, in joining coalitions we must be careful not to give implicit endorsement of views or behaviors we cannot accept. Accepting contributions from organizations tied to the Unification

Church, as some right-wing groups have done, may be an example of unacceptable coalition building, since much of Sun Myung Moon's wealth may have derived directly from the manipulative exploitation of church members.)

THE CHALLENGE OF SOWING PEACE

Along with the complexities of political action, Christians must beware of economic, social, and psychological factors that militate against the virtues of peace and gentleness in public witness. First, controversy sells, so anyone with an economic motivation—author, publisher, speaker, talk-show host—sees benefit in creating controversy, even among Christians. Second, writers and preachers know that colorful rhetoric makes a deeper impact than bland language, and in the heat of debate that rhetoric almost inevitably takes the form of denigrating one's adversary. Moreover, in making one's point clear one must define one's position over against the alternatives, and this requirement leads debaters to emphasize the differences and pay meager lip service to areas of agreement. On top of this, one who sincerely views certain competing opinions as dangerous will tend, in a spirit the speaker might term "righteous anger," to associate that revulsion with the *persons* holding those opinions as well, even if those persons are professing Christians. And in a market where sales, not theological precision, is the prime measure of success, there is little motivation for popular authors to commit themselves to hours of careful research that few book purchasers will care to notice.

In short, free-market economics and human nature push all analysts of contemporary issues, Christian and non-Christian alike, toward the journalistic, confrontational mode and away from diplomatic, peacemaking styles. For this reason responsible Christians must make a conscious effort to be different. To counteract the seductions of money and popularity, we must redirect our focus to more important questions of purpose and consequences.

Because Christians spend most of their time talking with each other, they usually exaggerate the significance of internal debates. I readily agree that doctrines have practical consequences and that Christians should remain on guard for error within the ranks, but when Christians in a secularized society spend most of their energy fighting each other, something is wrong.

What do we do then? We must certainly continue discussing heated issues like dominion theology, but we can reshape in several ways the context in which they are discussed. First, we can strive to emphasize areas of agreement; not only does this enhance mutual respect, but it helps to create an atmosphere in which each party is more disposed to listen to others, treating them as partners rather than simply adversaries and considering their insights more seriously. This guideline would not prohibit gifted writers like Gary North from unleashing their colorful pens, but it would foster a spirit of trust in which even North's rhetoric could provide much-needed comic relief rather than provoke rancor. Of course, if North and Chilton really do hate Ron Sider, or if conservative theologians personally detest independent charismatics, then mutual respect is impossible. But I think the trouble arises from the debate-oriented context, not from unbridgeable animosities.

Second, we can take more seriously the power of the spoken or printed word. This means, first and foremost, taking reasonable steps to make our words accurate. My personal interaction with Earl Paulk, Gary DeMar, and others has corrected many of my misconceptions and inaccuracies; why anyone would want to write about contemporary movements without speaking directly with at least some of their representatives mystifies me. Any attempt to promote firsthand dialogue also implies a responsibility for leaders not to isolate themselves, but to be receptive to the inquiries of reputable Christian researchers.

The power of public words also demands sensitivity to the unintended meanings words can communicate. One cannot rapidly turn dramatic sermons into widely distributed books in a culture that assumes written texts express carefully formed ideas. Earl Paulk may be readily forgiven for rough spots in his early books, but to publish and heavily advertise *That the World May Know* in 1987, explicitly entering the Dave Hunt-generated debate with unchecked statements that only increased the confusion, was a more avoidable error in judgment.

One member of Paulk's staff, when I recommended that Paulk have his manuscripts reviewed by respected theologians before publication, replied, "I can hardly imagine Isaiah submitting his prophecies to 'respected theologians' for review." I fully agree. I do not mean to suggest that Paulk should make his books conform to everything those theologians believe. What I do mean is that the wisdom of a multitude of prepublication counselors reveals to an author what impact a book will have and how its words will be interpreted. All reputable publishers use such a review process, with regard to both content and style, to make their books say what their authors mean and reduce the danger of misinterpretation. No Christian message is so urgent as to justify circumvention of these safeguards.

Every reader can contribute to making the world of Christian publishing genuinely Christian by refusing to patronize authors who specialize in stirring up controversy, critics who ridicule rather than openly interact with their opponents, and publishers who ignore established guidelines for responsible publishing. Only a substantial maturing of Christian buyers' tastes can harness the power of economic incentives and use it to create an environment in which Christian leaders talk *to*, rather than *past*, each other.

THE DOMINIONISTS' VALUABLE COMBINATION: OPTIMISM WITH DISTINCTIVENESS

We began this study by speaking of dominion theology as an evangelical ideology of resistance, both against what it perceives as a hostile secular culture and against evangelical accommodation to the norms of that culture. We have seen that it can at times go overboard in its unyielding antagonism to non-Christian cultural forces. We have also observed a discomforting triumphalism within dominion theology, especially its takeover rhetoric. Yet these two defining dominionist characteristics, cultural distinctiveness and optimism, also offer a positive contrast to the inconsistency and passivity that mark so much of both Christian and secular thought. It seems appropriate to conclude this examination of dominion theology with sympathetic remarks on these two points.

"If the world hates you," Jesus said, "keep in mind that it hated me first" (Jn 15:18). American evangelicals, on the other hand, often seem to have rewritten that verse as "If the world hates you, see if you can change your style." Or, to use James Hunter's phrase, the watchword today is "No offense, I am an evangelical" as the evangelical community seeks to exchange civility for social acceptance. But at some point the Gospel *will* offend, and those who wish to remain true to it must not negotiate away those points. Dominionists have unapologetically proclaimed Christ's lordship over every individual and over all of society, even in ways our society is anything but anxious to hear. One could perhaps charge dominionists with their own forms of cultural captivity—whether to free-market economics, or experience-centered charismatic spirituality, or political ambition. But their behavior echoes Paul's exhortation to "preach the Word . . . in season and out of season" (2Ti 4:2) and to be unashamed of the Gospel no matter how the crowds respond.

While seeking to present the Gospel without compromise, and while preparing for confrontation with unfriendly authorities, the dominionists have not fallen into the apocalyptic alienation typical of many unpopular preachers who consign this world to perdition and wait for Christ's return to bring judgment upon the scoffers. Rather, they proceed with vibrant optimism, confident that their efforts will make a difference. It might seem that men like Paulk, Gimenez, and Robertson, as heads of megaministries, have no reason to feel rejected or unsuccessful. But they have ventured far beyond the safe confines of their friendly home bases into active engagement with a less responsive society within which their faithful followers (as even Robertson discovered on Super Tuesday 1988) represent a small, outvoted minority. Nevertheless, they, along with the idealistic Dennis Peacocke, visionary Jay Grimstead, methodical Gary North, thundering R. J. Rushdoony, and others, tirelessly continue the work that has become the passion of their lives.

The dominionists' optimism also leads them to succeed in one area where Religious Right politics often fails miserably. Conservative Christians tend to focus virtually all their political energies on issues of public morality: abortion, pornography, sexuality, school prayer, religious freedom, parents' rights. These may be the most important issues for evangelicals, but they are not the most pressing ones for all Americans. In concentrating so heavily on sociomoral matters, evangelicals imply that they really do not care about other people's concerns—an unservantlike political style hardly befitting Christians, who should count it a privilege to make the needs of others their first priority (Php 2:3–4). The fact that candidates for major office often find it a liability to be associated with prominent evangelicals shows how poorly many Christians have lived out Jesus' message that he who would be greatest in the kingdom of God must become the servant of all (Mk 10:44).

How long can the dominionists remain both countercultural and optimistic? Probably not very long, if they are relying on their occasionally expressed hopes that the substantial social transformation toward which they toil will begin soon. But if their hope remains centered on the final victory Christ offers to every believer, that hope will sustain them for a lifetime, through cultural upturns and downturns alike. Insofar as they challenge modern America to consider the comprehensive, transformative Gospel of Jesus Christ, they are laying up treasures in heaven. And none of us can do anything more valuable than that.

• Notes •

Chapter 1

[1]Quoted by Gary North, "The Intellectual Schizophrenia of the New Christian Right," in *The Failure of the American Baptist Culture*, ed. James B. Jordan (Tyler, Tex.: Geneva Divinity School, 1982), 12.

[2]Gary North, *Backward, Christian Soldiers?* (Tyler, Tex.: ICE, 1984), 267; Rousas John Rushdoony, *Christianity and the State* (Vallecito, Calif.: Ross House, 1986), 3. For the Moral Majority position see Jerry Falwell with Ed Dobson and Ed Hindson, *The Fundamentalist Phenomenon* (Garden City, N.Y.: Doubleday, 1981), 190–91.

[3]For Robertson's disavowal, see Rodney Clapp, "Democracy as Heresy," *Christianity Today* (February 20, 1987): 21.

[4]In a broadcast of his "700 Club" television show on January 11, 1985, Robertson stated that Christians and Jews "are the only ones that are qualified to have the reign," because they alone are submitted to God. See Wayne King, "The Record of Pat Robertson on Religion and Government," *New York Times*, December 22, 1987. Other examples of Robertson's version of dominion thinking can be found in Fred Clarkson and Andy Lang, "What Makes Pat Robertson Run?" *Convergence* (Christic Institute, Washington, D.C.) (Spring 1988): 17–23.

[5]James Davison Hunter, *Evangelicalism: The Coming Generation* (Chicago: Univ. of Chicago Press, 1987).

[6]Paul Marshall, *Thine Is the Kingdom* (London: Marshall, Morgan and Scott, 1984; Grand Rapids: Eerdmans, 1986), 18, 20–22.

[7]Ibid., 18; *Pat Robertson's Perspective*, February 1977 and October 1989. See also Pat Robertson, *America's Dates with Destiny* (Nashville: Nelson, 1986), 300–304.

[8]Michael Cromartie, "The Emerging Debate Concerning Evangelical Political Involvement: Five Propositions" (unpublished paper, November 1989), 8.

[9]Richard John Neuhaus, quoted by Michael Cromartie, "The Story of an Encounter," in *The Bible, Politics, and Democracy*, ed. Richard John Neuhaus (Grand Rapids: Eerdmans, 1987), 129–30.

[10]Jeffrey K. Hadden and Anson Shupe, *Televangelism: Power and Politics on God's Frontier* (New York: Henry Holt, 1988), chap. 4. See also Peggy L. Shriver, *The Bible Vote: Religion and the New Right* (New York: Pilgrim, 1981).

[11]See Falwell, *Fundamentalist Phenomenon*, 191; on the effect of evangelical participation in coalitions beyond their own community, Steve Bruce, *The Rise and Fall of the New Christian Right* (Oxford: Clarendon, 1988), chap. 6; on the Christian

Right's ties to the Moonies, see "Baptist Pastor Resigns as Head of Religious Freedom Group," *Christianity Today* (June 16, 1985): 56.

[12]See Robert Wuthnow, "The Political Rebirth of American Evangelicals," *The New Christian Right*, ed. Robert Liebman and Robert Wuthnow (New York: Aldine, 1983), 167–85; James L. Guth, "The New Christian Right," in ibid., 31–45 (p. 41 for Jones's comment).

[13]The view of God's revealed law as the basis for government sometimes leaves the door open to acceptance of biblically oriented Jews as partners. Thus, for example, Pat Robertson could include Jews along with Christians as persons fit for political leadership (see note 4 above). However, Robertson's predilection for working with Christians appears in his choice of the name "Christian Coalition" for his new grass-roots political-action organization. "Christian Americans are tired of getting stepped on," its initial brochure proclaimed, but the coalition's executive director revealed that its goals went beyond having an equal say: "We think the Lord is going to give us this nation back one precinct at a time, one neighborhood at a time, and one state at a time." "Robertson Regroups 'Invisible Army' into New Coalition," *Christianity Today* (April 23, 1990): 35.

[14]Dave Hunt, *Whatever Happened to Heaven?* (Eugene, Ore.: Harvest House, 1988).

Chapter 2

[1]E.g., Gary North, foreword to Greg Bahnsen, *By This Standard: The Authority of God's Law Today* (Tyler, Tex.: ICE, 1985), xx; North, *Unconditional Surrender: God's Program for Victory*, 3d ed. (Tyler, Tex.: ICE, 1988), 8; North, *Liberating Planet Earth* (Ft. Worth, Tex.: Dominion, 1987), 157.

[2]Gary North, *Backward, Christian Soldiers?* (Tyler, Tex.: ICE, 1984), 267.

[3]Rousas John Rushdoony, *The Institutes of Biblical Law* (Nutley, N.J.: Craig, 1973), 14; cf. also p. 8, and North, *Unconditional Surrender*, 125.

[4]North, *Unconditional Surrender*, 57.

[5]Ibid., 76; cf. Rushdoony, *Institutes*, 308.

[6]David Chilton, *Paradise Restored: A Biblical Theology of Dominion* (Tyler, Tex.: Reconstruction Press, 1985), 219; cf. Rushdoony, *Institutes*, 277.

[7]Quotations from Rushdoony, *Institutes*, 725, citing 2Co 10:5; Chilton, *Paradise Restored*, 214; North, *Liberating Planet Earth*, 91–92, emphasis in original. Cf. also North, *Unconditional Surrender*, 233.

[8]North, *Backward, Christian Soldiers?*, 66; cf. Rushdoony, *Institutes*, 119.

[9]Quotations from Greg Bahnsen, *Theonomy in Christian Ethics*, 2d ed. (Phillipsburg, N.J.: Presbyterian and Reformed, 1984), 39; Bahnsen, *By This Standard*, 3, 41; Rushdoony, *Institutes*, 2, cf. also 653–54.

[10]Rushdoony, *Institutes*, 8; North, *Unconditional Surrender*, 98.

[11]North, *Unconditional Surrender*, 125, 143; however, he offers the qualifier that this general promise does not guarantee individual prosperity for every believer, *Liberating Planet Earth*, 119.

[12]David Chilton, *Productive Christians in an Age of Guilt-Manipulators*, 3d ed. (Tyler, Tex.: ICE, 1985), 39, cf. 94; Gary North, *Political Polytheism* (Tyler, Tex.: ICE, 1989), 31–35.

[13]Bahnsen, *By This Standard*, 7; Greg L. Bahnsen and Kenneth L. Gentry, *House Divided: The Break-Up of Dispensational Theology* (Tyler, Tex.: ICE, 1989), 31, 41–42.

[14]Bahnsen, *By This Standard*, 135–38, 168, 288–89, 317–18.

[15]Ibid., 71–76, 184, 190–91; Rushdoony, *Institutes*, 732–38.

[16]Bahnsen, *By This Standard*, 201.

[17]Rushdoony, *Institutes*, 9; cf. 651–54, 679–83. Bahnsen (*House Divided*, 46) argues that Calvin in this passage rejects not the Mosaic standard for moral law but only its use as a pretext for revolution.

[18]Rushdoony, *Institutes*, 1; cf. Bahnsen, *By This Standard*, 50–52. North, *Political Polytheism*, 51, calls the Reconstructionists "neo-Puritans."

[19]Chilton, *Productive Christians*, 156, 41.

[20]The separability of theonomy from postmillennialism is noted by Bahnsen and Gentry, *House Divided*, 21; Greg L. Bahnsen, "The Theonomic Position," in *God and Politics: Four Views on the Transformation of Civil Government*, ed. Gary Scott Smith (Phillipsburg, N.J.: Presbyterian and Reformed, 1989), 28. North says the theonomy-postmillennialism link is "fundamental," even though not logically necessary: "Theonomy is utopian unless postmillennialism is true" (*Political Polytheism*, 55–57).

[21]North, *Unconditional Surrender*, 357, 362; Chilton, *Productive Christians*, 213; North, *Political Polytheism*, 612–13.

[22]North, *Unconditional Surrender*, 307; cf. Chilton, *Productive Christians*, 238–41.

[23]Rushdoony, *Institutes*, 494.

[24]North, *Unconditional Surrender*, 144; Chilton, *Paradise Restored*, 204.

[25]Chilton, *Paradise Restored*, chaps. 9–13; cf. also David Chilton, *The Days of Vengeance* (Ft. Worth, Tex.: Dominion, 1987), and Kenneth L. Gentry, Jr., *Before Jerusalem Fell: Dating the Book of Revelation* (Tyler, Tex.: ICE, 1987). For a more recent exposition, see Bahnsen and Gentry, *House Divided*, part 2.

[26]Chilton, *Paradise Restored*, 24–25, 146–47; North, *Unconditional Surrender*, 110–15; Rushdoony, *Institutes*, 14.

[27]North, *Unconditional Surrender*, 309–29.

[28]North, *Liberating Planet Earth*, 138; cf. also North, *Unconditional Surrender*, 152–59; Rushdoony, *Institutes*, 659; cf. 676.

[29]Chilton, *Paradise Restored*, 221; Gary DeMar, *Ruler of the Nations* (Ft. Worth, Tex.: Dominion, 1987), 157; North, in Chilton, *Productive Christians*, 439 (the quotation also appears in North's brochure describing the ICE). Cf. Gary North, *The Sinai Strategy* (Tyler, Tex.: ICE, 1986), 86–92, for his optimism; *Backward, Christian Soldiers?*, 232–34, for his expectations of defeat.

[30]North, *Backward Christian Soldiers?*, 55; cf. 14, 55–58, 266. Cf. also Rushdoony, *Institutes*, 621: "Men will not obey a law which lacks moral structure."

[31]North, *Liberating Planet Earth*, 10; North heavily stresses the connection between obedience and external blessing in *Political Polytheism*, 31–32, 58, 140–47.

[32]Chilton, *Paradise Restored*, 222; North, *Unconditional Surrender*, 387. Joe Kickasola, similarly, says the motivation for Christians in this world should be "duty, sweet duty"; see his essay "The Bible, Ethics, and Public Policy," *Journal of Christian Reconstruction* 11, 1 (1985): 122.

[33]North, *Backward, Christian Soldiers?*, chap. 20; Gary North, ed., *Theology of Christian Resistance* and *Tactics of Christian Resistance* (both Tyler, Tex.: Geneva Divinity School, 1983).

³⁴Bahnsen, *By This Standard*, 322.

³⁵James B. Jordan, "Editor's Introduction," in *The Failure of the American Baptist Culture*, ed. James B. Jordan (Tyler, Tex.: Geneva Divinity School, 1982), vii.

³⁶North, *Liberating Planet Earth*, 153; cf. Rushdoony, *Institutes*, 241.

³⁷Russell Chandler, "Chalcedonians Seek to Tailor U.S. Religion to Precepts of Far Right," *Los Angeles Times*, March 29, 1986.

³⁸North, foreword to Bahnsen, *By This Standard*, xx; North, *Liberating Planet Earth*, 185–86.

³⁹Rushdoony, *Institutes*, 747; Gary North, *75 Questions Your Bible Instructors Hope You Won't Ask* (Tyler, Tex.: Spurgeon, 1984), 224–27.

⁴⁰Chilton, *Paradise Restored*, 216; North, *Unconditional Surrender*, 98; cf. North, *Liberating Planet Earth*, 93.

⁴¹DeMar, *Ruler of the Nations*, 144, 217; Randy Frame, "The Theonomic Urge," *Christianity Today* (April 21, 1989): 38.

⁴²North, "In Defense of Biblical Bribery," appendix 5 in Rushdoony, *Institutes*, 845–46; North, *Unconditional Surrender*, 340.

⁴³David Chilton on Bill Moyers's television documentary, "God and Politics" (Public Broadcasting Service, 1987), cited by H. Wayne House and Thomas D. Ice, *Dominion Theology: Blessing or Curse?* (Portland, Ore.: Multnomah, 1988), appendix C.

⁴⁴North, *Backward, Christian Soldiers?*, 140.

⁴⁵Ibid., 275.

⁴⁶Quotations are from North, *Liberating Planet Earth*, 142; Rousas John Rushdoony, *The Foundations of Social Order* (1968; Fairfax, Va.: Thoburn, 1978), 161. See also Rousas John Rushdoony, *The Nature of the American System* (Nutley, N.J.: Craig, 1965; Fairfax, Va.: Thoburn, 1978), 77; Rushdoony, *The Messianic Character of American Education* (Nutley, N.J.: Craig, 1963), 313.

⁴⁷Rushdoony, *Institutes*, 10; cf. 679–80, and also North, *Unconditional Surrender*, 59; DeMar, *Ruler of the Nations*, 47–50.

⁴⁸Gary North, "The Intellectual Schizophrenia of the New Christian Right," in *The Failure of the American Baptist Culture*, ed. James B. Jordan (Tyler, Tex.: Geneva Divinity School, 1982), 28, 39; the "humanistic myths" are discussed by Kevin Craig, "Social Apologetics," in ibid., 47–58. In *Political Polytheism*, 215, North accepts political pluralism, but only "as a temporary system during which all sides are mobilizing to capture the system permanently."

⁴⁹DeMar, *Ruler of the Nations*, 30–33.

⁵⁰Rousas J. Rushdoony, *This Independent Republic* (Nutley, N.J.: Craig, 1964), 33–35; Rushdoony, *Nature of the American System*, 72–75.

⁵¹Rushdoony, *Institutes*, 772; Rushdoony, *Foundations*, 125.

⁵²Quotation from Rushdoony, *Institutes*, 68; cf. also 541, citing Madison's statement that American civilization depended "upon the capacity of mankind for self-government . . . according to the Ten Commandments of God"; see also North, *Liberating Planet Earth*, 64, 69–70; North, *Unconditional Surrender*, 224; DeMar, *Ruler of the Nations*, 9, 25.

⁵³North, *Unconditional Surrender*, 180.

⁵⁴North, *Liberating Planet Earth*, 78–86; Rushdoony, *Institutes*, 179–82, 451, 493; North, *Unconditional Surrender*, 184–93.

⁵⁵Rushdoony, *Institutes*, 21; cf. p. 185, and also North, *Backward, Christian Soldiers?*, 138–41.

⁵⁶North, *Liberating Planet Earth*, 74–78; Chilton, *Productive Christians*, 113–21; Rousas John Rushdoony, *The Myth of Overpopulation* (Fairfax, Va.: Thoburn, 1969, 1973).

⁵⁷On church and state, Bahnsen, *By This Standard*, 290, 292; North, *Liberating Planet Earth*, 88, and Rousas J. Rushdoony, *Christianity and the State* (Vallecito, Calif.: Ross House, 1986), 47, both citing the punishment of King Uzziah in 2 Chronicles 26 as a warning against attempts to mix civil justice and religious ministry; Rushdoony, *Institutes*, 241. On expositing of law, Rushdoony, *Institutes*, 617–19. On settling of disputes, North, *Liberating Planet Earth*, 96. On responsibility to the needy, Rushdoony, *Institutes*, 249–53; Chilton, *Productive Christians*, 8, 46, 168, 199.

⁵⁸DeMar, *Ruler of the Nations*, 74–81; Rushdoony, *Institutes*, 281–84, 514, 643; Chilton, *Productive Christians*, 42–43; North, *Unconditional Surrender*, 237–39. First Samuel 8 is normally cited to prove that the state may not demand more money than the amount to which the church is entitled.

⁵⁹See Chilton, *Productive Christians*, passim; North, *Unconditional Surrender*, 244–50; North, *Liberating Planet Earth*, chap. 8; Rushdoony, *Institutes*, 487, 507–10, 640, 649.

⁶⁰Chilton, *Paradise Restored*, 49; see also Rushdoony, *Institutes*, 678–79; Chilton, *Productive Christians*, 220–24, 313–15.

⁶¹Rushdoony, *Institutes*, 123–24; North, *Liberating Planet Earth*, 103–8; Chilton, *Productive Christians*, 85.

⁶²Rushdoony, *Foundations*, 63–82.

⁶³Bahnsen, *By This Standard*, 323.

⁶⁴Chilton, *Productive Christians*, 242–43; see Rushdoony, *Nature of the American System*, chaps. 3, 4. George Grant, *The Changing of the Guard* (Ft. Worth, Tex.: Dominion, 1987), 40, 120–21, praises the American system as not only "decentralized" but "theocratic" in acknowledging "the sovereignty of God and the rule of His law." In this regard Grant is perhaps closer to the "constitutionalist" group discussed in the next chapter than are most Reconstructionists. On the other hand, North blasts the Constitution for denying religious tests for office (*Political Polytheism*, 311, 379–90, 410, 653) and regrets Rushdoony's affirmation of it (ibid., 657, 681).

⁶⁵Rushdoony, *Institutes*, 580–81; Rushdoony, *Christianity and the State*, 6–7. Connecticut kept its state-level establishment of religion until 1818, Massachusetts until 1833. Sydney Ahlstrom, *A Religious History of the American People* (New Haven, Conn.: Yale Univ. Press, 1972), 380.

⁶⁶Rushdoony, *Institutes*, 89.

⁶⁷Ibid., 228–29, 570–71; Rushdoony, *Messianic Character of American Education*, 5.

⁶⁸Rushdoony, *Institutes*, 515; cf. 187–88, 235, 425, 514–20; North, *Unconditional Surrender*, 115–20; Bahnsen, *By This Standard*, chap. 27.

⁶⁹Quotations from Rushdoony, *Institutes*, 326–27; DeMar, *Ruler of the Nations*, 99. See also Rushdoony, *Foundations*, 203; DeMar, *Ruler of the Nations*, chap. 4.

⁷⁰The essential primary source for Kuyper's thought is his *Lectures on Calvinism* (New York: Revell, [1898]). James Bratt, *Dutch Calvinism in Modern America* (Grand Rapids: Eerdmans, 1984), 14–27, succinctly summarizes Kuyper's central points and their sociopolitical importance. See also Frank Vanden Berg, *Abraham Kuyper* (Grand Rapids: Eerdmans, 1960).

[71]See Kuyper, *Lectures*, 102–15 on the state, 116–27 on sphere sovereignty. Bratt, *Dutch Calvinism*, 24–25, discusses Kuyper's openness, in guarded fashion, to state-directed reform.

[72]See Mark Noll, "Introduction," in *The Princeton Theology 1812–1921*, ed. Mark Noll (Grand Rapids: Baker, 1983); Jack B. Rogers and Donald K. McKim, *The Authority and Interpretation of the Bible: An Historical Approach* (New York: Harper and Row, 1979), chap. 4.

[73]B. B. Warfield, book review of *The Certainty of Faith*, by Herman Bavinck, *Princeton Theological Review* 1 (January 1903), reprinted in Noll, *Princeton Theology*, 306.

[74]Kuyper, *Lectures*, 4. Bratt, *Dutch Calvinism*, 271, concisely contrasts Kuyper and Warfield; see also George Marsden, *Fundamentalism and American Culture* (New York: Oxford Univ. Press, 1980), 115.

[75]William White, *Van Til: Defender of the Faith* (Nashville: Nelson, 1979), 29–40, 63, 71.

[76]Marsden, *Fundamentalism and American Culture*, 114–16, 218–21.

[77]White, *Van Til*, 84–90.

[78]Cornelius Van Til, *The Defense of the Faith*, 3d ed. (Nutley, N.J.: Presbyterian and Reformed, 1967), 112.

[79]Citations are from Van Til, *Defense of the Faith*, 108, 146, 151, 94, 100. For a summary of Van Til's apologetic see White, *Van Til*, 195–99.

[80]Van Til, *Defense of the Faith*, 100; cf. 82–86.

[81]Van Til does fault Kuyper and his colleague Bavinck for at times deviating from their own presuppositionalist principles and argues that at these points the Dutchmen have also deviated from Calvin and the apostle Paul. See *Defense of the Faith*, 163, 208, 285–97.

[82]Van Til, *Defense of the Faith*, 154–55, 201; the quotation is from p. 169.

[83]On Christian schools see White, *Van Til*, 183; on the other points see pp. 214–33, the transcript of a 1969 message in which Van Til creatively presented his philosophy, devoting considerable attention to Kuyper.

[84]Rodney Clapp, "Democracy as Heresy," *Christianity Today* (February 20, 1987): 22, recounts Rushdoony's emphasis, when interviewed by Clapp, on how Armenians continue to observe Old Testament sacrifices in Christian form (for example, slaying an animal as a symbol of Christ's atonement). Clapp also notes two other facets of Armenian Christianity that had an important impact on Rushdoony. First, Armenia was the first nation to accept Christianity as its state religion. Second, the Armenian church became schismatic by refusing to accept the fifth-century Chalcedon Creed, whereas the Armenian Protestant minority (a product of nineteenth-century Calvinist missionary outreach) whom Rushdoony's father served as pastor affirmed Chalcedon.

[85]David K. Watson, "Theonomy: A History of the Movement and an Evaluation of Its Primary Text" (M.A. thesis, Calvin College, 1985), 6, citing Rousas J. Rushdoony, "Christian Missions and Indian Culture," *Westminster Theological Journal* 12 (1949): 1–12. Watson's thesis is the primary written work on the history of Reconstruction. It is generally reliable though occasionally, due to its reliance on oral and unofficial sources, imprecise in deriving interpretations; for a key correction see Bahnsen and Gentry, *House Divided*, 1.

[86]Watson, "Theonomy," 8–16. Rushdoony's first book was *By What Standard? An Analysis of the Philosophy of Cornelius Van Til* (Nutley, N.J.: Presbyterian and Reformed, 1959).

[87]Gary North, "Confessions of a Washington Reject," *Journal of Christian Reconstruction* 5 (Summer 1978): 54–65; Watson, "Theonomy," 13–14, 19–20; Gary North and Gary DeMar, *Christian Reconstruction: What It Is, What It Isn't* (Ft. Worth, Tex.: ICE, 1991), ix–xiv.

[88]Gary North, *Honest Reporting as Heresy: My Response to "Christianity Today"* (Tyler, Tex.: ICE, 1987), 6. The essay has been reprinted as Appendix B in Gary North, *Westminster's Confession: The Abondonment of Van Til's Legacy* (Tyler, Tex.: ICE, 1991).

[89]See *Productive Christians*, 3d ed., 352–56, on North and Chilton's work in rushing the first edition into print in time for the 1981 debate, which took place at Gordon-Conwell Seminary in Massachusetts. Steve Crowe, "Reducing Poverty: Christians Debate Government's Role," *Christianity Today* (May 8, 1981): 46, describes the debate.

[90]See John M. Frame, review of Rushdoony's *Institutes, Westminster Theological Journal* 38 (November 1975): 195–217; Meredith G. Kline, "Comments on an Old-New Error" (review of Bahnsen, *Theonomy in Christian Ethics*), *Westminster Theological Journal* 41 (Fall 1978): 172–89; G. Aiken Taylor, "Postmillennialism Revisited," *Presbyterian Journal* (September 6, 1978): 9–11, and "Theonomy and Christian Behavior," *Presbyterian Journal* (September 13, 1978): 9–10, 18–19; "Theonomy Revisited," *Presbyterian Journal* (December 6, 1978): 12–13, 22. Harold O. J. Brown did call Rushdoony's *Institutes* "the most impressive theological work of 1973" in "Theology, Apologetics and Ethics," *Christianity Today* (May 1, 1974): 70.

[91]Francis Schaeffer, *A Christian Manifesto* (Westchester, Ill.: Crossway, 1981), 120.

[92]Carl F. H. Henry, *Twilight of a Great Civilization* (Westchester, Ill.: Crossway, 1988), 30. The comments were initially spoken in January 1987.

[93]Clapp, "Democracy as Heresy"; [Richard John Neuhaus], "The Theocratic Temptation," *Religion and Society Report* (May 1987): 2–3; House and Ice, *Dominion Theology*; Rob Boston, "Thy Kingdom Come," *Church and State* (September 1988): 6–12; Anson Shupe, "Prophets of a Biblical America," *Wall Street Journal*, April 12, 1989; Anson Shupe, "The Reconstructionist Movement on the New Christian Right," *Christian Century* (October 4, 1989): 880–82. Bill Moyers, in his three-part "God and Politics" documentary (Public Broadcasting Service, 1987), devoted one of the programs primarily to Reconstruction. Other, earlier published critiques included David A. Rausch and Douglas Chismar, "The New Puritans and Their Economic Paradise," *Christian Century* (August 3–10, 1983), 712–15; Robert P. Lightner, "Theonomy and Dispensationalism," *Bibliotheca Sacra* (January–March 1986): 26–36; Robert P. Lightner, "A Dispensational Response to Theonomy," *Bibliotheca Sacra* (July–September 1986): 228–45.

[94]Carl Henry, "The New Coalitions," *Christianity Today* (November 17, 1989): 26–28; Will S. Barker and W. Robert Godfrey, eds., *Theonomy: A Reformed Critique* (Grand Rapids: Zondervan, 1990).

[95]Clapp, "Democracy as Heresy," 18; Watson, "Theonomy," 13, 17–19; North, "Publisher's Foreword," in Bahnsen and Gentry, *House Divided*, xl.

[96]Watson, "Theonomy," 1–2, 20–21, 23; North and DeMar, *Christian Reconstruction*, xiv; Gary DeMar, *God and Government*, 3 vols. (Atlanta: American Vision, 1982–1986); Gary DeMar, *Surviving College Successfully* (Atlanta: American Vision, 1988).

[97]"A Local Church Thrives on Theonomy," *Presbyterian Journal* (December 6, 1978): 6–8 (on Morecraft); George Grant's books on poverty include *Bringing In the Sheaves: Turning Poverty into Productivity* (Atlanta: American Vision, 1985); *In the Shadow of Plenty: The Biblical Blueprints for Welfare* and *The Dispossessed: Homelessness in America* (both Ft. Worth, Tex.: Dominion, 1986).

[98]Bahnsen and Gentry, *House Divided*, 69–70; James Jordan, unpublished review of House and Ice's *Dominion Theology* (1988), 1.

[99]Jordan, review of House and Ice, 2–4. The Tyler stance became clear with the publication of James B. Jordan, ed., *The Reconstruction of the Church* (Tyler, Tex.: Geneva Divinity School, 1985).

[100]Joe Kickasola, interview with author, Virginia Beach, Va., December 18, 1989; Jordan, review of House and Ice, 1; Bahnsen and Gentry, *House Divided*, 70.

[101]See Greg L. Bahnsen, "Christ and Civil Government: The Theonomic Position Reviewed and Applied," paper presented to the Consultation on Civil Government (Geneva College, Beaver Falls, Pa., June 1–3, 1989): 43–47.

[102]Rushdoony, by including sympathetic charismatics, has claimed there are 20 million Reconstructionists (Clapp, "Democracy as Heresy," 21); North has retorted that the estimate is about 19,975,000 too high (*Remnant Review* [Ft. Worth, Tex.], April 21, 1989). For a more sober assessment of Reconstruction's growth, see Frame, "Theonomic Urge."

[103]Greg L. Bahnsen, *No Other Standard: Theonomy and Its Critics* (Tyler, Tex.: ICE, 1991), chap. 6, further addresses issues related to categories of Old Testament law but does not appear to address the criticisms that follow here.

[104]James B. Jordan, "The 'Reconstructionist Movement,' " *Geneva Review* (Tyler, Tex.), March 1985, shares this concern. In expressing his willingness to accept state aid in "extreme situations," he states, "Before I became a pastor, it was easy for me to take a harder line on this type of thing, but in the day to day life of the Church, God has brought me face to face with reality."

[105]See Douglas A. Oss, "The Influence of Hermeneutical Frameworks in the Theonomy Debate," *Westminster Theological Journal* 51, 2 (Fall 1989): 227–58. Oss concludes that the key issue is not *whether* Mosaic law should be applied to Christian ethics, but *how*.

[106]On the differentiation of modern society and its relevance to Christian political philosophy, see James Skillen, *The Scattered Voice: Christians at Odds in the Public Square* (Grand Rapids: Zondervan, 1990).

[107]James B. Jordan, "Tithing: Financing Christian Reconstruction," in *Tactics of Christian Resistance*, ed. Gary North (Tyler, Tex.: Geneva Divinity School, 1983), 355.

[108]Rushdoony, *Institutes*, 307.

[109]Ibid., 401–15.

[110]Chilton, *Paradise Restored*, 7.

[111]Ibid.

[112]The classic exposition of this theme is Max Weber, *The Protestant Ethic and the Spirit of Capitalism,* trans. Talcott Parsons (New York: Charles Scribner's Sons, 1958).

[113]See especially Gary North, *Healer of the Nations* (Ft. Worth, Tex.: Dominion, 1987). The motto appears in North and DeMar, *Christian Reconstruction,* 34.

[114]Donald Kraybill, in his marvelous work *The Riddle of Amish Culture* (Baltimore: Johns Hopkins Univ. Press, 1989), notes that the Amish in America have grown from four thousand to one hundred thousand members since 1900, almost totally due to high birth and retention rates.

[115]The Amish have qualified for religious exemption from social security under a 1965 law, but Amish businesses must still pay their portion of the social security tax, and Amish who work for non-Amish employers still have social security deducted from their pay. Kraybill, *Riddle of Amish Culture,* 220–22.

[116]DeMar interview, November 14, 1989.

Chapter 3

[1]Gary Amos, *Defending the Declaration* (Brentwood, Tenn.: Wolgemuth and Hyatt, 1989), 60. See also Herbert W. Titus, "The Law of Our Land," *Journal of Christian Jurisprudence* 6 (1986): 57–75.

[2]This debate between original-intent advocates and constitutional relativists leaped from the law schools to the public stage during the fierce battle over the unsuccessful nomination of Robert Bork to the Supreme Court in 1987. See also Stephen H. Galebach, "The Declaration of Independence and Original Intent," *Journal of Christian Jurisprudence* 6 (1986): 113–15.

[3]The ideological similarities between the two groups are further underscored by the fact that Rushdoony appears to have been a constitutionalist before he was a Reconstructionist. Two of his earliest works, *This Independent Republic* (1964) and *The Nature of the American System* (1965), enthusiastically endorse the form of government set forth in the Constitution while making no reference to biblical law.

[4]Amos, *Defending the Declaration,* 59, 61–62; Gary T. Amos, "A Limited National Congress: The Law of Nature and Constitutional Limitations," *Journal of Christian Jurisprudence* 7 (1988): 112–13.

[5]Herb Titus, interview with author, Virginia Beach, Va., December 15, 1989; Francis Wilkinson, "Divine Instruction," *American Lawyer* (March 1987): 89; Amos, "Limited National Congress," 114.

[6]Titus interview; "Oral Roberts University Gives Its Law School to CBN University," *Christianity Today* (February 7, 1986).

[7]Herbert W. Titus, *God, Man, Law, and Liberty* (unpublished manuscript, May 1984), 2.

[8]Ibid., 7.

[9]Ibid., 49–50.

[10]Ibid., 29–34.

[11]"The Biblical Covenants: An Introductory Overview" (xeroxed materials for Constitutional Law class, Regent University), viii–ix.

[12]Gary Amos, "Returning from the Fringes of Culture: Evangelical Efforts to Stimulate a New Great Awakening," paper presented to the meeting of the Society for the Scientific Study of Religion, Virginia Beach, Va., November 10, 1990.

[13]Regent University Catalog (1989–1990), iv.

[14]Steven W. Fitschen, "Paradoxes of Christian Public Policy Making: Reactionary and Radical Elements of the Vision of Regent University's School of Public Policy," paper presented to the meeting of the Society for the Scientific Study of Religion, Virginia Beach, Va., November 10, 1990. I am grateful to Fitschen for providing the first draft of the remainder of this section.

[15]For more detail on this battle, see Bruce Barron, "Bible-Based Law: CBN Law School Versus the American Bar Association," paper presented to the meeting of the Society for the Scientific Study of Religion, Virginia Beach, Va., November 10, 1990.

[16]Herb Titus, Appeal of CBN University College of Law to the Council of the ABA's Section of Legal Education and Admissions to the Bar (hearing manuscript, February 3, 1990), 51.

[17]Thomas Atwood, "Through a Glass Darkly," *Policy Review* (Fall 1990): 44.

[18]Titus, Appeal of CBN University College of Law, 68.

[19]Russell Chandler, "Robertson Moves to Fill Christian Right Vacuum," *Los Angeles Times*, May 15, 1990. The quotation is from a Christian Coalition Leadership Seminar I attended in September 1990.

[20]"Robertson Regroups 'Invisible Army' into New Coalition," *Christianity Today* (April 23, 1990): 35.

[21]Clapp, "Democracy as Heresy," *Christianity Today* (February 20, 1987): 21; see also Pat Robertson, *America's Dates with Destiny* (Nashville: Nelson, 1986), 28, 36.

[22]Robertson, *America's Dates*, 305.

[23]Ibid., 64–72, on the Declaration; 91–92 on the Constitution, whose "ultimate authority" he defends against the legal relativists on p. 261; 75–84, 92, 287 on pluralism; the quotation is from p. 299.

[24]Published in fall 1986, as Robertson was embarking on his drive to collect three million signatures in support of his proposed campaign, *America's Dates With Destiny* places the Reagan presidency alongside Washington for Jesus 1980 (on which see chapter 4 below) as the two signs that America may be emerging from a century of decline. Robertson bestows unqualified praise on Reagan, warns that his work "must be continued in 1988 or all that we have gained as a nation may be lost," describes the 1988 election as the next date with destiny, and urges all Americans— but especially evangelicals— to become politically involved. Robertson was shrewdly, subtly maximizing the importance of his readership's mobilization for a specific campaign in which he expected to be among the candidates. See *America's Dates With Destiny*, 283–304; the quotation is on p. 287.

[25]See Mark G. Toulouse, "Pat Robertson: Apocalyptic and American Foreign Policy," *Journal of Church and State* 31 (Winter 1989): 73–99, and two unpublished papers by Jim Castelli of the advocacy group People for the American Way: "Pat Robertson: Extremist" (1986) and "Pat Robertson: Still an Extremist" (1987).

[26]*Pat Robertson's Perspective* (March–April 1991): 6–7.

[27]Gary DeMar described the general Reconstructionist view of Robertson's campaign in this way (interview with author, Atlanta, Ga., November 14, 1989).

Chapter 4

[1]Information for these paragraphs, and on many aspects of Paulk and Chapel Hill Harvester Church's ministry, comes from my visit to the church on November

11–15, 1989. I spent forty hours interacting with Chapel Hill leaders and members, including formal interviews with Earl Paulk and seven of his associate pastors.

[2]Tricia Weeks, *The Provoker* (Atlanta: K Dimension, 1986), 147.

[3]Ibid., 137–64.

[4]Ibid., 168–92.

[5]Amazingly, the one Church of God congregation in the nation with larger attendance than Chapel Hill is the one Paulk left. Under the leadership of Paul Walker, whom Paulk recommended as his successor in 1960, Hemphill Church (now renamed Mt. Paran Church of God and relocated on Atlanta's north side) has grown to an average Sunday attendance of eight thousand. Both churches were among the largest ten in the nation according to a chart in Lyle E. Schaller, "Megachurch!" *Christianity Today* (March 5, 1990): 22.

[6]Earl Paulk, *That the World May Know* (Atlanta: K Dimension, 1987), 175; Earl Paulk, *Thrust In the Sickle and Reap* (Atlanta: K Dimension, 1986), 36, 98–99.

[7]Earl Paulk, *Held in the Heavens Until . . .* (Atlanta: K Dimension, 1985), 44–48.

[8]Earl Paulk, *Satan Unmasked* (Atlanta: K Dimension, 1984), 64.

[9]Earl Paulk, *Ultimate Kingdom*, rev. ed. (Atlanta: K Dimension, 1986), 66, 70; *Satan Unmasked*, 16; *That the World May Know*, 186–87.

[10]Quotations, in order, from Earl Paulk, *20/20 Vision: A Clear View of the Kingdom of God* (Atlanta: K Dimension, 1988), 12; *That the World May Know*, xiii, 36; *Satan Unmasked*, 117. On rejection of postmillennialism, see *That the World May Know*, 133; on witness in every area, Weeks, *Provoker*, 309; on dealing with world systems, Paulk, *Ultimate Kingdom*, 95, 123; *20/20 Vision*, 7; *Satan Unmasked*, 179.

[11]Weeks, *Provoker*, 145.

[12]Paulk, *Satan Unmasked*, 73–82. The text suggests that Paulk expects the last generation to be superior to all preceding ones; however, in an interview with the author on November 15, 1989, Paulk sought to correct this impression, stating that the last generation will be more complete only because it will have incorporated the truths revealed to previous ages. This is one of many places where Paulk's hastily produced books convey impressions that Paulk disclaimed during our personal conversations. For more information on these misperceptions and the role they have played in intraevangelical debates, see chap. 6 below.

[13]Ibid., xiii (foreword by Tom Skinner), 138, 187–88.

[14]Paulk, *Ultimate Kingdom*, 53–54, 182. Some of Paulk's comments have caused critics to charge him with anti-Semitism; to counter this label he has sought counsel from Dan Juster, a messianic Jewish leader who authored the foreword to the second edition of *Ultimate Kingdom*.

[15]Paulk, *20/20 Vision*, 22–23, 36–38.

[16]Paulk, *That the World May Know*, 72; *20/20 Vision*, 17–18. On Paulk's approach to the unbelieving world, see *That the World May Know*, 3; *Ultimate Kingdom*, 122.

[17]Paulk, *Satan Unmasked*, 134.

[18]Paulk, *That the World May Know*, 10.

[19]Earl Paulk, *Spiritual Megatrends* (Atlanta: K Dimension, 1988), 74–79.

[20]Paulk, *That the World May Know*, 126.

[21]Paulk, *Ultimate Kingdom*, 186, 225; see also *That the World May Know*, chap. 5, where he discusses in detail his seven principles of interpretation. For passages that

appear to equate modern revelations with Scripture (or even seem to imply that the former are more essential for today), see *Satan Unmasked*, 3–4, 8, 132. William Griffin, "Kingdom Now: New Hope or New Heresy?" (paper presented to the Society for Pentecostal Studies, Virginia Beach, Va., November 12–14, 1987), discusses Paulk's change in wording.

[22]Paulk, *20/20 Vision*, 3.

[23]Paulk, *Ultimate Kingdom*, 120.

[24]Paulk, *Satan Unmasked*, 264, 255.

[25]Paulk, *That the World May Know*, 186–87; similar statements can be found in Pat Robertson with Bob Slosser, *The Secret Kingdom* (Nashville: Nelson, 1982), 17, 74.

[26]See especially Paulk, *Spiritual Megatrends*, chap. 6, in which Paulk warns that the United States will "fall in total moral corruption and social devastation" (p. 160) within twenty-five years if Christians do not act politically.

[27]Paulk, *Satan Unmasked*, 35.

[28]Ibid., 217, 313.

[29]Paulk, *20/20 Vision*, 24.

[30]Paulk, *That the World May Know*, 124; *Satan Unmasked*, 96–97, 288. On the "ongoing incarnation of Christ" see also Paulk, *Thrust In the Sickle*, 9, 70, 103, 132. At times Paulk appears to treat Jesus more as a model for humanity than as a unique divine figure: "Just as Jesus was in the world, so also are we"; "His example shows the very real possibility of some generation fully demonstrating God's plan" (*Satan Unmasked*, 106, 275). In discussing these statements, Paulk hastened to disclaim any intent to deviate from the traditionally orthodox view of Christ's divinity (interview, November 15, 1989).

[31]Paulk, *That the World May Know*, 26–28, 131–40. Paulk's clarifications remain less than fully consistent and were anything but satisfactory to the California-based Christian Research Institute; see Craig S. Hawkins, review of *That the World May Know*, *Christian Research Journal* 10, 1 (Summer 1987): 30.

[32]For a representative reflection of the common charismatic attitude that biggest is best, see E. S. Caldwell, "Trend Toward Mega Churches," *Charisma* (August 1985): 30–38.

[33]Paulk told both Assemblies of God archivist Wayne Warner in 1987 and this author in November 1989 that he did not learn of the Latter Rain Movement until after he had begun to adopt the views that have caused observers to connect him with Latter Rain. Cf. Warner, letter to author, August 23, 1989.

[34]The main source on the movement is Richard M. Riss, *Latter Rain* (Mississauga, Ont.: Honeycomb Visual Productions, 1987). See also Tom Craig Darrand and Anson Shupe, *Metaphors of Social Control in a Pentecostal Sect* (Lewiston, N.Y.: Edwin Mellen, 1983), 34–50.

[35]Riss, *Latter Rain*, 103, 119, 127–30; Faith Campbell, *Stanley Frodsham: Prophet with a Pen* (Springfield, Mo,: Gospel Publishing House, 1974).

[36]Riss, *Latter Rain*, 140–44.

[37]For these ideas in their original Latter Rain context, see Riss, *Latter Rain*, 57, 70, on progressive revelation; 64, 71, 86, 93 on present-day apostles and prophets and the importance of heeding their words; 114 on unity; 57, 96, 141–43 on end-times views. See also Darrand and Shupe, *Metaphors of Social Control*, 76–91.

³⁸[George Hawtin], *Sharon Scripture Studies* ([North Battleford, Sask.: Sharon Bible School, 1948]), Series B, 5–13. I am grateful to David Adams for providing copies of this material.

³⁹Bill Hamon, *The Eternal Church* (Phoenix: Christian International, 1981), 159–61. Riss, *Latter Rain*, 141, refers to the role of "the foundational truths of Hebrews 6:1–2" in the Latter Rain Movement.

⁴⁰Hamon, *Eternal Church*, 158, 309–10, 320, 365–69. The concept of Christians executing righteous judgment on earth has frightened some observers who fear that a subset of Latter Rain descendants, known as Manifest Sons of God believers, expects to be spiritually empowered to physically destroy the unrighteous in the last days. See Pauline Griego MacPherson, *Can the Elect Be Deceived?* (Denver: Bold Truth Press, 1986).

⁴¹Hamon, *Eternal Church*, 290, 389, 394–95.

⁴²Hamon, *Eternal Church*, 321, 336, 340–43, 389. During the past decade Hamon has become a recognized leader in charismatic circles as both a prophet and a trainer of prophets; thus he was one of the eleven spokespersons *Charisma* magazine asked for a prophetic word at the threshold of the 1990s. His response shows how the expectation of an impending unveiling of the kingdom through believers has continued to take priority in his thinking: "The church of the 1990s must arise as the army of the Lord and become the 'Joshua generation' to execute God's judgments and dispossess the enemies of God from the church's prophetically promised 'Canaan land.' " Quoted in Michele Buckingham, "1990 Prophecy: What Is the Spirit Saying to the Church?" *Charisma* (January 1990): 76.

⁴³Hamon, *Eternal Church*, 274, spews disgust for "the humanistic denominational structured church system" and predicts that charismatics will have to leave the denominations in order to remain true to their faith. In contrast, Paulk participated in a groundbreaking dialogue between Pentecostal and Catholic leaders, and he says God told him to wear a collar as an explicit attack on antidenominational prejudice.

⁴⁴John Meares, *Bind Us Together* (Old Tappan, N.J.: Revell, 1987); see especially pp. 98–99 on his disfellowshipping and pp. 122–23 on his Bethesda connection, which he says alarmed some of his Pentecostal friends. Meares graciously refrains from naming the Church of God in his autobiography but does name its Bible school, Lee College, as his alma mater (p. 66).

⁴⁵Hamon, *Eternal Church*, 362–63.

⁴⁶The quotation is from John Gimenez, interview with author, Virginia Beach, Va., December 19, 1989. Robert Paul Lamb, *Upon This Rock* (n.p.: Souls Books, 1979; reprint, Virginia Beach, Va.: Rock Church Productions, 1983), is a popular biography of the Gimenezes.

⁴⁷Steven Lawson, "John Gimenez Challenges Us Again," *Charisma* (April 1988), 32–37, includes the quotation from Bright; Pat Robertson, June 1986 speech, quoted in Hubert Morken, *Pat Robertson: Where He Stands* (Old Tappan, N.J.: Revell, 1988), 200; Fred Clarkson, "Washington for Jesus II," *Christianity and Crisis* (July 6, 1987): 230.

⁴⁸See "Rock Church Lobbies Hard for Project," *Virginian-Pilot and Ledger Star* (Virginia Beach, Va.), December 18, 1983; "Founders of Rock Church Not Afraid to Make Waves," *Richmond News Leader*, March 5, 1985; "Church Maintains High Hopes for City of Refuge," *The Beacon* (Virginia Beach, Va.), October 23, 1988.

[49]The primary fact connecting them is that Paulk took Reid with him to his much-publicized meeting with two of his harshest critics, Jimmy Swaggart and Dave Hunt. On the meeting see Steven Lawson, "Swaggart, Paulk Meet," *Charisma* (February 1987): 63, and Paulk, *That the World May Know*, chap. 1.

[50]Tommy Reid, *Kingdom Now . . . But Not Yet* (Buffalo: IJN, 1988) 19; Tommy Reid, interview with author, Orchard Park, N. Y., December 27, 1989. On the success of his church see Tommy Reid with Doug Brendel, *The Exploding Church* (Plainfield, N.J.: Logos, 1979).

[51]Reid, *Kingdom Now*, 1, 8.

[52]Ibid., 8–9, 35–36.

[53]Quotations from ibid., 38, 13, 39, 71, 103.

[54]Gordon Spiller, interview with author, Orchard Park, N.Y., December 27, 1989.

[55]Quoted from the ACBS 1989 course catalogue, course number 740. While Reid stresses that use of a text does not imply complete endorsement of it, it is nevertheless noteworthy that Chilton's *Paradise Restored* is one of the two course texts (Paul Billheimer's equally controversial *Destined for the Throne* [Ft. Washington, Pa.: Christian Literature Crusade, 1975] being the other) and that the five recommended books are all by Gary North. Reid also notes (letter to author, March 28, 1991) that although this course is available for distribution to other schools, it is not taught at his own Buffalo Bible College because it differs from the eschatological view of the Assemblies of God.

[56]Reid, *Kingdom Now*, xix–xx.

[57]Robert Nolte, "Siege on Abortion," *Charisma* (January 1989): 46. Operation Rescue leader Randall Terry responded to Paulk by angrily branding him an "enemy of the pro-life movement." Paulk, *Spiritual Megatrends*, 195, also discusses his nonpartisanship.

[58]Reid interview.

[59]Gimenez interview.

[60]Dan Juster, in the appendix to Reid, *Kingdom Now*, describes Weiner as a postmillennialist, and others who know Weiner personally have confirmed this. Bob and Rose Weiner, "The Conquering Power of Christianity," *The Forerunner* (December 1987): 12–14, 20, 23, implies, though it does not state directly, that he subscribes to a confident eschatology regarding world transformation.

[61]Bob Weiner with David Wimbish, *Take Dominion* (Old Tappan, N.J.: Revell, 1988), 157, 158, 166; see also pp. 243–44 on the Providence Foundation.

[62]Quoted from a Providence Foundation brochure (P.O. Box 6579, Charlottesville, VA 22901). My understanding of the foundation comes primarily from an interview with its director, Stephen McDowell (Charlottesville, Va., December 14, 1989).

[63]John Fialka, "Maranatha Christians, Backing Rightist Ideas, Draw Fire over Tactics," *Wall Street Journal*, August 16, 1985. Maranatha's Bob Nolte (phone conversation with author, June 6, 1989) characterized this article as an inaccurate and overly political assessment of the ministry, but Maranatha did have a reputation as a source of Republican activists before the article appeared.

[64]"Where Do the Candidates Stand on Moral Issues?" *The Forerunner* (October 1984): 10–11, 20. The same issue's front cover greeted a conservative election victory in Canada as "good news."

65"Pat Robertson Has Discovered Private-Sector Solutions to American's [*sic*] Problems," *The Forerunner* (December 1987): 4–5.

66Lee Grady, "Being Prophetic in a Right-Wing/Left-Wing Society," *The Forerunner* (March 1987): 19–21.

67Randy Frame, "Maranatha Disbands as Federation of Churches," *Christianity Today* (March 19, 1990): 40–42; "Maranatha Revamps Church Structure," *Charisma* (March 1990): 21–22.

68Weiner, *Take Dominion*, 167.

69Clarkson, "Washington for Jesus II," 230, attributes the statement quoted to John Gimenez. On Robertson's commitment to the power of prayer, including the hurricane incident, see Morken, *Pat Robertson*, 195–205.

70Pat Robertson with Bob Slosser, *The Secret Kingdom* (Nashville: Nelson, 1982) 15, 74.

71 Robertson, 1986 commencement speech at Oral Roberts University, quoted in Morken, *Pat Robertson*, 178–79.

72Robertson, *Secret Kingdom*, 115.

73Connie Daigle, letter to author, January 1990. See also Mark Andrews, "Pat's People," *Charisma* (March 1988): 26–36.

Chapter 5

1Earl Paulk, *20/20 Vision: A Clear View of the Kingdom of God* (Atlanta: K Dimension, 1988), 32, 34.

2Gary North, *Backward, Christian Soldiers?* (Tyler, Tex.: ICE, 1984), 46, 55–58; Paulk, *20/20 Vision*, 40.

3North, *Backward, Christian Soldiers?*, 31; Don Paulk, interview with author, Decatur, Ga., November 13, 1989.

4Gary North, *Unconditional Surrender: God's Program for Victory*, 3d ed. (Tyler, Tex.: ICE, 1988), x.

5In a few cases, these similarities may have been a product of cross-pollination between the two groups. Reconstructionist thought has had considerable influence on Bob Weiner and may have helped convince Paulk to revise his vision of the church's role in kingdom demonstration so as to include development of Christian schools. See Earl Paulk, *Thrust In the Sickle and Reap* (Atlanta: K Dimension, 1987), 63, 111; Tricia Weeks, *The Provoker* (Atlanta: K Dimension, 1986), 355.

6Joe Morecraft made this prediction in Rob Boston, "Thy Kingdom Come," *Church and State* (September 1988): 9. See also Bill Alnor, "Is Reconstructionism Merging with 'Kingdom Now'?" *Christian Research Journal* 11, 2 (Fall 1989), 6, 26.

7Earl Paulk, *Spiritual Megatrends* (Atlanta: K Dimension, 1988), 117.

8Dennis Peacocke, phone interview with author, December 9, 1989.

9Dennis Peacocke, "Voting Booth Realities," *Rebuilder*, November 1988; Peacocke, "The Art of Change," *Rebuilder*, November 1989. Sara Diamond, in *Spiritual Warfare: The Politics of the Christian Right* (Boston: South End, 1989), 127–30, also discusses Peacocke's activities, stating that Anatole's goal was "to gain influence within the Republican Party" and documenting its connection with Republican leaders.

10Peacocke interview.

11Dennis Peacocke, *Winning the Battle for the Minds of Men* (Santa Rosa, Calif.: Alive and Free, 1987), 68.

[12]Ibid., 107, 124, 132.

[13]David Hazard, "Taking Back the Leadership of Our Cities," *Bridgebuilder* (March–April 1988): 17.

[14]Peacocke, *Winning the Battle*, 18–22 on spheres; 98–102, 115–18, 141 on economics; 147–58 on the coming collapse of humanism. Of the thirty-three books in Peacocke's bibliography, thirteen are by Reconstructionists and another seven by writers who have had ties to Reconstructionists.

[15]Gary North, *Unholy Spirits* (Tyler, Tex.: ICE, 1986), 392–93; H. Wayne House and Thomas D. Ice, *Dominion Theology: Blessing or Curse?* (Portland, Ore.: Multnomah, 1988), appendix A; Gary DeMar, interview with author, Pittsburgh, Pa., June 6, 1989.

[16]Diamond, *Spiritual Warfare*, 263, notes that Earl Paulk, John Meares, and R. J. Rushdoony were among the speakers at a January 1987 Anatole seminar.

[17]See especially *The Forerunner's* December 1987 issue, which includes Bob Weiner's "The Conquering Power of Christianity" and excerpts from books by North and DeMar. In an October 1982 letter to his ICE mailing list, North said Maranatha had ordered 750 copies of David Chilton's *Productive Christians*.

[18]North, *Unholy Spirits*, 388–92. The first edition of this book, entitled *None Dare Call It Witchcraft* (New York: Arlington House, 1976), included Rushdoony's "Power from Below," which had initially appeared in *Journal of Christian Reconstruction* 1 (Winter 1974), as an appendix. North tells of his change of heart and his wife's healing in "Reconstructionist Renewal and Charismatic Renewal," *Christian Reconstruction* (May–June 1988).

[19]House and Ice, *Dominion Theology*, 384–89. Greg L. Bahnsen and Kenneth L. Gentry, *House Divided: The Break-Up of Dispensational Theology* (Tyler, Tex.: ICE, 1989), 326–40, mock House and Ice's methodology by presenting their own list of parallels between dispensationalists and Jehovah's Witnesses. See also Gary DeMar, *The Debate Over Christian Reconstruction* (Atlanta: American Vision, 1988), 175–78.

[20]Paulk, *Thrust In the Sickle*, 70; Tommy Reid, in *Seduction?? A Biblical Response* (New Wilmington, Pa.: Son-Rise, 1987), 5.

[21]Rousas John Rushdoony, *The Foundations of Social Order* (1968; Fairfax, Va.: Thoburn, 1978), 152–54.

[22]Paulk, *Thrust In the Sickle*, 134; cf. North, *Unholy Spirits*, 388–92.

[23]Rousas John Rushdoony, *The Institutes of Biblical Law*, (Nutley, N.J.: Craig, 1973), 509–10; Paulk, *Spiritual Megatrends*, 174; John Meares, *Bind Us Together* (Old Tappan, N.J.: Revell, 1987), 158.

[24]Paulk, *20/20 Vision*, 31.

[25]*Pat Robertson's Perspective*, February 1977.

[26]*Pat Robertson's Perspective*, April 1978.

[27]*Pat Robertson's Perspective*, April, November, and September 1980.

[28]Bob Slosser, interview with author, Virginia Beach, Va., December 15, 1989.

[29]*Pat Robertson's Perspective*, March and June 1979. These were two of many examples. See also Mark G. Toulouse, "Pat Robertson: Apocalyptic and American Foreign Policy," *Journal of Church and State* 31 (Winter 1989): 73–99.

[30]Georgie Anne Geyer, "Evangelical as Chief?" *Washington Times*, August 27, 1985; Kirk De Smet, "Rev. Mr. President?" *Detroit News*, October 10, 1985; Jon Margolis and Bruce Buursma, "Evangelist Listens for Presidential Call," *Chicago Tribune*, November 3, 1985.

[31]Mark G. Toulouse makes this suggestion in "Robertson, Pat," *Dictionary of Christianity in America* (Downers Grove, Ill.: InterVarsity, 1990).

[32]Slosser interview; Paul Weyrich, "Conservatism's Future: Pat Robertson," *Conservative Digest* (August 1985): 13.

[33]Jeffrey K. Hadden and Anson Shupe, *Televangelism: Power and Politics on God's Frontier* (New York: Henry Holt, 1988).

[34]R. H. Melton, "Pat Robertson Returns to Shaken Empire," *Washington Post*, May 16, 1988; Slosser interview. Hubert Morken, *Pat Robertson: Where He Stands* (Old Tappan, N.J.: Revell, 1988), 23, points out that Robertson embarked on his campaign stating that he definitely would never return to the "700 Club."

[35]Hadden and Shupe, *Televangelism*, 280.

[36]See Rob Gurwitt, "The Christian Right Has Gained Political Power. Now What Does It Do?" *Governing* 3, 1 (October 1989): 52–58.

[37]*Pat Robertson's Perspective*, October 1989.

[38]Diamond, *Spiritual Warfare*, 128; COR conference invitation, 1985.

[39]Norman Geisler, then of Dallas Theological Seminary, resigned from COR because of "the dominance of a theonomy/reconstructionist perspective"; see *Moody Monthly*, January 1986, 110. See also Al Dager, "Balsiger Resigns from COR," *Media Spotlight* 10, 3 (1989), 3.

[40]Coalition on Revival, *Manifesto for the Christian Church* (1986), 16.

[41]Brochure advertising the 1986 COR Washington assembly.

[42]COR, *Manifesto*, 19.

[43]Ibid., 13, 14, 19.

[44]Gary DeMar and Marshall Foster, *The Christian World View of Government* (Mountain View, Calif.: Coalition on Revival, 1986), 13. COR has been accused of promoting unchecked ecclesiastical authoritarianism, but its worldview document on pastoral renewal does stipulate counterchecks on the pastor's authority.

[45]COR statement of faith.

[46]Randy Frame, "The Theonomic Urge," *Christianity Today* (April 21, 1989): 39.

[47]Virginia C. Armstrong and Michael Farris, ed., *The Christian World View of Law* (Mountain View, Calif.: Coalition on Revival, 1986), 12.

[48]COR, *Manifesto*, 7.

[49]Armstrong and Farris, *Christian World View of Law*, 24–25 (affirmations 78–83); DeMar and Foster, *Christian World View of Government*, 6–7 (affirmations 6–12).

[50]Armstrong and Farris, *Christian World View of Law*, 19 (denial 59), 24–25 (affirmation 80); DeMar and Foster, *Christian World View of Government*, 9 (denial 21).

[51]E. Calvin Beisner and Daryl S. Borgquist, eds., *The Christian World View of Economics* (Mountain View, Calif.: Coalition on Revival, 1986), 17–19, 23 (affirmations 29, 34, 35, 38, 40, and "Concrete Steps" #15); Jay Grimstead, letter to COR supporters, November 1989.

[52]Armstrong and Farris, *Christian World View of Law*, 12, 16 (affirmations 28–29, 47–49); see also DeMar and Foster, *Christian World View of Government*, 5, 9 (affirmations 3, 23).

[53]Michael Cromartie, interview with author, Washington, D. C., December 13, 1989.

[54]Randy Frame, "Plan Calls for Doing Away with Public Schools, IRS," *Christianity Today* (November 19, 1990): 57–58.

Chapter 6

[1]For a careful discussion of how to define the term *evangelical* usefully — a problem all too many pollsters have overlooked — see Corwin Smidt and Lyman Kellstedt, "Evangelicalism and Survey Research: Interpretative Problems and Substantive Findings," in *The Bible, Politics, and Democracy*, ed. Richard John Neuhaus (Grand Rapids: Eerdmans, 1987), 81–102; Lyman A. Kellstedt, "The Meaning and Measurement of Evangelicalism: Problems and Prospects," in *Religion and Political Behavior in the United States*, ed. Ted G. Jelen (New York: Praeger, 1989), 3–21.

[2]See James F. Maclear, "The 'True American Union' of Church and State: The Reconstruction of the Theocratic Tradition," *Church History* 28 (1959): 41–62; Clifford S. Griffin, *Their Brothers' Keepers: Moral Stewardship in the United States, 1800–1865* (New Brunswick, N.J.: Rutgers Univ. Press, 1960); Charles C. Cole, *The Social Ideas of the Northern Evangelists, 1826–1860* (New York: Octagon, 1954).

[3]The essential work on this period is George M. Marsden, *Fundamentalism and American Culture* (New York: Oxford Univ. Press, 1980). See also Ferenc Morton Szasz, *The Divided Mind of Protestant America, 1880–1930* (University, Ala.: Univ. of Alabama Press, 1982); Paul Carter, *The Spiritual Crisis of the Gilded Age* (DeKalb: Northern Illinois Univ. Press, 1971); William R. Hutchison, *The Modernist Impulse in American Protestantism* (Cambridge, Mass.: Harvard Univ. Press, 1976); J. Gresham Machen, *Christianity and Liberalism* (New York: Macmillan, 1923).

[4]For a discussion of the problem, citing this instance and others, see Mark Noll, "Evangelicals and the Study of the Bible," in *Evangelicalism in Modern America*, ed. George Marsden (Grand Rapids: Eerdmans, 1984), 109–16.

[5]See Gary North, *Unconditional Surrender: God's Program for Victory*, 3d ed. (Tyler, Tex.: ICE, 1988), 14–17, 36–41, on Genesis; Rousas J. Rushdoony, *The Institutes of Biblical Law* (Nutley, N.J.: Craig, 1973), 20, 697 on neo-orthodoxy.

[6]Gary North, "Publisher's Preface," in Ray R. Sutton, *That You May Prosper: Dominion by Covenant* (Tyler, Tex.: ICE, 1987), xii.

[7]Gary North, "Editor's Introduction," in Gary DeMar, *Ruler of the Nations* (Ft. Worth, Tex.: Dominion, 1987), xiii–xiv; North, "Editor's Introduction," in George Grant, *The Changing of the Guard* (Ft. Worth, Tex.: Dominion, 1987), xxx.

[8]See North, "Publisher's Preface," in Sutton, *That You May Prosper*, xi.

[9]Earl Paulk, *Ultimate Kingdom*, rev. ed. (Atlanta: K Dimension, 1986), 225.

[10]On the Puritan background see Iain Murray, *The Puritan Hope* (London: Banner of Truth, 1971), especially chap. 3.

[11]For Edwards's eschatological theories see Stephen J. Stein, ed., *Apocalyptic Writings*, vol. 5 of *The Works of Jonathan Edwards* (New Haven, Conn.: Yale Univ. Press, 1977); for his more immediate hopes see Jonathan Edwards, *Thoughts on the Revival of Religion in New England* (New York: American Tract Society, n.d.).

[12]See Keith Hardman, *Charles Grandison Finney, 1792–1875: Revivalist and Reformer* (Syracuse, N.Y.: Syracuse Univ. Press, 1987).

[13]Alan Heimert, *Religion and the American Mind from the Great Awakening to the Revolution* (Cambridge, Mass.: Harvard Univ. Press, 1966), e.g., p. 341; Timothy L. Smith, *Revivalism and Social Reform in Mid-Nineteenth-Century America* (Nashville, Tenn.: Abingdon, 1957).

[14]This thesis regarding the spread of dispensationalism is pursued most fully in Douglas Frank, *Less Than Conquerors: How Evangelicals Entered the Twentieth Century*

(Grand Rapids: Eerdmans, 1986). On dispensationalism itself see Timothy P. Weber, *Living in the Shadow of the Second Coming: American Premillennialism 1875–1925* (New York: Oxford Univ. Press, 1979), chap. 1, and C. Norman Kraus, *Dispensationalism in America: Its Rise and Development* (Richmond, Va.: John Knox, 1958).

[15]Almost the sole identifiable defender was Loraine Boettner, in *The Millennium* (Phillipsburg, N.J.: Presbyterian and Reformed, 1957) and in Robert G. Clouse, ed., *The Meaning of the Millennium: Four Views* (Downers Grove, Ill: InterVarsity, 1977). The other two postmillennial works frequently cited by Reconstructionists (excluding their own writings) are Roderick Campbell, *Israel and the New Covenant* (Phillipsburg, N.J.: Presbyterian and Reformed, 1954; reprint Tyler, Tex.: Geneva Divinity School, 1981) and Marcellus Kik, *An Eschatology of Victory* (Nutley, N.J.: Craig, 1971), to which Rushdoony wrote the introduction.

[16]See Steve Schlissel's appendix, addressed to those who think Reconstruction is anti-Semitic, in David Chilton, *Paradise Restored: A Biblical Theology of Dominion* (Tyler, Tex.: Reconstruction Press, 1985); Dan Juster, foreword to Paulk, *Ultimate Kingdom*, 2d ed.

[17]Hal Lindsey, *The Road to Holocaust* (New York: Bantam, 1989), 78.

[18]Wayne House, letter to Gary DeMar, March 17, 1989. DeMar and Gary North had sought to use House as a mediator through whom to reach Lindsey.

[19]The dynamics of the Christian book-publishing scene are analogous to those documented for Christian television in Razelle Frankl, *Televangelism* (Carbondale and Edwardsville: Southern Illinois Univ. Press, 1987). To my knowledge, no one has studied in detail the impact of economic incentives in Christian publishing. However, the issue gained a higher profile after the debate over Lauren Stratford, *Satan's Underground* (Eugene, Ore.: Harvest House, 1988), whose author claimed to have been an active satanist and even to have participated in child sacrifice. Harvest House withdrew the best-selling book and a sequel after several Christians who attempted to verify her story concluded that it was fabricated. See Ken Sidey, "Publisher Withdraws Satanism Story," *Christianity Today* (February 19, 1990), 34–35.

[20]Dave Hunt, *The Seduction of Christianity* (Eugene, Ore.: Harvest House, 1985); Hunt, *Whatever Happened to Heaven?* (Eugene, Ore.: Harvest House, 1988).

[21]Hunt, *Whatever Happened to Heaven?*, 8.

[22]H. Wayne House and Thomas D. Ice, *Dominion Theology: Blessing or Curse?* (Portland, Ore.: Multnomah, 1988).

[23]Marsden, *Fundamentalism and American Culture*, 124–38, surveys the variety of American evangelical views of cultural involvement in the early twentieth century. Carl Henry, *The Uneasy Conscience of Modern Fundamentalism* (Grand Rapids: Eerdmans, 1947), marked the beginning of the postwar new evangelicals' concern for social action; see also George Marsden, *Reforming Fundamentalism: Fuller Seminary and the New Evangelicalism* (Grand Rapids: Eerdmans, 1987), 75–82.

[24]Pat Robertson with Bob Slosser, *The Secret Kingdom* (Nashville: Nelson, 1982), 155. Premillennialists have traditionally recalled that Matthew 24:14 specifies that the Gospel must be preached to all nations before the end can come, but they carefully distinguish worldwide preaching from worldwide acceptance; they also avoid Robertson's confident expectations of improvement in areas like technology and international relations.

[25]Robertson, *Secret Kingdom*, 213–18; see also Andy Lang and Fred Clarkson, "What Makes Pat Robertson Run?" *Convergence* (Spring 1988): 20. It is important to recall that Robertson believes in a *post*tribulation rapture; therefore, unlike Lindsey and Hunt, he expects that Christians will have to live through the Tribulation.

[26]Gary North, *Backward, Christian Soldiers?* (Tyler, Tex.: ICE, 1984), 31. More recently North seems to have hardened his insistence on postmillennialism: "The historic Christian creeds either do not discuss eschatology, or else establish eschatological tolerance within the Church. The historic creeds are wrong on this point." See Gary North, *Political Polytheism* (Tyler, Tex.: ICE, 1989), 57.

[27]"A Summary of Some Kingdom Now Doctrines Which Differ from the Teaching of the Assemblies of God" (unpublished paper adopted by the Assemblies of God General Presbytery, 1987), 5–7. Other attacks include Jimmy Swaggart, "The Coming Kingdom," *The Evangelist* (September 1986): 4–12; [Peter Lalonde], "Kingdom Theology," *Omega-Letter* (North Bay, Ontario) (April 1987), who states that Kingdom Now "visualizes a day when Christians will take over this world and present it as a trophy to the Lord"; Albert James Dager, *Vengeance Is Ours: The Church in Dominion* (Redmond, Wash.: Crown, 1990).

[28]Paulk says he unsuccessfully sought dialogue with Assemblies of God leaders before that denomination produced its paper critical of him; he subsequently invited David Lewis, a primary contributor to the paper, to speak in the Chapel Hill pulpit. See "Paulk Answers," *Thy Kingdom Come* (Paulk's newspaper), November 1987, 1.

[29]Gary DeMar and Peter Leithart, *The Reduction of Christianity* (Atlanta: American Vision, 1988). DeMar shared with me a copy of Harvest House's letter to Dominion Press.

[30]Gary DeMar, *The Debate over Christian Reconstruction* (Atlanta: American Vision, 1988); Greg L. Bahnsen and Kenneth L. Gentry, Jr., *House Divided: The Break-Up of Dispensational Theology* (Tyler, Tex.: ICE, 1989); the responses to Lindsey are *House Divided*, 367–79, and Gary DeMar and Peter Leithart, *The Legacy of Hatred Continues: A Response to Hal Lindsey's "The Road to Holocaust"* (Tyler, Tex.: ICE, 1989).

[31]Earl Paulk, *That the World May Know* (Atlanta: K Dimension, 1987), e.g., 1–3, 96, 121.

[32]Maranatha's basic Bible study guide is Bob and Rose Weiner, *Bible Studies for a Firm Foundation* (Gainesville, Fla.: Maranatha Publications, 1980, rev. 1983). In the 1980 edition, the lesson entitled "God's Predetermined Purpose versus Man's Free Will" includes several questions on the passage in 1 Samuel 15 where, after Saul's disobedience, God rejects him as king. The last of these questions is "Do you think from these scriptures that God knew how Saul was going to respond to the task given him when he chose him?" (p. 93). The correct answer, according to the answer guide in the back of the book, is *no* (p. 135). In the 1983 edition of the study guide, this question was omitted. Also dropped were an implication that without water baptism "our salvation experience is not complete" and a statement that Jesus spent three days in hell after the Crucifixion (cf. pp. 9–11 of both editions).

[33]Robert M. Bowman, Jr., with Craig S. Hawkins and Dan R. Schlesinger, "The Gospel according to Paulk: A Critique of 'Kingdom Theology' " (part 2), *Christian Research Journal* 11, 1 (Summer 1988): 15–20.

[34]Before my visit to Chapel Hill Harvester Church in November 1989 I submitted a summary of Paulk's theology, based on five of his books, for his examination. To my surprise, on point after point he disavowed the teachings I had

attributed to him, even though I had carefully documented my work. It would be both uncharitable and bad scholarship, especially in view of how the books have been produced, not to accept Paulk's explicit disavowals at face value.

[35]Earl Paulk, *Unity of Faith* (Decatur, Ga.: Chapel Hill Harvester Church, n.d.), 4. For the criticisms, see Hunt, *Whatever Happened to Heaven?*, 191–92, and House and Ice, *Dominion Theology*, appendix A.

[36]Robert M. Bowman, Jr., with Craig S. Hawkins and Dan R. Schlesinger, "The Gospel according to Paulk" (part 1), *Christian Research Journal* 10, 3 (Winter–Spring 1988): 9; Paulk, "Paulk Answers," 2–3.

[37]This was Paulk's later reflection on his use of "little gods" terminology; see "Paulk Answers," 1, and *That the World May Know*, 26–28.

[38]Earl Paulk, *Spiritual Megatrends* (Atlanta: Kingdom Publishers, 1988), 70.

[39]Paulk, Ibid., 86.

[40]Paulk, Ibid., 218.

[41]Paulk, Ibid., 41, 37.

[42]The Jesus Only (or "oneness") movement divided Pentecostalism by dogmatically insisting, in opposition to traditional Trinitarianism, that God is one person with three modes of expression rather than one God in three persons. The movement denied the validity of baptisms performed "in the name of the Father, Son, and Holy Spirit" and rebaptized its followers in the name of Jesus only—thus the name of the movement. A substantial sector of Pentecostalism, primarily represented by the United Pentecostal Church, still holds this view. See David Reed, "Aspects of the Origins of Oneness Pentecostalism," in *Aspects of Pentecostal-Charismatic Origins*, ed. Vinson Synan (Plainfield, N.J.: Logos, 1975), 145–68.

[43]Margaret Poloma, *The Assemblies of God at the Crossroads* (Knoxville: Univ. of Tennessee Press, 1989), examines these sociological dilemmas skillfully and in detail.

[44]See, e.g., Paulk, *Spiritual Megatrends*, 51–53.

[45]Kevin Shanahan, "Patterns of Sect Maturation in a Pentecostal Denomination" (paper presented to the Society for the Scientific Study of Religion, Salt Lake City, Utah, October 27–29, 1989), insightfully examines this conflict in the context of the Pentecostal Assemblies of Canada. Tommy Reid, in *Kingdom Now . . . But Not Yet* (Buffalo: IJN, 1988), xiii–xv, sees the battle over Latter Rain as a precedent for the current conflict and deplores AG rigidity in both cases.

[46]See Shanahan, "Patterns of Sect Maturation," and Poloma, *Assemblies of God*.

[47]"Summary of Some Kingdom Now Doctrines," 1, 5, 11. The Commission on Doctrinal Purity, like CRI, worked strictly from Paulk's books and did not speak with him directly.

[48]Reid, *Kingdom Now*, xviii–xix, 1, 14.

[49]Ibid., 107.

[50]Shanahan, "Patterns of Sect Maturation"; William Griffin, "Kingdom Now: New Hope or New Heresy?" (paper presented to the Society for Pentecostal Studies, Virginia Beach, Va., November 12–14, 1987).

[51]Abraham Kuyper, *Lectures on Calvinism* (New York: Revell, 1898), 94.

[52]Rockne M. McCarthy et al., *Society, State and Schools* (Grand Rapids: Eerdmans, 1981), 46–50.

[53]This is the main argument of Rockne M. McCarthy, James W. Skillen, and William A. Harper, *Disestablishment a Second Time: Genuine Pluralism for American Schools*

(Grand Rapids: Eerdmans, 1982), especially 124–26; see also McCarthy et al., *Society, State and Schools*, 174–88.

[54]Os Guinness, "Reaffirming Founding Truths," *Richmond Times-Dispatch*, June 26, 1988. A reprint of this article and a brief summary of the Williamsburg Charter Foundation's plans appear in *Report on the "First Liberty" Summit* (Washington, D.C.: Williamsburg Charter Foundation, 1988).

[55]The signers are listed in *Report on the "First Liberty" Summit*, 34–37. Richard John Neuhaus, "Genuine Pluralism and the Pfefferian Inversion," *This World* (Winter 1989): 72, notes that "obviously" neither the ACLU, which wants to see religious-based morality "relentlessly excluded" from public life, nor the theonomists supported the charter.

[56]*The Williamsburg Charter* (Washington, D.C.: Williamsburg Charter Foundation, 1988), 10, 15. The document also appears in *This World* (Winter 1989): 40–53.

[57]George Weigel, "Achieving Disagreement: From Indifference to Pluralism," *This World* (Winter 1989): 56–57, 61. Neuhaus, "Genuine Pluralism," 72, uses similar language, misleadingly saying that theonomists "believe that democracy is a heresy and that the present Constitution must be replaced."

[58]Weigel, "Achieving Disagreement," 60, 63.

[59]*Williamsburg Charter*, 9.

[60]Herb Titus, interview with author, Virginia Beach, Va., December 15, 1989.

[61]*Williamsburg Charter*, 10; Os Guinness, phone conversation with author, April 11, 1991.

[62]Herbert W. Titus, "The Law of Our Land," *Journal of Christian Jurisprudence* 6 (1986): 67–68.

[63]William Bentley Ball, "What's Not Wrong with the Williamsburg Charter," *This World* (Winter 1989): 66; Weigel, "Achieving Disagreement," 59, cites Tribe.

[64]Ball, "What's Not Wrong," 67.

[65]*Williamsburg Charter*, 14, emphasis added.

[66]Herbert W. Titus, "Righteousness, Power, Liberty, and Authority" (paper presented to the Williamsburg Charter Symposium, Charlottesville, Va., April 11–13, 1988).

[67]Quotations are from Gordon Spykman, "The Principled Pluralist Position," 94, and "The Principled Pluralist Major Response," 248, both in *God and Politics: Four Views on the Transformation of Civil Government*, ed. Gary Scott Smith (Phillipsburg, N.J.: Presbyterian and Reformed, 1989).

[68]William S. Barker, "A Response to Greg L. Bahnsen's 'Christ and Civil Government: The Theonomic Position Reviewed and Applied,'" paper presented to the Geneva College Consultation on Civil Government, Beaver Falls, Pa., June 1–3, 1989.

[69]Gary North, *Political Polytheism* (Tyler, Tex.: ICE, 1989), 265.

[70]Ed Dobson and Ed Hindson, "Apocalypse Now? What Fundamentalists Believe about the End of the World," *Policy Review* (Fall 1986): 16–22. Rushdoony responded candidly in a letter to the editor, *Policy Review* (Winter 1987): 88: "I learned things about myself from reading the article that I never knew!"

[71]Carl Henry, "The New Coalitions," *Christianity Today* (November 17, 1989): 26–28.

Chapter 7

[1]The phrase comes from David Moberg, *The Great Reversal* (Philadelphia: Lippincott, 1972), chap. 8. Richard V. Pierard, "The New Religious Right in American Politics," in *Evangelicalism and Modern America*, ed. George Marsden (Grand Rapids: Eerdmans, 1984), 161–74, traces the rise of evangelical politics through an extensive review of literature on the topic.

[2]Tim Stafford, "The Abortion Wars," *Christianity Today* (October 6, 1989): 19–20, describes the (in retrospect) surprising diversity of evangelical views on abortion before, and the hardening of a consensus after, the *Roe v. Wade* decision.

[3]See the essays collected in Robert C. Liebman and Robert Wuthnow, eds., *The New Christian Right* (New York: Aldine, 1983), for further discussion of the Christian Right's rise and its causes.

[4]J. A. Carper, "Schools, Protestant Day," *Dictionary of Christianity in America* (Downers Grove, Ill.: InterVarsity, 1990), estimates that eight thousand to ten thousand such schools have been launched in the United States in the last twenty years.

[5]Matthew Moen, *The Christian Right and Congress* (Tuscaloosa: Univ. of Alabama Press, 1989), 26–28, describes the IRS crackdown and its significance in arousing evangelicals.

[6]Robert Thoburn, *The Christian and Politics* (Fairfax, Va.: Thoburn, 1984), xi–xii. The foreword to this book acknowledges Thoburn's reliance on Rushdoony and North.

[7]David K. Watson, "Theonomy: A History of the Movement and an Evaluation of Its Primary Text" (M.A. thesis, Calvin College, 1985), 10, notes the role of Rushdoony's speaking engagements, primarily on educational issues, in broadening his reputation. Rushdoony's book *Intellectual Schizophrenia* (Philadelphia: Presbyterian and Reformed, 1961) is a collection of several of these speeches.

[8]Jeffrey Hadden and Anson Shupe, *Televangelism: Power and Politics on God's Frontier* (New York: Henry Holt, 1988); Steve Bruce, *The Rise and Fall of the New Christian Right* (Oxford: Clarendon, 1988).

[9]The evangelicals are not as monolithic, in either their voting or their lobbying, as is often assumed; for recent discussions on this topic see Clyde Wilcox, "The New Christian Right and the Mobilization of the Evangelicals," in *Religion and Political Behavior in the United States*, ed. Ted G. Jelen (New York: Praeger, 1989), 149–55, and Allen Hertzke, *Representing God in Washington: The Role of Religious Lobbies in the American Polity* (Knoxville: Univ. of Tennessee Press, 1988). However, the evidence that evangelicals have voted heavily Republican since 1980 is unquestionable, and Democrats generally have made little effort to change the situation.

[10]See Jerome L. Himmelstein, "The New Right," in Liebman and Wuthnow, *New Christian Right*, 13–30.

[11]Anne Kincaid, a prominent evangelical strategist within the Virginia Republican party, called Coleman's loss "probably the most avoidable election defeat in Virginia's history." See "Politicians Reconsider Their Prolife Positions," *Christianity Today* (January 15, 1990): 46.

[12]Andrew Rosenthal, "GOP Leaders Urge Softer Line about Abortion," *New York Times*, November 10, 1989.

[13]Kim A. Lawton, "Promises to Keep," *Christianity Today* (February 3, 1990): 44–45.

[14]Kim A. Lawton, "Evangelicals Still Not Sure about Bush," *Christianity Today* (January 15, 1990): 44–45; for Pat Robertson's comments see *Pat Robertson's Perspective*, October 1989. My Washington interviews in December 1989 confirmed the prevalence of this trend among evangelicals.

[15]Kim A. Lawton, "It's 'Dog Days' in D.C.," *Christianity Today* (September 10, 1990): 60, 62.

[16]Herbert Schlossberg, *Idols for Destruction* (Nashville: Nelson, 1983), 321, 333.

[17]Carl F. H. Henry, *Twilight of a Great Civilization* (Westchester, Ill.: Crossway, 1988), 23.

[18]Ibid., 40, 41, 181–82.

[19]Ibid., 141, 172; see especially pp. 115–24 on Henry's worldview emphasis.

[20]Charles Colson with Ellen Santilli Vaughn, *Against the Night: Living in the New Dark Ages* (Ann Arbor, Mich.: Servant, 1989); quotations are from pp. 23, 161–62. Earl Paulk made this book required reading for his staff. For another illustration, see the January 1990 issue of *Tabletalk*, the devotional monthly from Reformed theologian R. C. Sproul's Ligonier Ministries in Orlando, Florida, which seeks to reach laypersons on a daily basis with intellectually substantial Christian thinking. Sproul's lead article, "A New Dark Age?" is followed by an interview with Carl Henry and an excerpt from Colson's book.

[21]Frank Peretti, *This Present Darkness* (Westchester, Ill.: Crossway, 1988) and *Piercing the Darkness* (Westchester, Ill.: Crossway, 1989); the quotation is from *Piercing the Darkness*, 71. John Seel, interview with author, Burke, Va., December 11, 1989.

[22]Henry dismisses Hebrew theocracy in *Twilight of a Great Civilization*, 30, 69, 116; he supports religious liberty on pp. 175–76. Colson states, "I don't suggest that we can simplistically apply Old Testament civil law to modern circumstances; that is the error of the theonomist" (*Against the Night*, 168). See also Charles Colson, *Kingdoms in Conflict* (Grand Rapids and New York: Zondervan/Morrow, 1987), 117, 291, 305.

[23]Francis Schaeffer, *A Christian Manifesto* (Westchester, Ill.: Crossway, 1981). Gary North and David Chilton, "Apologetics and Strategy," in *Tactics of Christian Resistance*, ed. Gary North (Tyler, Tex.: Geneva Divinity School, 1983), 118–31, while praising Schaeffer's critique of humanism, point out his inability to offer a credible alternative. In a typically Reconstructionist dichotomy, they blame Schaeffer's fuzziness on his unwillingness to accept either humanism or theocracy and his failure to recognize that there is no third option.

[24]Henry, *Twilight of a Great Civilization*, 134; see also pp. 145–60 for his dissection of modern, transcendentless notions of law and human rights, in a fashion reminiscent of Regent University's College of Law and Government.

[25]See, e.g., ibid., 116–18.

[26]George Grant, *The Changing of the Guard* (Ft. Worth: Dominion, 1987), 11.

[27]Ibid., 154.

[28]Rob Gurwitt, "The Christian Right Has Gained Political Power. Now What Does It Do?" *Governing* 3, 1 (October 1989): 52–58, discusses the hostility in Georgia, North Carolina, and Washington, while citing Oregon, Minnesota, and Arizona as cases where intra-GOP strife has helped the Democrats.

[29]Robert Hartley, "The Role of the Religious Right in the Republican Party: A Case Study of the Religious Right in Two U.S. Congressional Districts" (B.A. thesis, Rollins College, Orlando, Fla., 1991).

Chapter 8

[1]"Guns: Should They Be in Christian Homes?" *Christianity Today* (August 18, 1989): 42–43, 47.

[2]For Sider's basic principles see his book *Completely Pro-Life* (Downers Grove, Ill.: InterVarsity, 1987), 20–28. See also Lawrence D. Pratt, "Tools of Biblical Resistance," in *Tactics of Christian Resistance*, ed. Gary North (Tyler, Tex.: Geneva Divinity School, 1983), 432–48.

[3]Robert K. Johnston, *Evangelicals at an Impasse: Biblical Authority in Practice* (Atlanta: John Knox, 1979), 2.

[4]Dave Hunt, *Whatever Happened to Heaven?* (Eugene, Ore.: Harvest House, 1988), 8; see also pp. 41–44, 79, 205.

[5]Dennis Peacocke, *Winning the Battle for the Minds of Men* (Santa Rosa, Calif.: Alive and Free, 1987), 3. His use of the same passage on pp. 149–50 indicates that he knows the biblical meaning of the term. See also Pratt, "Tools of Biblical Resistance," 442: "Christ told us to 'occupy till I come' (Luke 19:13). It's hard for Christians to occupy while crooks, murderers, and tyrants are running around loose."

[6]See, e.g., Gary DeMar and Peter Leithart, *Reduction of Christianity*, 179, 182; David Chilton, *Paradise Restored, 1985),* 213.

[7]Rousas John Rushdoony, *The Institutes of Biblical Law* (Nutley, N.J.: Craig, 1973), 730.

[8]Ibid., 3.

[9]Ibid., 725.

[10]Hunt, by working with this narrower definition, concludes that humanity never lost its God-given dominion, despite the Fall. See *Whatever Happened to Heaven?*, 224.

[11]Ibid., 257.

[12]Earl Paulk, *Held in the Heavens Until . . .* (Atlanta: K Dimension, 1985), 44–46, 221–22.

[13]Hunt, *Whatever Happened to Heaven?*, 205–8.

[14]Ibid., 79; cf. pp. 38, 57.

[15]Paulk, *Held in the Heavens Until . . .*, 234.

[16]See Robert M. Bowman, Jr., with Craig S. Hawkins and Dan R. Schlesinger, "The Gospel According to Paulk: A Critique of 'Kingdom Theology' " (part 2), *Christian Research Journal* 11, 1 (Summer 1988): 19.

[17]Chilton, *Paradise Restored*, 87–91.

[18]See, e.g., Gary North, *Unconditional Surrender: God's Program for Victory*, 3d ed. (Tyler, Tex.: ICE, 1988), 144–46.

[19]Chilton, *Paradise Restored*, 74; cf. North, *Unconditional Surrender*, 315–19.

[20]North, *Unconditional Surrender*, 104.

[21]See, e.g., DeMar and Leithart, *The Reduction of Christianity*, 214, 226–27; Chilton, *Paradise Restored*, 73, 146–47.

[22]North, *Unconditional Surrender*, 110–14.

[23]Ibid., 320; cf. pp. 343–44, 370.

[24]See Robert M. Bowman, Jr., "The New Puritanism: A Preliminary Assessment of Reconstructionism," *Christian Research Journal* 10, 3 (Winter–Spring 1988): 27.

[25]DeMar and Leithart, *Reduction of Christianity*, 297.

[26]Sider, *Completely Pro-Life*, 17, 25; Ronald A. Sider, *Rich Christians in an Age of Hunger* (Downers Grove, Ill.: InterVarsity, 1977), 205.

[27]Sider, *Completely Pro-Life*, 19.

[28]David Chilton, *Productive Christians in an Age of Guilt-Manipulators*, 3d ed. (Tyler, Tex.: ICE, 1985), 43, 45.

[29]Sider, *Completely Pro-Life*, 23.

[30]See John Frame, "Toward a Theology of the State," *Westminster Theological Journal* 51, 2 (Fall 1989): 202–3.

[31]Rushdoony, *Institutes*, 742.

[32]Rousas J. Rushdoony, *Christianity and the State* (Vallecito, Calif.: Ross House, 1986), 47.

[33]Greg L. Bahnsen, "Christ and Civil Government: The Theonomic Position Reviewed and Applied" (paper presented to the Geneva College Consultation on Civil Government, Beaver Falls, Pa., June 1–3, 1989), 1–3. William S. Barker, in his response to Bahnsen, stated that Psalm 2's "application to unbelieving rulers is evangelistic, not the sort of political application that Dr. Bahnsen is claiming" (p. 5).

[34]Douglas A. Oss, "The Influence of Hermeneutical Frameworks in the Theonomy Debate," *Westminster Theological Journal* 51, 2 (Fall 1989): 255–58.

[35]Kenneth A. Myers, "Biblical Obedience and Political Thought: Some Reflections on Theological Method," in *The Bible, Politics, and Democracy*, ed. Richard John Neuhaus (Grand Rapids: Eerdmans, 1987), 23.

[36]See Mark A. Noll, *One Nation Under God? Christian Faith and Political Action in America* (San Francisco: Harper and Row, 1988), especially chap. 10, and Myers, "Biblical Obedience," 21–25.

[37]Charles Colson with Ellen Santilli Vaughn, *Against the Night: Living in the New Dark Ages* (Ann Arbor, Mich.: Servant, 1989), 167–68.

Chapter 9

[1]The Jehovah's Witnesses provide a contemporary example of such rigidity. See Raymond Franz, *Crisis of Conscience* (Atlanta: Commentary, 1983).

[2]This process of accommodation has been extensively documented for American evangelicalism in James Davison Hunter, *Evangelicalism: The Coming Generation* (Chicago: Univ. of Chicago Press, 1987), and for the charismatic movement in Margaret Poloma, *The Charismatic Movement: Is There a New Pentecost?* (Boston: Twayne, 1982) and Richard Quebedeaux, *The New Charismatics II* (San Francisco: Harper and Row, 1983).

[3]See Everett Emerson, *Puritanism in America* (Boston: Twayne, 1977), chaps. 2–4.

[4]See James Reichley, *Religion in American Public Life* (Washington, D.C.: Brookings Institution, 1985), chap. 6; Charles Colson, *Kingdoms in Conflict* (Grand Rapids and New York: Zondervan/Morrow, 1987), 288–89; John Whitehead, *True Christianity* (Westchester, Ill.: Crossway, 1989), 42.

[5]See Glenn Tinder, *The Political Meaning of Christianity: An Interpretation* (Baton Rouge: Louisiana State Univ. Press, 1989), 186–94. Tinder argues that "equality can in some circumstances be destructive of community," which he considers a higher virtue.

[6]Robert Handy, *A Christian America: Protestant Hopes and Historical Realities*, 2d ed. (New York: Oxford Univ. Press, 1984), chap. 6, provides a pertinent review of these social gospel tendencies, also linking them with the growth of ecumenism. Perry Miller, *The Life of the Mind in America from the Revolution to the Civil War* (Cambridge: Harvard Univ. Press, 1965), 82–84, discusses the same process as active in earlier nineteenth-century evangelicalism.

[7]This is the central point Dave Hunt (though greatly overstressing it) accurately makes in *Whatever Happened to Heaven?* (Eugene, Ore.: Harvest House, 1988).

[8]Bob Weiner with David Wimbish, *Take Dominion* (Old Tappan, N.J.: Revell, 1988), 167. It is interesting that Weiner stood by this prediction as late as 1988.

[9]Herbert Schlossberg, *Idols for Destruction* (Nashville: Nelson, 1983), 325–33. Schlossberg and Marvin Olasky have since articulated more fully a positive agenda for Christians in *Turning Point: A Christian Worldview Declaration* (Westchester, Ill.: Crossway, 1987).

[10]Tinder, *Political Meaning*, 154.

[11]J. Philip Wogaman, *Christian Perspectives on Politics* (Philadelphia: Fortress, 1988), 13, cf. 231. Wogaman is aware of the danger of totalitarianism, but his moderately liberal stance leads him to overestimate the harmlessness of state solutions to social problems.

[12]See Reinhold Niebuhr, "The Weakness of the Modern Church," in *Essays in Applied Christianity*, ed. D. B. Robertson (Cleveland, Ohio: World, 1959), 71–75.

[13]See Richard John Neuhaus, *The Naked Public Square* (Grand Rapids: Eerdmans, 1984).

[14]The Old Testament prohibition of blasphemy would seem justifiable only in cases where the nation's adult members unanimously covenant to such a law and where all citizens, including succeeding generations, are freely and openly granted the opportunity to move to a nontheonomic society if they so choose. Since I am not a postmillennialist, however, I do not expect that any society will ever reach the point where it could justly consider civil sanctions against religious blasphemy anyhow (unless flag desecration be interpreted as blasphemy against our civil religion!). Thus I tend not to debate ivory-tower issues like this one but to concentrate on questions of greater practical relevance.

[15]See John Stott, *Involvement* (Old Tappan, N.J.: Revell, 1984), 1:34–50, for an excellent discussion of the biblical basis for social concern.

[16]Mark Noll, *One Nation Under God? Christian Faith and Political Action in America* (San Francisco: Harper and Row, 1988), chap. 3.

[17]Dennis Peacocke, *Winning the Battle for the Minds of Men* (Santa Rosa, Calif.: Alive and Free, 1987), 56.

• Glossary •

Amillennialism. The belief that the millennium of Revelation 20 is symbolic, not literal, representing the continuing and ultimate triumph of good over evil and not any particular events that will happen at the end of history. This interpretation is compatible with either the optimism of postmillennialists or the pessimism of premillennialists regarding the final result of human progress.

Antichrist. Generally, one who opposes Christ; when capitalized, refers to a single person, the embodiment of evil, who (according to some interpreters) will lead the opposition to God's people in the time just before Christ's second coming.

Antinomianism. A theological stance that holds biblical law, especially civil law, to be no longer applicable in the Christian era. Reconstructionists, with their strong commitment to the binding nature of Old Testament law, often use this term with a negative connotation to describe those who, in their opinion, have no adequate standards for law.

Armageddon. The great last battle between the forces of good and evil, as described in Revelation 16:14–16.

Apologetics. Defense of the truth of Christianity by reasoned argument. Among evangelicals, apologetics has taken two primary forms: evidentialism and presuppositionalism.

Calvinism. A theological tradition, dating back to sixteenth-century Protestant reformer John Calvin, that heavily emphasizes God's sovereignty and predestination of human affairs, the sinfulness of humankind, and the unique authority of the Bible.

Charismatic. One who believes that the gifts of the Holy Spirit described by the apostle Paul in 1 Corinthians 12 (including miracle healings, prophecy, and speaking in tongues) should continue to occur in the Christian church today. Generally, charismatics report having experienced the gift of speaking in tongues.

Charismatic movement. A renewal movement, beginning among mainline American denominations in the 1960s and subsequently leading to the creation of independent churches as well, which emphasizes charismatic gifts, especially speaking in tongues, as a means of attaining deeper spirituality.

Christian Right. A movement, beginning in the late 1970s, among evangelicals and conservative Roman Catholics who sought greater political influence. The Christian Right generally focused its attention on family and moral issues, such as opposing abortion and homosexual rights and supporting school prayer and tuition tax credits for private schools. Often referred to as the New Christian Right to distinguish it from other manifestations of conservative Christian political action earlier in the century.

Constitutionalist. As used in this book, one who believes that America's founding documents described the appropriate role and limits of government, in accordance with God's absolute standards, and that these standards should be protected (or, where necessary, restored) in today's society.

Dispensationalism. The belief that human history is comprised of a series of ages (dispensations), usually seven, that can be distinguished by changes in God's ways of dealing with humankind. Dispensationalists expect Christians to be removed from the earth ("raptured") before the final years of human history, during which unbelievers will remain and suffer through the Tribulation. Their pessimism regarding social progress has led them to be generally uninterested in social and political action.

Dominion theology. A term used to describe various groups of evangelical Christians who believe Christians are called to transform society in a way that is self-consciously defined as exclusively Christian, and dependent specifically on the work of Christians, rather than based on a broader consensus.

Eschatology. The study of, or one's belief as to, how the closing events of human history will take place. There are three major eschatological positions: premillennial (of which dispensationalism is a subset), amillennial, and postmillennial.

Evangelical. A Protestant Christian who believes that spiritual salvation can be received only through personal commitment to Jesus Christ and that the Bible is the fully inspired, infallible Word of God.

Evidentialism. The type of apologetics that seeks to convince unbelievers of the truth of Christianity by presenting historical, psychological, sociological, scientific, or other forms of evidence. It is opposed to presuppositionalism.

Exegesis. Explanation of the original meaning of a biblical text.

Fundamentalist. One who holds strictly to the absolute inerrancy of the Bible, usually in militant opposition to those who would moderate or call into question this belief. While close to evangelicalism in its basic theological convictions, fundamentalism has usually been distinguished by its strict moral conservatism, antipathy to higher scholarship, and avoidance of social or political involvement.

Hermeneutics. The interpretation of biblical texts, especially their application to life in our own day.

Holiness movement. A Christian movement that arose in America in the latter half of the nineteenth century, stressing the importance of the complete sanctification of Christians, often through a second experience subsequent to initial salvation (justification). From this background the Pentecostal movement derived much of its theology (as well as its emphasis on personal holiness), adding a belief in speaking in tongues.

Humanism (or Secular humanism). An ideology that rejects the existence of God, the supernatural, or any higher order to which humanity is responsible beyond humanity itself. Politically conservative evangelicals frequently blame secular humanism for the erosion of Judeo-Christian values they believe has taken place in American society.

Kingdom Now. A movement among charismatics that emphasizes Christians' responsibility to demonstrate the Kingdom of God on earth now. While many charismatics hold to some form of this view, the specific title *Kingdom Now* is seldom applied other than to Earl Paulk and his close associates.

Millennium. The thousand-year reign of Christ, during which perfect peace and righteousness will prevail, described in Revelation 20.

Moral Majority. The most visible organization within the Christian Right, formed in 1979 by Baptist pastor Jerry Falwell and disbanded in 1989.

Neo-orthodoxy. A twentieth-century theological movement, most closely associated with Swiss theologian Karl Barth, that reacted against liberal Protestant theology by reasserting the sinfulness of humanity and the unique nature of Jesus Christ as the revelation of God. Though neo-orthodoxy has recovered these facets of traditional orthodoxy, evangelicals have often faulted it for inadequately affirming the objective and complete truth of Scripture.

New Christian Right. See **Christian Right**.

Pentecostal movement. A movement, dating from the beginning of the twentieth century, among Christians who emphasized the importance of an additional experience, subsequent to salvation, accompanied by speaking in tongues. While akin in this respect to the charismatic movement, the Pentecostal movement has usually remained (though less so in recent years) closer to fundamentalism in its moral rigidity, theological conservatism, and cultural withdrawal.

Pietism. Term used to describe a variety of Christian movements that have stressed personal piety and devotion as the most important parts of the Christian life. Dominionists and other socially active Christians often criticize pietism for its relative lack of attention to public or political issues.

Pluralism. A state of civil order in which all citizens, of any religion or no religion, hold equal status and have equal rights to participate in society and lawmaking; or, the belief that society should operate in this way.

Postmillennialism. The belief that the millennium of Revelation 20 will occur as a result of gradual, divinely inspired improvement of the human condition and that Christ's second coming will not take place until after the millennium.

Premillennialism. The belief that the millennium of Revelation 20 must be preceded by Christ's second coming. This belief usually leads to skepticism about human ability to produce lasting, positive social change before Christ's return.

Presuppositionalism. The type of apologetics that argues that all of a person's beliefs are governed by that person's presuppositions regarding God, humanity, and nature. It is opposed to evidentialism.

Rapture. According to dispensationalists, the event in which all Christians will be removed from the earth before the Tribulation.

Reconstruction. A contemporary Christian movement that aims at the eventual restructuring of society in accordance with the guidelines of the Bible, especially the first five books of the Old Testament.

Reformed. The Christian tradition that derives from the Calvinist branch of the Protestant Reformation. Most of the American denominations in this stream of Protestantism use the title *Presbyterian*, though some use *Reformed* in their name. The Reformed churches have usually been the branch of Protestantism most concerned with participating actively in the transformation of society.

Sphere sovereignty. The philosophy, developed primarily by Dutch statesman Abraham Kuyper, that divides society into multiple, interlocking spheres (usually four: the individual, family, church, and state), each of which is sovereign in its own area of concern and none of which should dominate any other.

Theonomy. From the Greek *theos* (God) and *nomos* (law), a belief that biblical law (especially as detailed in the first five books of the Old Testament) remains binding for society today. Often used as a synonym for Reconstruction, though actually Reconstruction encompasses other concepts beyond theonomy.

Tribulation. The seven-year period of great distress that, according to premillennialists, will take place on earth just before the return of Christ.

• Select Bibliography •

Amos, Gary. *Defending the Declaration*. Brentwood, Tenn.: Wolgemuth and Hyatt, 1989.

—————. "A Limited National Congress: The Law of Nature and Constitutional Limitations." *Journal of Christian Jurisprudence* 7 (1988): 99–125.

Armstrong, Virginia C., and Michael Farris, eds. *The Christian World View of Law*. Mountain View, Calif.: Coalition on Revival, 1986.

Assemblies of God, General Presbytery. "A Summary of Some Kingdom Now Doctrines Which Differ From the Teaching of the Assemblies of God." Unpublished paper, 1987.

Atwood, Thomas. "Through a Glass Darkly." *Policy Review* (Fall 1990): 44–52.

Bahnsen, Greg L. *By This Standard: The Authority of God's Law Today*. Tyler, Tex.: ICE, 1985.

—————. *Theonomy in Christian Ethics*. 2d ed. Phillipsburg, N. J.: Presbyterian and Reformed, 1984.

Bahnsen, Greg L., *House Divided: The Break-Up of Dispensational Theology*. Translated by Kenneth L. Gentry. Tyler, Tex.: ICE, 1989.

Bandow, Doug. *Beyond Good Intentions: A Biblical View of Politics*. Westchester, Ill.: Crossway, 1988.

Barker, Will S., and W. Robert Godfrey, eds. *Theonomy: A Reformed Critique*. Grand Rapids: Zondervan, 1990.

Beisner, E. Calvin, and Daryl S. Borgquist, eds. *The Christian World View of Economics*. Mountain View, Calif.: Coalition on Revival, 1986.

Boettner, Loraine. *The Millennium*. Phillipsburg, N. J.: Presbyterian and Reformed, 1957.

Bowman, Robert M., Jr. "The New Puritanism: A Preliminary Assessment of Reconstructionism." *Christian Research Journal* 10, 3 (Winter–Spring 1988): 21–25.

Bowman, Robert M., Jr., with Craig S. Hawkins and Dan R. Schlesinger. "The Gospel According to Paulk: A Critique of 'Kingdom

Theology.' " *Christian Research Journal* 10, 3 (Winter–Spring 1988): 9–14 (part 1); 11, 1 (Summer 1988): 15–20 (part 2).

Bratt, James. *Dutch Calvinism in Modern America.* Grand Rapids: Eerdmans, 1984.

Bruce, Steve. *The Rise and Fall of the New Christian Right.* Oxford: Clarendon, 1988.

Campbell, Roderick. *Israel and the New Covenant.* Phillipsburg, N. J.: Presbyterian and Reformed, 1954. Reprint. Tyler, Tex.: Geneva Divinity School, 1981.

Chilton, David. *The Days of Vengeance.* Ft. Worth: Dominion, 1987.

————. *Paradise Restored: A Biblical Theology of Dominion.* Tyler, Tex.: Reconstruction Press, 1985.

————. *Productive Christians in an Age of Guilt-Manipulators.* 3d ed. Tyler, Tex.: ICE, 1985.

Clapp, Rodney. "Democracy as Heresy." *Christianity Today* (February 20, 1987): 19–23.

Coalition on Revival. *Manifesto for the Christian Church.* Mountain View, Calif.: Coalition on Revival, 1986.

Colson, Charles. *Kingdoms in Conflict.* Grand Rapids and New York: Zondervan/Morrow, 1987.

Colson, Charles, with Ellen Santilli Vaughn. *Against the Night: Living in the New Dark Ages.* Ann Arbor: Servant, 1989.

Dager, Albert James. *Vengeance Is Ours: The Church in Dominion.* Redmond, Wash.: Sword, 1990.

Darrand, Tom Craig, and Anson Shupe. *Metaphors of Social Control in a Pentecostal Sect.* Lewiston, N. Y.: Edwin Mellen, 1983.

DeMar, Gary. *The Debate Over Christian Reconstruction.* Ft. Worth: Dominion, 1988.

————. *God and Government.* 3 vols. Atlanta: American Vision, 1982–1986.

————. *Ruler of the Nations.* Ft. Worth: Dominion, 1987.

DeMar, Gary, and Marshall Foster. *The Christian World View of Government.* Mountain View, Calif.: Coalition on Revival, 1986.

DeMar, Gary, and Peter Leithart. *The Reduction of Christianity: A Biblical Response to Dave Hunt.* Ft. Worth: Dominion, 1987.

Diamond, Sara. *Spiritual Warfare: The Politics of the Christian Right.* Boston: South End, 1989.

Eidsmoe, John. *Christianity and the Constitution: The Faith of Our Founding Fathers.* Grand Rapids: Baker, 1987.

Fialka, John. "Maranatha Christians, Backing Rightist Ideas, Draw Fire Over Tactics." *Wall Street Journal,* August 16, 1985.

First Principles. Rev. ed. Virginia Beach: Rock Ministerial Fellowship, 1989.

Frame, John M. "Toward a Theology of the State." *Westminster Theological Journal* 51, 2 (Fall 1989): 199–226.

Grant, George. *Bringing in the Sheaves: Turning Poverty Into Productivity.* Atlanta: American Vision, 1985.

──────. *The Changing of the Guard: Biblical Blueprints for Political Action.* Ft. Worth: Dominion, 1987.

──────. *The Dispossessed: Homelessness in America.* Ft. Worth: Dominion, 1986.

──────. *In the Shadow of Plenty: The Biblical Blueprints for Welfare.* Ft. Worth: Dominion, 1986.

Griffin, William. "Kingdom Now: New Hope or New Heresy?" Paper presented to the meeting of the Society for Pentecostal Studies, Virginia Beach, November 12–14, 1987.

Gurwitt, Rob. "The Christian Right Has Gained Political Power. Now What Does It Do?" *Governing* 3, 1 (October 1989): 52–58.

Hadden, Jeffrey K., and Anson Shupe. *Televangelism: Power and Politics on God's Frontier.* New York: Henry Holt, 1988.

Hamon, Bill. *The Eternal Church.* Phoenix: Christian International, 1981.

Henry, Carl F. H. "The New Coalitions." *Christianity Today* (November 17, 1989): 26–28.

──────. *Twilight of a Great Civilization.* Westchester, Ill.: Crossway, 1988.

Hertzke, Allen. *Representing God in Washington: The Role of Religious Lobbies in the American Polity.* Knoxville: Univ. of Tennessee Press, 1988.

House, H. Wayne, and Thomas D. Ice. *Dominion Theology: Blessing or Curse?* Portland, Ore.: Multnomah, 1988.

Hunt, Dave. *Whatever Happened to Heaven?* Eugene, Ore.: Harvest House, 1988.

Hunter, James Davison. *Evangelicalism: The Coming Generation.* Chicago: Univ. of Chicago Press, 1987.

Johnston, Robert K. *Evangelicals at an Impasse: Biblical Authority in Practice.* Atlanta: John Knox, 1979.

Jordan, James B., ed. *The Failure of the American Baptist Culture.* Tyler, Tex.: Geneva Divinity School, 1982.

Kline, Meredith G. "Comments on an Old–New Error." *Westminster Theological Journal* 41 (Fall 1978): 172–89.

Kraybill, Donald. *The Riddle of Amish Culture.* Baltimore: Johns Hopkins Univ. Press, 1989.

Kuyper, Abraham. *Lectures on Calvinism.* New York: Revell, [1898].

Lamb, Robert Paul. *Upon This Rock.* N.p.: Souls Books, 1979. Reprint. Virginia Beach: Rock Church Productions, 1983.

Liebman, Robert, and Robert Wuthnow, eds. *The New Christian Right*. New York: Aldine, 1983.

Lindsey, Hal. *The Road to Holocaust*. New York: Bantam, 1989.

Marsden, George. *Fundamentalism and American Culture*. New York: Oxford Univ. Press, 1980.

――――. *Reforming Fundamentalism: Fuller Seminary and the New Evangelicalism*. Grand Rapids: Eerdmans, 1987.

Marshall, Paul. *Thine Is the Kingdom*. London: Marshall Morgan and Scott, 1984; Grand Rapids: Eerdmans, 1986.

McCarthy, Rockne M., James W. Skillen, and William A. Harper. *Disestablishment a Second Time: Genuine Pluralism for American Schools*. Grand Rapids: Eerdmans, 1982.

McCarthy, Rockne M., et al. *Society, State and Schools*. Grand Rapids: Eerdmans, 1981.

McDowell, Stephen, and Mark Beliles. *America's Providential History*. Charlottesville, Va.: Providence Foundation, 1984.

Meares, John. *Bind Us Together*. Old Tappan, N. J.: Revell, 1987.

Moen, Matthew. *The Christian Right and Congress*. Tuscaloosa: Univ. of Alabama Press, 1989.

Morken, Hubert. *Pat Robertson: Where He Stands*. Old Tappan, N. J.: Revell, 1988.

Neuhaus, Richard John, ed. *The Bible, Politics, and Democracy*. Grand Rapids: Eerdmans, 1987.

――――. *The Naked Public Square*. Grand Rapids: Eerdmans, 1984.

Noll, Mark. *One Nation Under God? Christian Faith and Political Action in America*. San Francisco: Harper and Row, 1988.

――――, ed. *The Princeton Theology 1812–1921*. Grand Rapids: Baker, 1983.

North, Gary. *Backward, Christian Soldiers?* Tyler, Tex.: Institute for Christian Economics, 1984.

――――. "Confessions of a Washington Reject." *Journal of Christian Reconstruction* 5 (Summer 1978): 54–65.

――――. *Healer of the Nations*. Ft. Worth: Dominion, 1987.

――――. *Liberating Planet Earth*. Ft. Worth: Dominion, 1987.

――――. *Political Polytheism*. Tyler, Tex.: Institute for Christian Economics, 1989.

――――. *Unconditional Surrender: God's Program for Victory*. 3d ed. Tyler, Tex.: ICE, 1988.

North, Gary, and Gary DeMar. *Christian Reconstruction: What It Is, What It Isn't*. Tyler, Tex.: ICE, 1991.

Oss, Douglas A. "The Influence of Hermeneutical Frameworks in the Theonomy Debate." *Westminster Theological Journal* 51, 2 (Fall 1989): 227–58.

Paulk, Earl. *Held in the Heavens Until* . . . . Atlanta: K Dimension, 1985.

————. *Satan Unmasked*. Atlanta: K Dimension, 1984.

————. *Spiritual Megatrends*. Atlanta: K Dimension, 1988.

————. *That the World May Know*. Atlanta: K Dimension, 1987.

————. *Thrust In the Sickle and Reap*. Atlanta: K Dimension, 1986.

————. *20/20 Vision: A Clear View of the Kingdom of God*. Atlanta: K Dimension, 1988.

————. *Ultimate Kingdom*. Rev. ed. Atlanta: K Dimension, 1986.

Peacocke, Dennis. *Winning the Battle for the Minds of Men*. Santa Rosa, Calif.: Alive and Free, 1987.

Peretti, Frank. *Piercing the Darkness*. Westchester, Ill.: Crossway, 1989.

————. *This Present Darkness*. Westchester, Ill.: Crossway, 1988.

Reid, Tommy. *Kingdom Now . . . But Not Yet*. Buffalo: IJN, 1988.

Riss, Richard M. *Latter Rain*. Mississauga, Ont.: Honeycomb Visual Productions, 1987.

Robertson, Pat. *America's Dates With Destiny*. Nashville: Nelson, 1986.

Robertson, Pat, with Bob Slosser. *The Secret Kingdom*. Nashville: Nelson, 1982.

Rogers, Jack B., and Donald K. McKim. *The Authority and Interpretation of the Bible: An Historical Approach*. New York: Harper and Row, 1979.

Rushdoony, Rousas John. *By What Standard? An Analysis of the Philosophy of Cornelius Van Til*. Nutley, N. J.: Presbyterian and Reformed, 1959.

————. *Christianity and the State*. Vallecito, Calif.: Ross House, 1986.

————. *The Foundations of Social Order*. 1968. Reprint. Fairfax, Va.: Thoburn, 1978.

————. *The Institutes of Biblical Law*. Nutley, N. J.: Craig, 1973.

————. *The Messianic Character of American Education*. Nutley, N. J.: Craig, 1963.

————. *The Nature of the American System*. Nutley, N. J.: Craig, 1965; Fairfax, Va.: Thoburn, 1978.

————. *This Independent Republic*. Nutley, N. J.: Craig, 1964.

Schaeffer, Francis. *A Christian Manifesto*. Westchester, Ill.: Crossway, 1981.

Schlossberg, Herbert. *Idols for Destruction*. Nashville: Nelson, 1983.

Schlossberg, Herbert, and Martin Olasky. *Turning Point: A Christian Worldview Declaration*. Westchester, Ill.: Crossway, 1987.

Shupe, Anson. "Prophets of a Biblical America." *Wall Street Journal*, April 12, 1989.

Sider, Ronald A. *Completely Pro-Life*. Downers Grove, Ill.: InterVarsity, 1987.

—————. *Rich Christians in an Age of Hunger*. Downers Grove, Ill.: InterVarsity, 1977.

Skillen, James W. *The Scattered Voice: Christians at Odds in the Public Square*. Grand Rapids: Zondervan, 1990.

Smith, Gary Scott, ed. *God and Politics: Four Views on the Transformation of Civil Government*. Phillipsburg, N. J.: Presbyterian and Reformed, 1989.

Sutton, Ray R. *That You May Prosper: Dominion by Covenant*. Tyler, Tex.: ICE, 1987.

Thoburn, Robert. *The Christian and Politics*. Fairfax, Va.: Thoburn, 1981.

Tinder, Glenn. *The Political Meaning of Christianity: An Interpretation*. Baton Rouge: Louisiana State Univ. Press, 1989.

Titus, Herbert W. "God, Man, Law, and Liberty." Unpublished manuscript.

—————. "The Law of Our Land." *Journal of Christian Jurisprudence* 6 (1986): 57–75.

Toulouse, Mark G. "Pat Robertson: Apocalyptic and American Foreign Policy." *Journal of Church and State* 31 (Winter 1989): 73–99.

Van Til, Cornelius. *The Defense of the Faith*. 3d ed. Nutley, N. J.: Presbyterian and Reformed, 1967.

Watson, David K. "Theonomy: A History of the Movement and an Evaluation of Its Primary Text." M.A. thesis, Calvin College, 1985.

Weber, Max. *The Protestant Ethic and the Spirit of Capitalism*. Trans. Talcott Parsons. New York: Charles Scribner's Sons, 1958.

Weeks, Tricia. *The Provoker*. Atlanta: K Dimension, 1986.

Weiner, Bob, and Rose Weiner. *Bible Studies for a Firm Foundation*. Gainesville, Fla.: Maranatha Publications, 1980; rev. ed. 1983.

—————. "The Conquering Power of Christianity." *Forerunner* (December 1987): 12–14, 20, 23.

Weiner, Bob, with David Wimbish. *Take Dominion*. Old Tappan, N. J.: Revell, 1988.

White, William. *Van Til: Defender of the Faith*. Nashville: Nelson, 1979.

Whitehead, John. *The Second American Revolution*. Elgin, Ill.: David C. Cook, 1982.

—————. *True Christianity*. Westchester, Ill.: Crossway, 1989.

Williamsburg Charter Foundation. *Report on the "First Liberty" Summit*. Washington, D. C.: Williamsburg Charter Foundation, 1988.

—————. *The Williamsburg Charter*. Washington, D. C.: Williamsburg Charter Project, 1988.

• Subject Index •

Subject Index

SUBJECT INDEX

• Scripture Index •

Page numbers in parentheses denote references where precise verses are not specified in the main text.